© Fleurus Éditions, Paris – 2008
Original title: *Matières à créer*
ISBN 978-2-215-09512-5

Editorial director: Christophe Savouré
Series director and cover photograph: Franck Schmitt
Editor: Gaëlle Guilmard assisted by Adélaïde de Sade
Editorial contributions: Valérie Monnet, Isabelle Macé, Marie Pieroni and Catherine Talamoni
Art director: Laurent Quellet
Designer: Florence Le Maux

© 2013 for the English edition:
h.f.ullmann publishing GmbH

Translation from French: Anna Bennett, in association with First Edition Translations Ltd, Cambridge
Editing: Jenny Knight, in association with First Edition Translations Ltd, Cambridge
Typesetting: The Write Idea Ltd, in association with First Edition Translations Ltd, Cambridge

Project management for h.f.ullmann: Isabel Weiler

Overall responsibility for production: h.f.ullmann publishing GmbH, Potsdam, Germany

Printed in China, 2013

ISBN 978-3-8480-0531-4

10 9 8 7 6 5 4 3 2 1
X IX VIII VII VI V IV III II I

www.ullmann-publishing.com
newsletter@ullmann-publishing.com

Health and safety

When using this book care should be taken to keep to the procedures specified in it and to use only the materials stated. It is also essential to follow the advice regarding health and safety given by the manufacturers and suppliers of materials listed. Always use protective clothing – particularly gloves and/or goggles – when appropriate. The book is intended for adults and any children who use it should be supervised by an adult.

The publishers cannot take responsibility for any health problems or accidents resulting from making any of the items featured in the book.

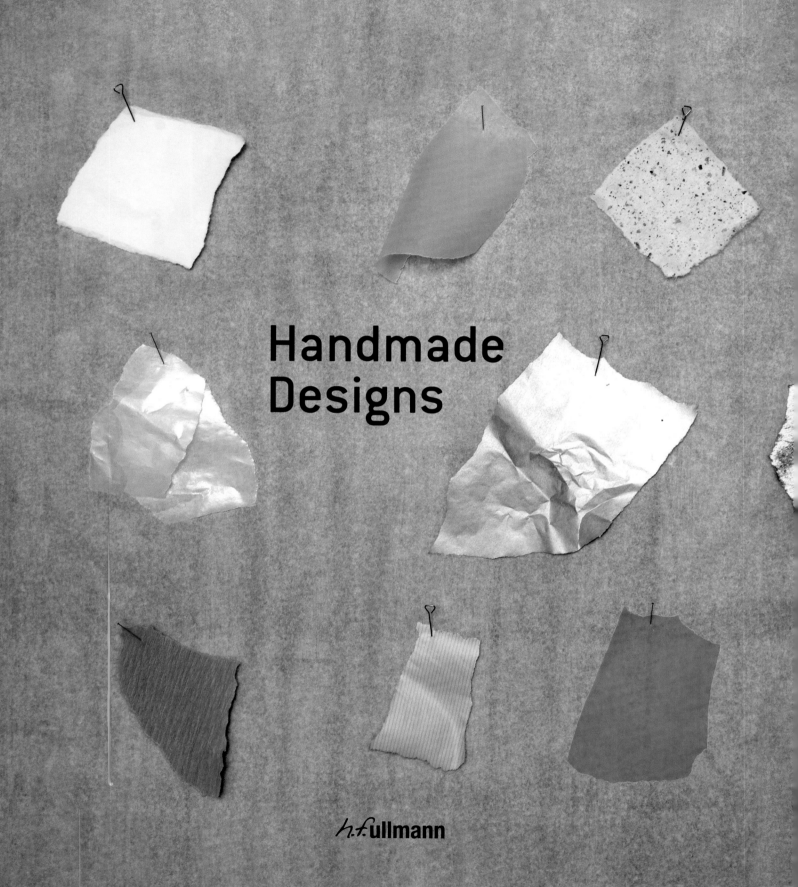

Handmade
Designs

h.f.ullmann

Contents

Fashions and trends

Floral bonnet	50
Green embroidered decoration	53
Felt bucket bag	54
Flower pins	56
Button jacket	61
Violet-colored mohair scarf	62
Seventies purse	64
Raffia brooch	69
Fun chain	70
Metallic belt and moneybag	72
Beads and drawer knobs	76
Pouch with flower	78
Openwork sandals	80
Seashell purse	82
Lily brooch	84
Embroidered hat decoration	86
Cake apron	88
Hot pink bead necklace	90
Leaf purses	92
A bouquet of flower decorations	94
String bag	98
Floral decorations for summer pumps	100
Milky Way	102
Propeller hat	104
Giraffe decoration	106
Mauve slippers	109
Doll and purse transfers	110
Patterns	112

Interior design projects

Floral frame	126
Lined beanbag	128
Decorated round vase	130
Special jigsaw puzzle	133
Theo and Leah	134
Taffeta decorations	136
Art Deco mirrors	141
Letters for pouffe	142
Drape tieback	144
Dried leaf frieze	148
Memory board	150
Woolen flowers	152
Country cushions	156
Springtime frame	159
Cream bedside table	160
Decorations for pouffe	164
Love those spots!	166
Vase with felt	168
Paper blind	170
Trompe-l'oeil cushion	172
Eastern mirror	174
Organdie net drape	176
Elegant quilted cushion	178
Small colored vases	182
Patterns	184

Beautiful lighting

Square candleholder	192
Garland paper lamp	194
String lamp	196
Magic chandelier lamp	198
Crocheted fern lamp	200
Hydrangea lamp	202
Cylindrical tartan lamps	204
Pale blue pleated lamp	206
Button candleholder	208
Tutti frutti candles	210
Glass and pebble lamp	214
Lace-effect lamps	216
Pearl candleholder	218
Button lamp	220
Duo of candleholders	222
Flying butterflies	225
Seed light	226
Rose net	228
Pink candleholder	231
Assorted candleholders	232
Patterns	236

Be practical and organized

Week organizer	242
Grocery pots	244
My personal mailbox	248
Ethnic photograph albums	250
Letter files	252
Old-fashioned key ring	254
Letters for your organizer	256
Memory hatbox	258
Fall leaf shelves	260
Corded plant pot	262
Linen organizers	264
Tool buckets	266
Bucolic notebooks	268
Linen pouch	270
Two-tone boxes	272
Decorated shelves	274
Cotton penholder	276
Ladybug hot water bottle	278
Cotton wool holder	280
Patterns	282

The art of fine dining

Floral tablecloth	286
Mint tea	288
Bamboo tray	292
Salad bowl and servers	294
Napkin rings	296
Ethnic table runner	300
Star plates	302
Bamboo bowl and saucer	304
Seafaring tablecloth	306
Romantic tray	308
Engraved glasses	310
Embellished placemat	313
Sage leaf transfers	314
Sunny bottle holder	316
Multicolored tray with wicker mugs	318
Beribboned table runner	322
Crocheted coasters	324
Personalized steak knives	326
Geometric table mats	328
Ethnic placemat	330
Coffee time	332
Delicate tablecloth	334
Decorated placemats	336
Patterns	338

Little ideas

Buttons, buttons, buttons!	346
Creative beads	350
Ideas with seeds	352
Inspirational raffia	354
A garden paved with good ideas	356

Techniques

Embroidery: instructions

Setting up

The pre-existing elements (clothing, beret, bag) and all the small elements (jewelry) are worked freehand, that is to say without any given pattern. The same applies to the table runner and netting.

For the other projects, the fabric is stretched on a large rectangular wooden frame. You will have to add enough extra fabric round the work to allow for the seam widths. It is only when you take the embroidery off the frame that you will recover the piece of fabric with the dimensions indicated.

If setting up takes a little time, the comfort achieved as you embroider is without compare. Place the frame on two trestles and adjust the height so it comes just below your chest. This is to avoid backache even if you embroider for hours on end. Use both hands: one should always be below, the other above. With the exception of a few stitches or applications, you will embroider much faster in this way. Only turn the frame to thread through. It is not necessary to knot each thread at the beginning and end of each stitch; you can leave some unfastened.

The frame will be particularly useful to embroider the projects on pages 72 and 82. For the project on page 82, a ring frame would also be suitable. If you have to move the work while you are embroidering it, take care to surround the ring frame on the underside with felt (or another fabric) to protect the parts you have already embroidered.

Finally, note that a piece of work embroidered on a frame needs hardly any ironing when completed.

Designs

To reproduce designs, use some dressmaker's carbon paper in a color similar to that of the support (first take a sample on a piece of fabric). Place the carbon paper face down on the fabric and the design on top. Using a ballpoint pen, draw round the outline of the design and push firmly without tearing the paper.

For some more "free" designs, trace them freehand with a pencil directly on the fabric. If you are not very sure of yourself, tack the outlines of the design through tissue paper. Remove the tissue paper afterward as and when required or at the end of embroidering. Special felt-tipped pens for fabric are available, either water soluble or air erasable.

Threads

Six-stranded cotton can be separated in order to embroider with just one, two, or three threads. Throughout the present book, how many strands to embroider with is specified. Unless otherwise stated, use all six strands.

Metallic six-stranded cotton requires short knots to avoid wear and tear on the strands. If you need to use only two strands, proceed as follows.

A

B

Threading metallic threads into the needle

1• Cut 1 strand of metallic thread double the length of the desired knot. Fold it in 2 and thread it into the eye of the needle.

2• Lengthen the thread so it is greater than the length of the needle.

3• Draw the needle in one direction and the metallic thread in the other.

4• The thread will be held at the end of the needle. You will have 2 strands of thread with which to embroider.

Pearl cotton #5 is ideal for post stitch, the French knot, and buttonhole stitch because it slides well and produces an attractive raised finish. It can also be used for basting stitch and back stitch, but not for satin stitch.

Originally intended for needlepoint, matt embroidery cotton is easy to sew with as long as you use a large-eyed needle and take somewhat short stitches.

Needles

Embroidery needles have a fairly long eye. Different sizes will be necessary, depending on the thread, the number of strands used, and the thickness of the fabric you intend to embroider. The greater the size of the eye, the greater the protection afforded to the thread. To sew on pearls, on the other hand, the finest needles are the most effective.

Tips and tricks

To transfer a photograph onto fabric, use special tissue paper and print your image on it using a photocopier or a computer with a scanner and printer. You can then make the transfer by ironing over the design.

This type of paper is widely available. Follow the manufacturer's instructions.

Do not make a knot at the start of the stitches. Insert your needle from the right to the wrong side of the fabric (¾ or 1¼ in [2 or 3 cm]) from the stitch you began with, leaving a short length of thread, then take it out a little bit farther down from the stitch you chose to start with. *(A)* Then embroider the thread which is not held by your finger. Once you have finished embroidering, turn the work inside out, draw the loose opening thread, and insert it into the first few embroidery stitches. *(B)*

If you have to sew a machine-stitched seam round the border of the embroidery stitches, use the asymmetrical presser foot with a zip so as not to damage it.

To iron an embroidered piece of work, place it embroidery side down against a very thick piece of flannel and iron it on the wrong side using a damping cloth. Let it cool before removing the piece of work from the ironing board. Ironing is not recommended for a few kinds of material.

The stitches used

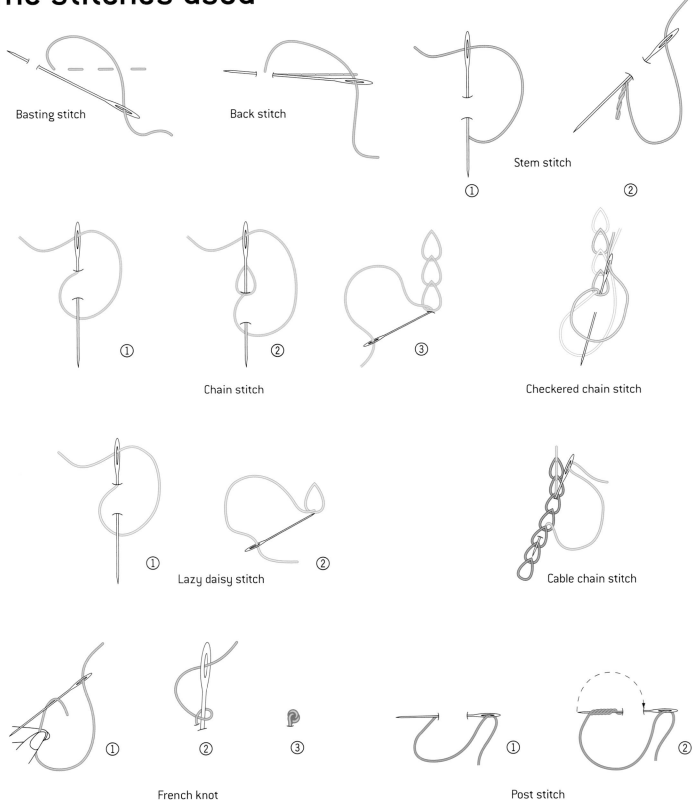

Basting stitch

Back stitch

Stem stitch
① ②

Chain stitch
① ② ③

Checkered chain stitch

Lazy daisy stitch
① ②

Cable chain stitch

French knot
① ② ③

Post stitch
① ②

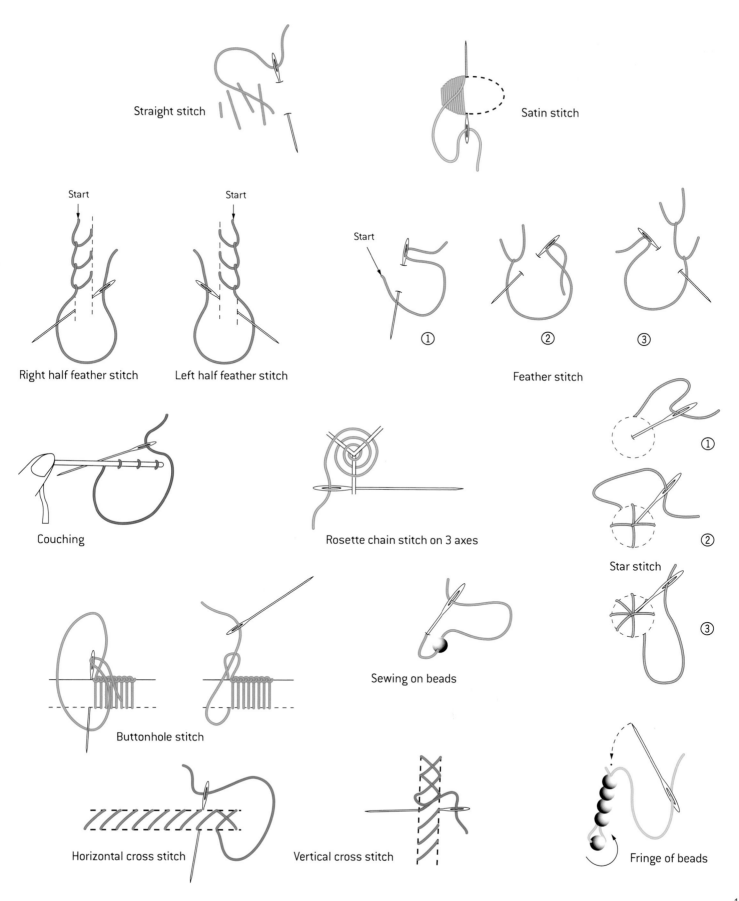

Straight stitch

Satin stitch

Right half feather stitch

Left half feather stitch

Feather stitch

① ② ③

Couching

Rosette chain stitch on 3 axes

Star stitch

① ② ③

Buttonhole stitch

Sewing on beads

Horizontal cross stitch

Vertical cross stitch

Fringe of beads

Crochet threads: basic techniques

This chapter summarizes all the techniques that are necessary for producing the crochet projects in this book. The decorative stitches are explained in the grids you will find in the pattern pages. Listed below are the abbreviations used.

The ideal thread with which to crochet is pearlized thread, most commonly known as pearl cotton; it twists in a particular way, which gives it a shiny appearance and this round thread does not split because the crochet hook catches it firmly. Pearl cotton is widely available in an attractive range of colors. There are also very interesting matt cotton threads with which to crochet. In truth, you can crochet with many often unexpected different threads and fabrics, as you will discover when you work some of these projects. You will have to adjust the size of the crochet hook depending on the thread you are using or on the effect you aim to achieve, airy or tight, and you will happily work with wool, linen, silk, viscose, lurex, mohair, and even leather threads. Ribbons, raffia strands, and strips of fabric can also be used. Only a thread with large irregularities, a very fluffy or bouclé thread for example, could be a problem in that it would get stuck as you stitch. Test any thread you find attractive—therein lies the pleasure of creation.

Stitch abbreviations and symbols

dc	double crochet		
ch	chain(s) or chain stitch(es)	○	ch(s) chain stitch(es)
cm	centimeter(s)	●	sl st slip stitch
col	color	+	single crochet(s)
beg	begin or beginning	±	rib stitch
cont	continue	⋎	2 single stitches in 1 stitch
croch	crochet	Т	half double crochet (hdc)
dec	decrease	Ŧ	double crochet (dc)
g	grams	⋀	double crochet two together
m	meters	⋔	double crochet three together
st(s)	stitch(es)	Ŧ	treble crochet (tr)
obt	obtain	⋀	treble crochet two together
prev	refers to chain(s) previously made/worked	⋔	treble crochet three together
rep	repeat		
foll	following	⊗	picot stitch
fo	finish off	⊖	single crochet
∅	diameter	⊖	with pearls

```
*  *
** **        repeat the instructions
             given between these
○  ○         signs
○○ ○○
```

14

Make a chain (chain stitch ◦)

1 • Make 1 loop, pass the yarn from the ball behind the crochet hook in order to pass it above. You will then have made 1 yarn over.
Draw the crochet hook from left to right to make the yarn over twist through the loop. Lightly secure the knot.

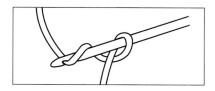

2 • To make up the chain, make a yarn over—draw the crochet hook from left to right in order to make the yarn over—twist through the loop and continue in this manner. You will end up with a foundation chain made up of chain stitches.

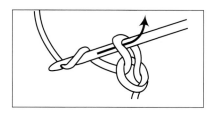

Slip stitch ●

Insert the crochet hook in 1 stitch of the foundation chain, and make 1 yarn over. Draw the yarn through the 2 loops.

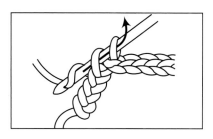

Single crochet +

1 • Insert the crochet hook in 1 stitch of the foundation chain, and make 1 yarn over. Draw the yarn over the stitch.

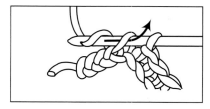

2 • Make 1 yarn over, and draw through the 2 loops. At the end of each row, make 1 chain stitch to turn.

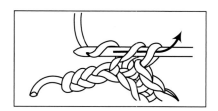

Rib stitch ±

1 • Uneven rows (the right way up for the fabric): work single crochets, inserting stitches from the previous row into the strand behind.
2 • Even rows (the wrong way up for the fabric): work single crochets, inserting stitches from the previous row underneath the strand in front of you. If you are working a circular piece, the work should be executed entirely on the right side of the fabric: crochet all turns as for uneven rows.

Half double crochet ⊤

1 • Make 1 yarn over on a foundation chain, insert crochet hook in 1 stitch of the chain, make up a further 1 yarn over, and draw through the stitch.

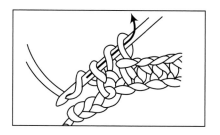

2 • Make another 1 yarn over and draw the yarn through the 3 loops. At the end of each row, make 2 chain stitches in order to turn.

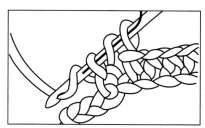

Double crochet ⊤

1 • Make 1 yarn over on a foundation chain, insert hook in 1 stitch of the chain, make up a further 1 yarn over, and draw the yarn through the stitch.

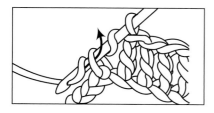

2 • Make another 1 yarn over and draw yarn through the first 2 loops.

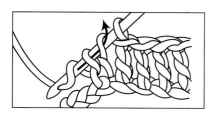

3 • Make another 1 yarn over and draw the yarn through the remaining 2 loops. At the end of each row, make 3 chain stitches in order to turn.

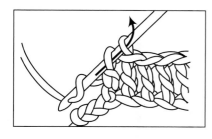

Double crochet two together ⋔

1 • Crochet 1 incomplete double crochet by executing only steps 1 and 2; you will obtain 2 loops.

2 • Crochet 1 incomplete double crochet in the same stitch or the stitch foll; you will obtain 3 loops.

3 • Make 1 yarn over and draw it through the 3 loops.

Double crochet three together ⋔

1 • Crochet 1 incomplete double crochet by executing only steps 1 and 2; you will obtain 2 loops.

2 • Crochet 1 incomplete double crochet in the same stitch or the stitch foll; you will obtain 3 loops.

3 • Crochet 1 incomplete double crochet in the same stitch or the stitch foll; you will obtain 4 loops.

4 • Make 1 yarn over and draw it through the 4 loops.

Treble crochet ⊤

1 • Make 2 yarn overs on a foundation chain.

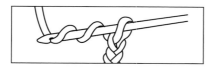

2 • Insert the hook in the 5th stitch, make 1 yarn over, and draw yarn through the stitch. You will obtain 4 loops.

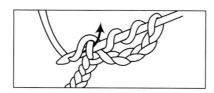

3• Make 1 yarn over and draw the yarn through 2 loops.

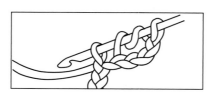

4 • Make 1 yarn over and draw the yarn through 2 loops.

5 • Make 1 yarn over and draw the yarn through the last 2 loops.

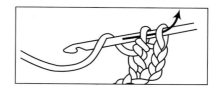

6 • The treble crochet is made.

7 • At the end of each row, make 4 chain stitches in order to turn.

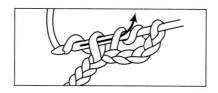

Treble crochet two together

1 • Crochet 1 incomplete treble crochet by executing only steps 1 to 3; you will obtain 2 loops.

2 • Crochet 1 incomplete treble crochet in the same stitch or the stitch foll; you will obtain 3 loops.

3 • Make 1 yarn over and draw it through the 3 loops.

Treble crochet three together

1 • Crochet 1 incomplete treble crochet by executing only steps 1 to 3; you will obtain 2 loops.

2 • Crochet 1 incomplete treble crochet in the same stitch or the stitch foll; you will obtain 3 loops.

3 • Crochet 1 incomplete treble crochet in the same stitch or the stitch foll; you will obtain 4 loops.

4 • Make 1 yarn over and draw it through the 4 loops.

Picot stitch

1 • Crochet the number of chain stitches indicated on the pattern (3, 4, or 6).

2 • Crochet 1 sl st in the first chain stitch of the picot stitch in order to enclose it.

To cast on a circular work

1 • Thread the yarn 2 times in a circle about 8 in (20 cm) from the end.

2 • Insert the crochet hook in the circle, take up the yarn that remains on the ball (=1 yarn over), and draw it through the circle.

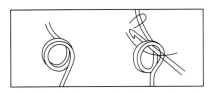

3 • Make 1 yarn over and draw it through the loop = 1 ch.

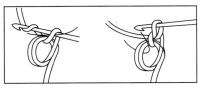

4 • Inserting into the circle, crochet the desired number of stitches for the 1st row (here, some single crochets).

5 • Draw 1 of the circle's loops toward the outside to adjust the latter's diameter.

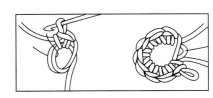

6 • Pull the end of the yarn in order to tighten the circle.

7 • Close up the first row by crocheting 1 sl st in the first stitch.

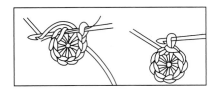

Assembly by oversewing

Align the 2 pieces to be assembled, the wrong way round, border to border.

1 • Insert a wool needle under the 2 strands of the stitch on 1 of the pieces.

2 • Insert the needle under the 2 strands of the stitch and have the pieces opposite each other.

3 • Repeat stages 1 and 2.

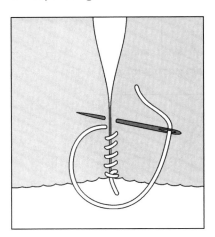

Assembly by *grafting*

Align the two pieces to be assembled, the right way round, border to border.

1 • Insert a wool needle under the 2 strands of the sl st on one of the pieces and take it out between the 2 strands of the foll stitch.

2 • Insert the needle under the 2 strands of the sl st and have the pieces opposite each other. Take it out between the 2 strands of the foll stitch.

3 • Repeat stages 1 and 2.

Back stitch

1 • Make a front loop. Let the needle come out on the left hand side; the space should be equal to the length of the front loop.

2 • Execute a back loop by inserting at the end of the previous loop. Let the needle come out on the left.

3 • Repeat stage 2.

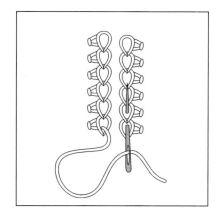
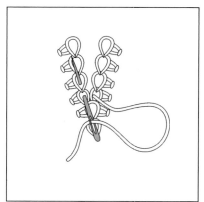
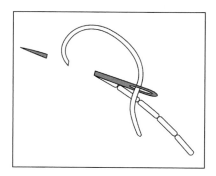

Buttons: threads and techniques

Be as creative as you like when working with buttons; use embroidery thread, scoubidou thread, wool, pearls, sequins, brass wire, and safety pins, and in order to multiply your props you will find that glue will be your best friend!

Threads to attach buttons
Sewing thread
Embroidery thread
Lurex thread
Woolen thread

To thread
Brass wire
Wire
Leather laces
Rat's tail
Plastic thread

To customize
Pearls
Sequins
Felt

Other methods for fastening
Plastic glue
Neoprene glue
Textile glue

Different kinds of button
You can find 2-hole and 4-hole buttons, and buttons with a shank:

2 holes   4 holes   shank

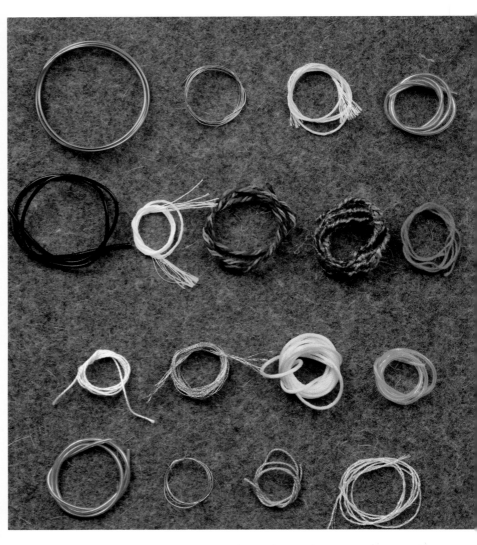

To sew on a button with thread

(sewing or embroidery thread)

To conceal the knot when the wrong side is visible, insert the needle at the spot where you want to place the knot. This will then be hidden by the button.

1. Insert needle on right of the fabric.
2. Push it through 2nd hole of button.
3. Take needle out on the wrong side of the fabric and repeat several times.

On the last stitch.

1. To finish sewing on button, take needle out under button, on the outside.
2. Wrap thread round the base of button (whether it has holes or buckle).
3. Insert the needle in the wrapped thread and make a loop. Cut off any excess thread.

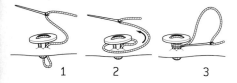

To thread a button, with thread

(brass wire, scoubidou thread, leather)

1. Thread it underneath the button (1A)... or above it (1B).

2. Pendant buttons: holed buttons; buttons with shank

Using a safety pin:
holed buttons; buttons with shank

Examples of attaching

Buttons with 2 holes. In the case of a functional button, push the thread through to the center of the underside.

Buttons with 4 holes.

Buttons with 4 holes.

On cord. The thread goes round the cord.

Customizing buttons

1. With pearls.

2. With sequins and a pearl.

3. With felt.

4. Tie a knot on the underside with the 2 ends of the thread.

Glueing buttons

1. Button sewn onto felt.

First sew the button onto the felt. Then glue the wrong side of the felt with textile glue.

2. Simple button.

In cases where it is difficult to attach a button, make a trompe-l'oeil seam; push the thread into the 2 holes in order to simulate sewing, tie a knot, and then glue the wrong side of the button with neoprene glue in order to fix it in place.

Wet felting

This technique requires very little in the way of materials—wool fibers, soap, and warm water are enough—and can be learned in an instant!

SUPPLIES
- Wool for felting
- Pure soap (bar or flakes)

EQUIPMENT
- Synthetic tulle
- Plastic bubble wrap or bamboo table mats
- Towel
- Sponge

1• Place the towel on the table, then place a piece of bubble wrap on top. Pull on the wool in order to detach the small fibers and lay these horizontally on top, so they slightly overlap and form a kind of "carpet." *(A)*

2• Next place a second layer perpendicularly in the opposite direction. *(B)* Repeat the layering 3 times, or more if you want to end up with a thicker piece of work.

3• Then cover the wool with a piece of tulle, to keep it still when you wet felt with soapy water. *(C)*

4• Moisten the wool with warm water and a sponge, then rub the bar of soap over it to lather (if you are using soap flakes, dilute them in a bowl of hot water before use). Sponge well so the soap soaks the wool thoroughly. *(D)*

5• Remove the tulle and cover the wool with another piece of bubble wrap. *(E)* Rub it vigorously with your hands for about 20 min. *(F)* You are thus massaging the wool through the plastic bubble wrap. Afterward roll the entire thing—towel, bubble wrap, and wool—in one direction for 5 min, then in the opposite direction for the same amount of time (10 min in all).

6• Separate the piece of wool you have obtained from the bubble wrap and beat it (that is to say, bang it against the base of the sink or a receptacle) for a few mins.
Then rinse the wool thoroughly in clear water to remove all traces of soap. *(G)* Let dry.

A

B

C

D

E

F

G

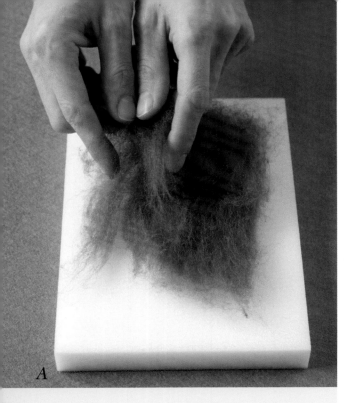

A

Needle felting

This technique enables you to felt carded wool without using water. It is generally used to make smaller projects, or to decorate a piece of fabric with designs.

SUPPLIES
• Wool

EQUIPMENT
• Foam board about 1¼ to 2 in (3 to 5 cm) thick
• 3 single felting needles (1 fine, 1 medium, and 1 thick)
• 1 medium double felting needle
• 1 large quadruple felting needle
• Thimble (for protection, especially for beginners)

1• Lay the thick foam board on the table. Pull on the wool in order to detach the small fibers and lay these horizontally on top, so they slightly overlap and form a kind of "carpet". *(A)* Next place a second layer perpendicularly in the opposite direction. *(B)* Repeat the layering if you want to end up with a thicker piece of work.

2• Work the wool by inserting a suitable carding needle *(B)*; use a quadruple needle to work large surfaces, a single or double needle for finer work. The more you pierce the wool, the more it will amalgamate.

3• Begin by working the piece of wool by separating it from time to time from the foam board to check its progress. *(C)* Turn it occasionally in order to work the two sides thoroughly.

4• Next work its edges more precisely by using a double needle this time. *(D)* Alternate between working the whole and the shapes. *(E)*

5• To make a ball of felt, roll the amalgamated wool on the foam board while pricking it with a needle: the ball will thus become increasingly thicker. *(F)* To create an airy effect at the bottom of a piece of felted wool on the other hand, lay it on the foam board and "paint" (that is, pierce and pull) the lower part of the piece of wool with a double felting needle. The ply will split a bit and create a filmy effect.

6• To create a design on a piece of felted wool, take up a small amount of wool in your chosen color and lay it in the same position as the design. Now shape it using a single fine needle (a long one is shown here to make the stem, a round one to make the flower). *(G)* By pricking them, these small colored wool fibers will blend into the felt background.

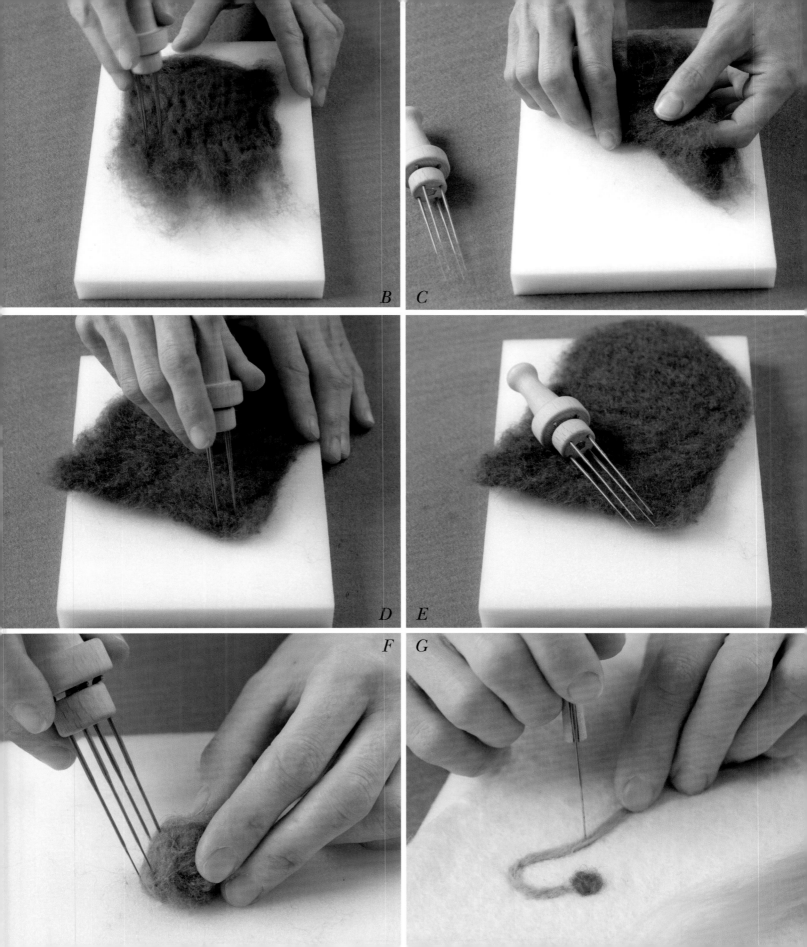

B

C

D

E

F

G

Glued paper technique

To avoid it curling when it comes into contact with the glue, use thin paper: silk paper, crystal paper, photocopying paper, tracing paper, craft paper, gift wrapping paper, crêpe paper. You can also use tissue paper, and even cotton wool.

SUPPLIES
- Paper
- Saran wrap
- Adhesive tape
- Wallpaper paste

EQUIPMENT
- Shape to be molded
- Flexible silk bristle paintbrush
- Glass pot

1 • Wrap the shape to be molded in Saran wrap, securing it if necessary with adhesive tape. *(A)*

2 • Tear the paper into small pieces of approximately the same size.

3 • Thin down the glue in the glass pot. Glue the shape to be molded using a paintbrush.

4 • Cover the shape with small pieces of paper, then apply wallpaper paste over everything. Repeat this step twice in order to obtain 3 layers of paper pieces, always superimposing them in the same direction.

5 • Let dry for 2 or 3 days before unmolding.

A

Papier mâché technique

This technique enables you to recycle paper, either plain or printed (advertising leaflets, newspaper, envelopes...), and also cellulose egg cartons. Sort out your chosen materials according to dominant colors.

SUPPLIES
• Recycling paper with the same dominant color
• Saran wrap
• Adhesive tape
• Wallpaper paste
• 4 x ¾ in (18 mm) batons of wood, 9¾ in (246 mm) long
• 4 x ¾ in (18 mm) batons, 13 ⅛ in (333 mm) long
• Plastic screen

EQUIPMENT
• Saw
• Miter box
• Wall stapler
• Stick blender
• Salad bowl, bowl, glass pot
• Small square washing-up bowl
• Ladle
• Sponge
• Kitchen knife
• Flexible silk bristle paintbrush

Make a sheet of paper

1 • Cover your work surface with Saran wrap and secure this with adhesive tape.

2 • Saw the ends of the batons at an angle of 45°. Staple them so as to build 2 frames with an inner window A4 in size. Staple the screen to 1 of these; *(A)* it should act as a sifter.

3 • Tear the paper into small pieces into the salad bowl. *(B)* Add water and blend using a stick blender until you have a smooth paste. *(C)*

4 • Superimpose the 2 frames, that with the sifter below, and place them in the washing-up bowl.

5 • Ladle a little paste into 1 frame, *(D)* and absorb any excess water by sponging over the sifter, then let the sifter drain out into the washing-up bowl. Repeat this step until the entire sifter is covered, slightly overlapping each application to obtain an even surface. Keep the 2 frames perfectly superimposed as you work so that the paste does not spill out.

 *A*

 *B*

C D

E

6• Remove the lower frame, then place the one with the sifter back on the work surface. Sponge off any excess water.

7• Gently release the sifter from the paste using a knife and gradually lift up the frame by its corners. *(E)*

8• Thin down the wallpaper paste in the pot. Using a paintbrush, apply a layer of it on the sheet of paper.

9• Let dry for 2 or 3 days before detaching the sheet of paper from the work surface.

To make a papier mâché mold

SUPPLIES
• Recycling paper with the same dominant color
• Saran wrap
• Adhesive tape
• Wallpaper paste

EQUIPMENT
• Shape to be molded
• Stick blender
• Salad bowl, bowl, glass pot
• Sponge
• Flexible silk bristle paintbrush

1• Wrap the shape to be molded in Saran wrap, securing it if necessary with adhesive tape.

2• Tear the paper into small pieces into the salad bowl, add water, and blend using a stick blender until you have a fairly thick paste.

3• Apply a small amount of paste onto the shape to be molded, and immediately absorb any excess water with the sponge and let the sponge drain out into the washing-up bowl. Repeat this step until the entire shape is covered, slightly overlapping each application to obtain an even surface.

4• Thin down the wallpaper paste in the pot. Using a paintbrush, apply a layer of it on the sheet of paper.

5• Let dry for 2 or 3 days before unmolding.

To engrave on glass

Despite its difficult appearance, nothing could be simpler than engraving on glass. An engraving implement is used in the same way as a pencil, and you go over the lines of previously traced or drawn designs on the support.

You will find manual engravers in craft stores. For greater speed, however (for once you are into this you will not want to stop), use an electric mini-engraver, which is sold with a few diamond burrs. Ideally you would then practice on all kinds of yogurt pots, jam jars, fruit juice bottles, or medicine containers.

Getting started

First of all clean your support with a cloth that has been soaked in alcohol (90 or 60% proof) or in white spirit. This will get rid of all traces of grease and make it easier for you to engrave. Choose your design.

Trace it, then position it inside the support. You can make several nicks all round the object you are engraving, so it can adopt the shapes and curves of a glass better, for example.

If you are unable to slide your design into the inside of the support (the neck of the bottle or the vase may be too tight), use some carbon paper to transfer the design onto the glass.

It is of course always possible to draw the design to be engraved directly onto the glass. Use a fine felt-tipped pen for this. Afterward you need only go over your drawing with the engraver. Erase the last traces of ink with cotton wool soaked in nail polish remover.

Always start by executing the outline of the designs, pressing down only lightly the first time to avoid any mistakes. When you go over with the burr afterward, you will follow these first outlines, no matter how faint they are. Then fill in the surfaces, using a burr in a larger size. To trace straight lines, you can use masking tape as a ruler. Remove the glass dust regularly with a cloth, in order to see your work more clearly.

Always sit in a comfortable position to engrave. Work next to a window or choose good lighting to avoid any reflection. Put your support on your lap or on a folded piece of cloth, and keep it firmly in position to ensure even strokes.

Pyrography: nibs and accessories

There are many nibs that can be used on the handle of a pyrography machine. The machine is usually sold with a **no. 21** or "universal" nib (no. 2 in the photograph). Bevelled in shape, it is very useful for tracing fine or thick lines, curves, downstrokes, and thin strokes, and it can also darken the wood.

Nib no. 22 (no. 1 in the photograph) is needle shaped, and it will produce thinner lines and strokes with good depth.

Nib no. 25 (no. 3 in the photograph) is generally used for pyrosculpture (on expanded polystyrene). When used on wood it traces thick lines and triangles.

Nib no. R20 (no. 4 in the photograph) can make medium-thick bevels and other triangle shapes.

Nib no. F20 (no. 5 in the photograph) is fork shaped and will enable you to mark out parallel lines or evenly spaced points.

Nib no. C23 (no. 6 in the photograph) will outline circles or straight round shapes in greater detail. You can also make semicircles by turning the handle of the pyrography machine.

Nib no. B24 (no. 7 in the photograph), with a rounded tip, will mark out strokes $1/4$ in (4 mm) in diameter and lines of the same size. There are also nibs B21, $1/16$ in (1 mm) in diameter, B22, $1/16$ in (2 mm) in diameter, and B23, $1/8$ in (3 mm) in diameter.

Nib no. 24 (no. 8 in the photograph) is for working on velvet and will darken wood. You can also choose nib no. P20 for the latter operation; this is easier to use and does not require you to press down in order to mark the support.

Other pyrography nibs are sold, each with their own individual characteristics, depending on their shape and the support to be engraved. You do not need to buy a large number of tools at first, however. Nibs 21, 22, 24, 25, B24, and C23 will make a good basic kit.

Before pyrographing your design, practice, test out the nibs on a piece of wood, and choose the one that is best suited to your work.

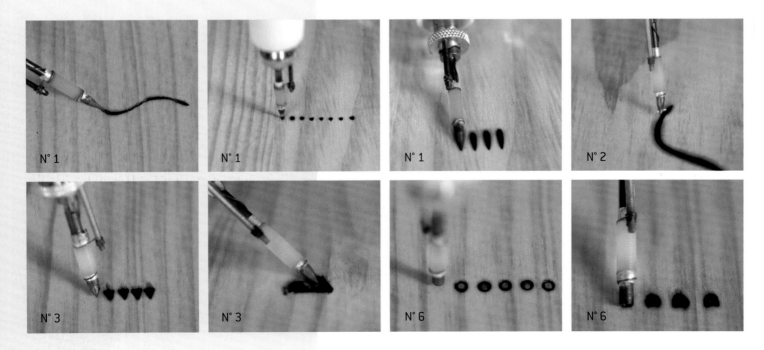

N° 1 N° 1 N° 1 N° 2

N° 3 N° 3 N° 6 N° 6

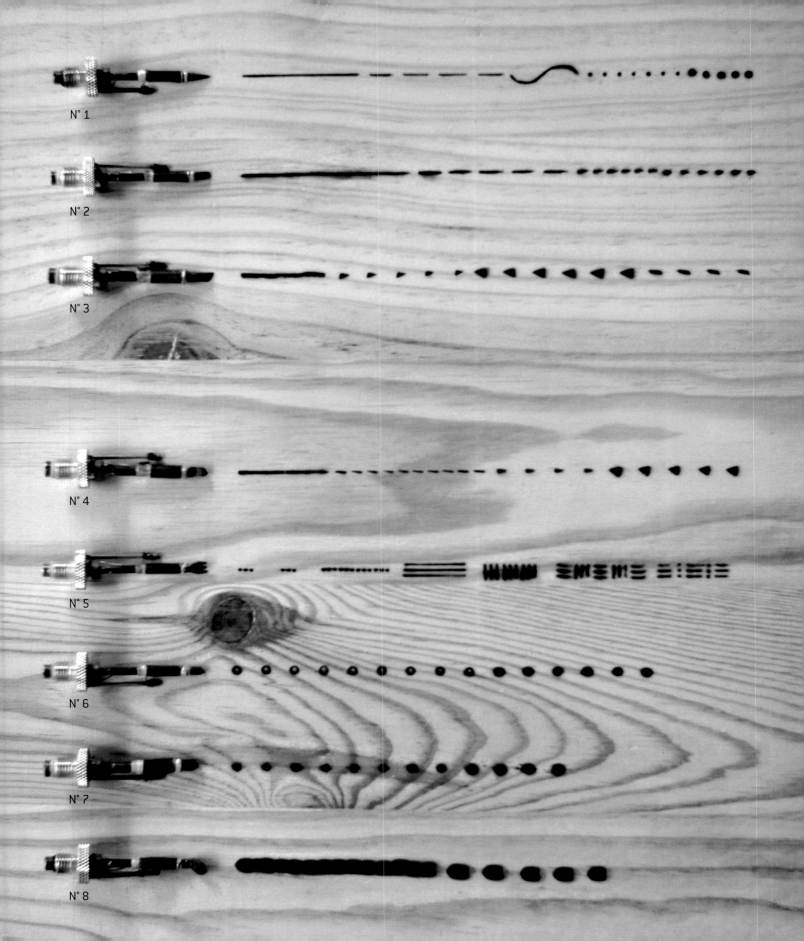

N° 1

N° 2

N° 3

N° 4

N° 5

N° 6

N° 7

N° 8

How to use a pyrography machine...

The pyrography machine is an electric tool composed of a pen with which to burn different shapes on wood. When heated, the nibs leave a burn mark in the wood (or other material to be pyrographed). The softer the wood, the easier it is to pyrograph it; the harder it is, the more complicated the job. The first few times you use it, we would recommend that you pyrograph objects made of pine.

Proceed in stages

When you have the hang of the pyrography machine, you could work pieces in oak or beech. Do not get bogged down trying to reproduce designs that are too complicated at first; some traced outlines demand a fairly great degree of precision which you will probably not have acquired in the beginning but which you will master quite quickly.

Good equipment

Invest in a reasonably priced pyrography machine and buy it preferably in a craft or DIY store. You will thus be spared the disappointment of a sale object that no longer works or a poor-quality pyrography machine which will not take other nibs, for example. Once you have bought it, read the accompanying instructions carefully; they will be very useful to you and will help you avoid damaging your machine or burning yourself. It is usually recommended that the temperature be at the lowest setting when you use it for the first time as well as before disconnecting it. Depending on the type of machine you are using, it will be fitted with a control button going from − to +, or from 6 to 12 V, and the temperature should be regulated according to the hardness of the wood. Basically, the softer the wood, the lower the temperature will need to be; the same goes for fabrics. On the other hand, if you are working with oak or beech the temperature should be set to the highest.

Before you start working screw on a nib, squeezing tightly, then turn the machine on.

Safety tips...

When changing nibs, always cut off the electricity supply and wait for the machine to cool down completely. Screw in a new nib and turn the pyrography machine on again. You can wrap the machine's pen in a piece of cloth or similar insulating material to avoid burning your fingers. If pyrographing with children, take all necessary safety precautions, and do not leave the machine unattended.

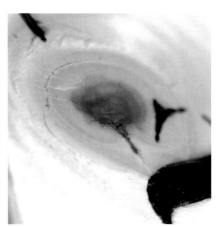

Transfer: techniques

Selecting and preparing pictures

Before your start choose a good-quality photograph, engraving, or drawing with sufficient contrasts. If you wish to lighten or darken your images, make them sepia colored, turn them black and white, play about with the contrasts, or correct small flaws such as red eyes or undesirable blemishes, modify these with a photocopying machine—or, better, with a computer which has a scanner, software with which to retouch photographs, and a printer. Once the picture has been corrected, you can either enlarge or reduce it according to the desired size of the transfer.

How to use transfers

You can produce transfers at home up to A4 format ($11^3/_4$ x $8^1/_4$ in [29.7 x 21 cm]) using special transfer paper on which you will print your photograph using a photocopying machine or a computer with a printer. To avoid wasting paper, group several small images together on the same sheet. For the larger A3 format ($16^1/_2$ x $11^3/_4$ in [42 x 29.7 cm]), photocopying stores produce transfers on cloth from your photographs. All you have to do is provide the picture and your chosen fabric. The present book suggests 2 kinds of transfer: on fabric and on objects. Depending on which you choose, different types of transfer paper are available (see

below). You will find them in hypermarkets, craft stores, paper stores, and specialist stores.

Transfers on fabric

You can transfer pictures onto natural fabrics such as cotton, silk, woolens, or linen, but it is best to avoid synthetic fabrics. Depending on your chosen fabric and the effect desired, it is recommended throughout this book that you use transfer paper suitable for light or dark fabrics. There are two kinds of papers for light-colored fabric: one calls for the printing of the photograph on the wrong side (mirror image), and the other does not. Both papers are of the same quality. The paper on which the printing is done on the right side is simpler to use, but sometimes less easy to get hold of.

A

EQUIPMENT FOR TRANSFERS ON FABRIC
- Transfer paper for fabric
- Photocopying machine or computer with a scanner and printer
- Ironing board and iron
- Fabric
- Fine scissors

- **Before you start**

If your fabric is new, machine-wash it before you apply the transfer. Make the transfer and iron it on the same day.

- **Transfers on light-colored fabric, on the wrong side**

1• Choose and prepare your picture (see the previous page), and then print or photocopy it on the wrong side (mirror image) of the white side of the transfer paper. Let the ink dry thoroughly.

2• Cut out the picture, leaving a border of ¹/₄ in (5 mm) all round.

3• Iron your piece of fabric and lay it flat on a rigid support that is itself covered in fabric (like an ironing board). Place the printed image directly on the right side of the fabric.

4• Preheat the iron (take care not to use steam) and iron the transfer paper all over for 1 to 3 minutes, in circular movements and pressing down well. Don't forget to iron the borders and the

angles, especially if the design has an uneven shape.

5• Let the paper cool a little, then remove the protective paper, starting with a corner and pulling gently but constantly on it.

6• To remove any excess ink from the fabric, place some wax paper on the freshly applied design. Iron once again following step 4. Let cool for a few minutes before removing the wax paper.

- **Transfers on light-colored fabric, on the right side**

1• Choose and prepare your picture (see the previous page), and then print it on the right side of the white side of the transfer paper. Let the ink dry thoroughly.

2• Cut out the picture with a border, or without a border depending on the fineness and quality of the design.

3• Iron your piece of fabric and lay it flat on a rigid support that is itself

covered in fabric (like an ironing board). Remove the protective sheet that is situated behind the transfer paper and place the wrong side of the printed image on the right side of the fabric.

4• Preheat the iron (take care not to use steam), lay the protective wax paper on the transfer paper, then iron all over for 1 to 3 minutes, in circular movements and pressing down well. Don't forget to iron the borders and the angles, especially if the design has an uneven shape.

5• Let it cool for a few minutes, then remove the protective wax paper, starting with a corner and pulling gently but constantly on it. Do not throw away the wax paper, it can be used again.

Tip

If you do not cut out the outline of the image and leave a transparent background, the fabric will appear plastified.

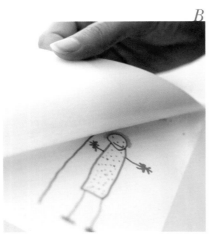

B

C

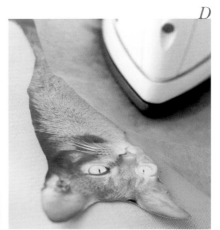

D

• Transfers on dark-colored fabric

The procedure is exactly the same as for an impression on the right side of light-colored fabric (see the previous page). Remember, though, that if you leave a border round the picture, it will appear white on the fabric. It is better to cut out the picture without a border.

• Care of transfers on fabric

Do not wash the fabric with the transfer for 24 hours after making the transfer. When you come to wash it for the first time, it is recommended that you machine-wash it separately, at 40° at most, turning it inside out. Dry-cleaning is not advisable, nor is the application of bleach. Do not dry it in a tumble-dryer but let it dry in the open air. Finally, never iron the printed image directly but iron the fabric on the wrong side.

Transfers on objects

You can transfer images onto wooden or metal objects with a flat surface, thanks to special outdoor adhesive paper which is water, sunlight, and stain resistant.

1 • Choose and prepare your picture (see before), and then print it on the right side of the white side of the transfer paper. Let the ink dry thoroughly.

2 • Cut out the picture, leaving no borders.

3 • Remove the protective paper behind the transfer paper and arrange the picture carefully on the previously cleaned object.

4 • Fix the image well, pressing gently with a dry cloth.

5 • To protect your transfer you can cover it with 1 or 2 thin layers of matt, satin, or brilliant acrylic varnish, applied with a paintbrush.

EQUIPMENT FOR TRANSFERS ON OBJECTS

• Special outdoor adhesive paper
• Photocopying machine with a scanner and printer
• Metal or wood object
• Fine scissors

A small lesson in knots

In the following instructions, the term "working end" designates the end of the thread that is free, and "dormant" that part of the thread that is attached to the work. The working end is shown in red in the illustrations.

Overhand or thumb knot

1• Make a loop by placing the working end on the dormant end.
2• Pass the working end through the loop, from back to front.
3• Tighten the knot by pulling both ends of the cord at the same time.

Half knot with two strands

Repeat the same operation as for the overhand knot, but this time use 2 parallel lengths.

Split knot

1• Make a flange, then make a double loop with the end of this.
2• Afterward make an overhand knot, keeping the cords parallel.

True lover's knot

1• Make an overhand knot with a cord.
2• Pass another cord through the overhand knot, from back to front.
3• Make an overhand knot with the second cord and leave it open.
4• Tighten the knot by pulling both cords simultaneously.

Figure-of-eight or Flemish knot

1• Make a flange, then make a loop by passing the working end behind the dormant end.
2• Pass the loop you have made in the previous step back on itself, from bottom to top.

3• Bring the working end over the dormant end, then slide it into the loop, from back to front.
4• Tighten the knot by pulling both ends of the cord simultaneously.

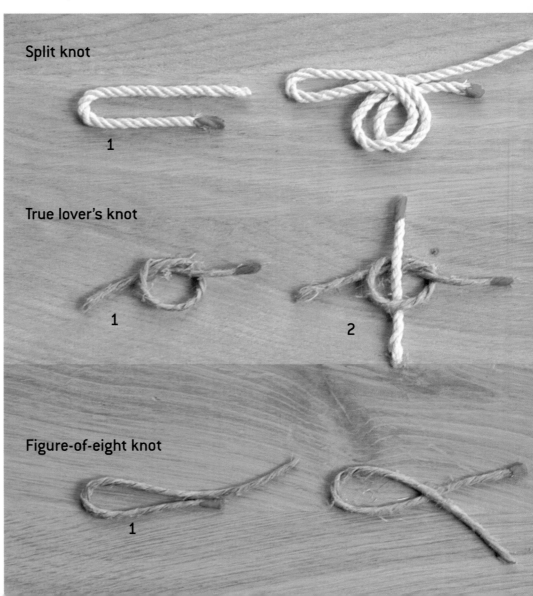

Split knot

1

True lover's knot

1

2

Figure-of-eight knot

1

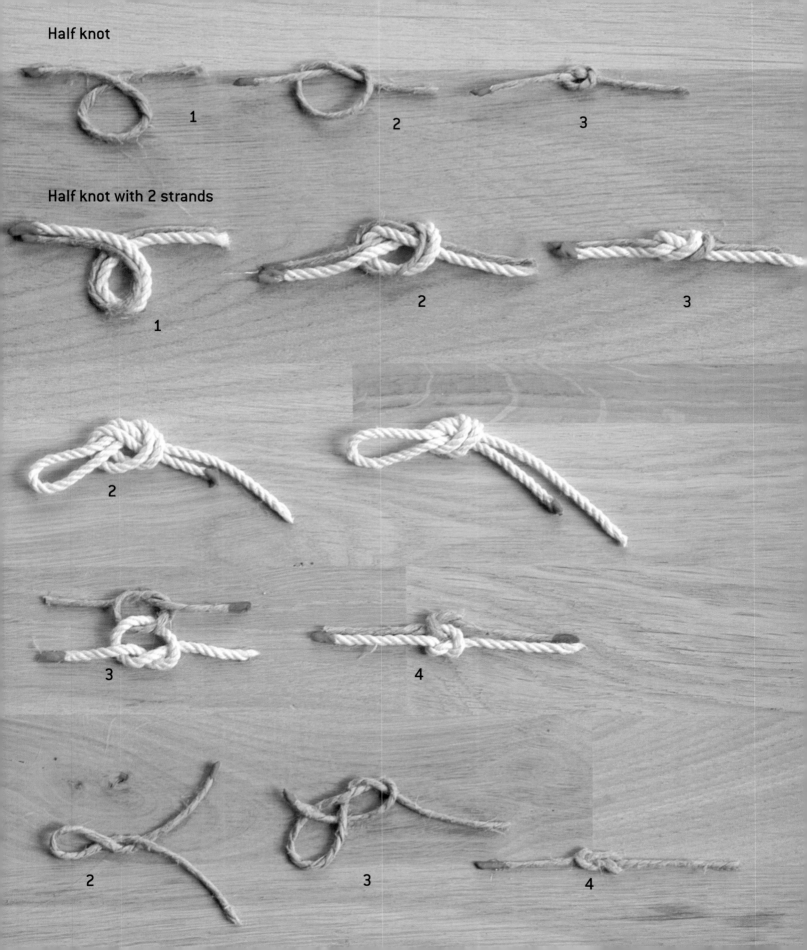

Half knot

1
2
3

Half knot with 2 strands

1
2
3

2

2

3
4

2
3
4

Pebbles in all their guises

There are many techniques used to create pebble projects in this book. Some are very straightforward, others call for greater dexterity. Here are a few tips to help you obtain the best results.

Glueing

There are many high-performance glues available nowadays. Products with 2 components (see page 214) are frequently the most effective, particularly when working on glass where quick adherence is necessary; they are, however, more difficult to work with than the classic glues. Each of the projects here gives the recommended glue in the list of supplies. In every case, though, it is worthwhile to test them out for compatibility, because the chemical nature of pebbles is very variable.

Always begin by carefully cleaning the sections you propose to glue, either with water or nail polish remover, and take care to handle objects and pebbles with gloves or very clean hands so as not to transmit any grease—most importantly not on glass.

Set yourself up with a suitable work surface for this activity and have within reach something with which to secure your work firmly until it dries (masking tape, jam jars, elastic bands...).

Last but not least, read the instructions carefully!

How to make a hole in a pebble

To make a hole in a pebble, use a power drill and a carbide drill bit. If you use an ordinary drill and a concrete drill bit the risk of breaking the pebble is much greater; if you do use one, take care not to run it at full speed.

In all cases, the best procedure is to put the pebble on the ground, between your feet, on an old carpet or a sand bed, in order to absorb the vibrations.

To engrave a pebble

To engrave a pebble, use a drill for classic glass and make a few drilling tests. Some pebbles lend themselves better to engraving than others; go for the flat, smooth, and rather dark ones.

To varnish and waterproof a pebble

Some pebbles are porous and can stain or absorb fats and liquids. In that case, it is advisable to apply a waterproof coating, or a product that is at once waterproof and oil repellent, which will also prevent any fats from penetrating the pebble. Varnishing enables you to give a satin or brilliant finish to a pebble, and to protect any inscriptions on it.

To write on a pebble

To write on a pebble, use some thin felt-tipped pens suitable for gouache. Let dry thoroughly and varnish the pebble, if you wish, especially if it is likely to be rubbed.

How to use clear epoxy resin

This product has to be mixed. It is clear and is very versatile: use a soft mold (such as a plastic food container). There too, read the instructions carefully.

To build up a covering of pebbles

You will find this technique very useful in your creative work. You are in effect producing a kind of mosaic with wallpaper paste, cement, mortar, or tile joints. The procedure is virtually the same as that for glueing mosaic or china. A waterproof product will make it easy to work the joints afterward.

Seeds: techniques and tools

The techniques used in this book do not pose any difficulties. Here are a few tips, nevertheless, to help you obtain the best results.

To make a hole in a seed

To make a hole in a small seed, lay it on a plank of wood and hold it steady with small pincers, without crushing it. Use a small hand drill, lighter than a classic drill.

Larger seeds (entada seeds, for example) can be laid flat on the plank of wood and carefully held steady by hand.

To paint and varnish a seed

Seeds happily take all kinds of paint and varnish. Always apply the latter in the same direction, and do not stray from this. Smaller seeds can be glued together and onto a surface (a frame, or balls) with matt varnish, which you should apply before dusting the seeds.

To thread a seed

For smaller seeds use an ordinary sewing needle and linen thread. For larger seeds (shea, entada, Hymenea courbaril) make a staple that is longer than the seed with wire, wedge the cord through it, across the seed, and pull in the opposite direction using small pincers.

To glue a seed

Glue guns are usually refilled from the back. The glue comes in small sticks. Every time you press the trigger a small stick heats up to 356 °F (180 °C) and makes the glue liquid as it comes out. Always handle this tool carefully to avoid burning yourself. You can also use superglue, especially for attaching the final knot in a fringe, and wallpaper paste, for objects made out of papier mâché.

Note finally that small wooden cocktail picks are very useful for taking hold of the smallest seeds one by one. All you have to do is to glue the end of the small stick and to lay it on the seed.

Trimming

The light (see page 226) is trimmed by circling it with seeds and passing these between the fastenings or fringes.

Candles

If you are using gel, keep the water simmering so you have a product that is always liquid when you are working. Let the first base layer harden before you add the seeds.

Epoxy resin

This product should be mixed with a hardening agent, which will be sold in the same department of the store. Blow gently on the bubbles which will form on the surface so they disappear.

Strips of plaster

The instructions for use on the packaging usually recommend that these be soaked. To work on the projects in this book, dampen each new layer, then spread the plaster with your fingers. To cover beans easily, cut the strips into squares.

Shea

Hevea

Khat

Seed husks

Hymenea courbaril

Entada

Calabash

Raffia

Drying techniques

There are several different techniques for drying flowers and leaves you have collected. Be advised that some of your finds may be difficult to keep because of their large size or because of other features they have. Even when dried, plants continue to evolve in time and the colors they sported when picked will not be lasting. Botanical objects could be highly useful to you; the texture of a plant, its perfume, coloring, and age give important information. For example, if you pick a flower at the beginning of its flowering period, before it is pollinated, you will see how its colors change less after drying; the more scented it is, the more its colors will continue to evolve. Leaves with a texture that is hard to the touch and which are highly breakable (such as holly and oleander) will keep more easily and will lose little of their color. In all cases, whatever the plant may be, it should be dried as soon as possible to ensure the quality of its preservation.

Pressing

You can buy a readymade press commercially or make your own with two squares of wood 3/4 in (20 mm) thick and 20 in (50 cm) on the sides. Make holes in all four corners of them with a wood drill bit 1/2 in (12 mm) in diameter and secure them with 1/2 in (10 mm) screws, flat washers, and wing nuts (see the photograph opposite). Put some sheets of newspaper between your plants. You can also dry the plants you have picked between sheets of newspaper (do not use the glazed paper found in magazines) and press them under piles of books.

The leaves and flowers should be spread out flat. Take care not to lay several thicknesses of plant on top of each other. After two or three weeks the plants will have dried completely, during which time you should watch out for nasty surprises. Inspect the press regularly and aerate the plants frequently (every two or three days), changing the sheets of newspaper if necessary. This is to avoid mold from forming and parasites from appearing. Should this happen, throw away the infected leaves and flowers.

Other methods

To preserve flowers such as hydrangeas, lavender, and tea roses and flowering tree branches, hang them upside down and secure the base with an elastic band (the size of the stems reduces in a dark and aerated place). Within a few days, the plants will have dried and the stems will keep their strength. To make potpourri, tear off rose petals and let them dry on a wooden tray or in a flat basket. Stir or mix occasionally to aerate the petals.

Preservation

Dried plants should preferably be preserved in paper bags or brown wrapping paper, and stored away from the light and the damp. Leave the paper open to ensure a good circulation of air, label the bags, and note their contents. To limit the appearance of parasites, place strips soaked in insecticide and bits of cedar wood next to them.

Fashions
and **trends**

Floral bonnet

A bonnet finds a new lease of life with the addition of these floral buttons, created according to your taste...

SUPPLIES
- 1 green bonnet
- 1 large dark wooden button
- 7 (plastic and metal) fancy buttons in tones of green
- small ½ in (1.2 cm) metallic buttons
- Pearl cotton # 5 in dark green
- Thick green mottled wool
- Medium bluish mottled wool

EQUIPMENT
- Tapestry needle with blunt tip
- Embroidery needle

1• With a length of moss-green wool of about 32 in (80 cm) make a flower with 8 petals—that is to say, 8 loops gathered together in a central point kept secure by a few stitches of pearl cotton. *(A)*

2• With a tapestry needle, sew on the metallic buttons with blue-green wool. Space them out, leaving about 2½ to 4 in (6 to 10 cm) between them. In the same way, gather up the wool in loops, positioning the buttons at the end of each petal, then form 4 additional, large 2 in (5 cm) loops. Secure everything in a central point with a few stitches in pearl cotton.

3• Lay the blue-green flower at the center of the moss-green flower and sew them together with a few stitches in pearl cotton. *(B)* Sew the flower, with the buttoned part toward the bottom, beneath the sides of the bonnet's base.

4• Having carefully arranged the petals, sew the large wooden button at the center of the flower and add a little fancy button. *(C)*

5• On the sides of the bonnet, starting from the flower and moving toward the front, sew on a series of 6 fancy buttons, leaving more space between them at the beginning if necessary (if they overlap a bit because of the bonnet's elasticity).

A

B

C

Green embroidered decoration

An easy to create embroidery with a touch of improvisation in different shades of green.

1• Cut about 60 in (150 cm) ribbon and fold it in 2 to obtain 2 unequal lengths.

2• Pin the ribbon at the fold at the sweater's shoulder. Let the 2 lengths fall and make 1 or 2 light knots at different heights, then pin them without pulling on the sweater.

3• Pin the remaining length of ribbon (about 20 in [50 cm]) underneath the first one. Baste everything with large stitches, then remove the pins.

4• On this sweater the pistachio green thread will be embroidered in back stitch, the teal green in basting stitch (work from top to bottom in both cases), and the Color Variations thread in feather stitch (working from bottom to top to join the rows of light green).

5• Do not tie a knot at the beginning of each stitch; push the needle in on the wrong side of the fabric, leaving a short length of thread, then take it out a little farther down, at your chosen starting point. *(A)*

6• Following the photograph, embroider curved lines on the left-hand side of the sweater, occasionally taking in the ribbons at the top and occasionally at the bottom, to secure them.

7• When you have finished a row, push in the thread in the wrong side of the fabric and slide it into the stitches. Do the same with the starting threads which remain on the right side of the fabric, having pulled them through to the wrong side. *(B)* On the rows in teal green, make a knot on the right side of the fabric before cutting the thread ³/₄ or 1¹/₄ in (2 or 3 cm) farther down.

8• Let the remaining ribbon strands hang down the sweater and cut them in different lengths on the slant. Take out the basting threads. If any lengths of ribbon remain hanging, leave them as they are or add a few embroidery stitches.

9• Ensure that the starting point of the small length of ribbon is well concealed and secured by the embroidery. If it is not, sew it or embroider on top. Do not iron!

SUPPLIES

• DMC cotton thread, 1 skein each in the following colors: Pistachio Green 164, Deep Teal Green 3847, and Color Variations 4050
• Bias-binding or soft ribbon in a color to match the sweater, ⅝ in (14 mm) wide, 80 in (200 cm)
• Thin green sweater

EQUIPMENT

• Embroidery and sewing needles
• Pins
• Tape measure
• Thimble
• Scissors

STITCHES USED

• Back stitch
• Basting stitch
• Feather stitch

A

B

Felt bucket bag

An elegant felt shopping bag in two shades is decorated with a flower in matching colors.

1• Enlarge the pattern for the main part of the shopping bag (see page 112), reproduce it on a sheet of paper, and cut it out. Using this template, trace the outline of each piece on the white felt in textile felt-tipped pen, then repeat the process on the green felt. Cut the 8 pieces.

2• Reproduce and cut out the background, then the handle, in the same way in the white and green felt (see page 112).

3• Overlay the identical pieces of white and green felt and baste them with large stitches.

4• After making a central hole, machine-stitch the 4 pieces that make up the outside of the bag, border to border and wrong side to wrong side.

5• Sew the rest of the shopping bag in the same way.

6• Pin the handle on both sides of the shopping bag by placing it astride the central seam. (A) Machine-stitch it afterward in order to backstitch it.

7• Cut 2 strips of felt ³/₄ x 12 in (2 x 30 cm) in each shade to make the flower.

8• Overlay the strips of felt. Fold them toward the center to make the petals' 6 loops, the green color toward the outside. Secure the petals with a few stitches to make the flower. (B)

9• Sew the flower onto the front of the shopping bag.

SUPPLIES
• White and pistachio green felt, ¹/₁₆ in (2 mm) thick:
– Front and back: 4 pieces in each color, 10 x 16 in (25 x 41 cm) each
– Handle: 2 pieces in each color, 1³/₄ x 15 in (4.5 x 38 cm) each
– Background: 2 pieces in each color, 4 x 8 in (10 x 20 cm) each
– Flower: 2 pieces in each color, 1 x 14 in (2.5 x 36 cm) each
• Sewing thread in white

EQUIPMENT
• Textile felt-tipped pen
• White paper
• Dressmaking scissors
• Sewing needle
• Pins
• Sewing machine

A

B

Flower pins

Here are two clever ideas for flower pins that can be fastened on a jacket, on the rim of a hat, or on the handle of a purse.

SUPPLIES

- 10 sheets embossed white paper
- 1 tube silver glass beads
- Sewing thread in white
- 2 squares cream-colored felt (2½ x 2½ in [6 x 6 cm] and 2 x 2 in [5 x 5 cm])
- 1 pin clasp to sew on
- Paste
- 1 diamond-effect rectangular sheet to sew on
- 12 iridescent glass beads

EQUIPMENT

- Embroidery needle for sewing on the beads, sewing needle no. 9
- Paintbrush no. 12
- Thimble, scissors, felt

White flower

1 • With an embroidery needle, stitch 5 silver glass beads on the ridge of each of the sheets of paper, spacing them out evenly.

2 • Trace and cut out the circle, using the pattern on page 113, on the 2½ in (6 x 6 cm) felt square. Sew the pin's clasp in the center of the circle with a no. 9 needle. Glue the sheets of paper onto the felt circle, opposite the pin. *(A and B)* Let dry.

3 • Sew the diamond-effect rectangular sheet onto the 2 x 2 in (5 x 5 cm) felt square. Embroider the iridescent glass beads all round.

4 • Cut off the excess felt. Glue the central part of the flower and let dry. Sew on the clasp. *(C)*

Note

The clasp can be replaced by a clip.

SUPPLIES

- Fuchsia-colored nonwoven fabric, 12 in (30 cm)
- Lilac nonwoven fabric, 12 in (30 cm)
- Fuchsia-colored felt
- 1 pin clasp
- 1 tube iridescent Plexiglas pink beads
- Sewing thread in fuchsia
- Paste

EQUIPMENT

- Sewing needle no. 9
- Paintbrush no. 12
- Scissors, felt

Fuchsia flower

1 • Trace and cut out 7 circles of fuchsia-colored and lilac nonwoven fabric (see patterns on page 113). Overlay them, alternating the 2 colors. *(A)*

2 • Using the pattern, trace and cut out 7 circles of fuchsia-colored felt. Sew the pin's clasp to 1 of these. Place the latter in the center of the nonwoven fabric circles and embroider the Plexiglas™ beads in such a manner as to create a pearly flower center. *(B)* Glue the felt circle with the clasp on the back of the flower. Let dry.

3 • Cut a fringed border with scissors in the nonwoven fabric. Crumple the flower with your hands in order to give it volume.

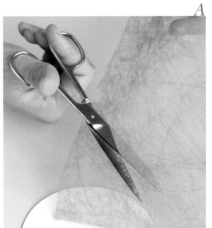

A

B

Note

The clasp can be replaced by a clip.

Button jacket

A khaki linen jacket is covered in odd buttons and fabric circles which create a trompe-l'oeil effect!

1 • With a compass trace 4 circles on the Bristol paper: 2¹/₂ in (6 cm), 2 in (5 cm), 1¹/₄ in (3 cm), and 1 in (2.5 cm). Cut out the circles.

2 • With a textile felt-tipped pen, draw the outlines of the 2¹/₂ in (6 cm) and 2 in (5 cm) circles on the wrong side of the fabric pieces, then cut out the 8 circles.

3 • To make the yo-yos, draw points all round the fabric circles, ¹/₄ in (5 mm) from the edge. *(A)* In the center of the wrong side of a 2¹/₂ in (6 cm) fabric circle place a 1¹/₄ in (3 cm) outline of Bristol paper, and in the center of a 2 in (5 cm) circle place an outline of 1 in (2.5 cm). Pull on both ends of the thread on each circle; the excess fabric will tighten in a central point. *(B)* Flatten with the iron, then remove the Bristol paper outlines. Proceed in the same way for the other 6 fabric circles.

4 • With small running stitches, sew the yo-yos (gathers at the bottom) onto the jacket by arranging them as you like, without forgetting the sleeves. Embroider a large cross stitch in yellow-green metallic thread in the center of the fabric yo-yos to suggest buttons.

5 • Afterward sew the buttons onto the jacket. The most basic buttons are sewn on with mottled red metallic thread by inserting the needle in the wrong side in a button-hole and drawing it out on the right side, outside the button itself, at the starting point (see page 112). Sew the star button on in the same way. Sew the other buttons on normally with sewing thread.

Note

Attach the buttons and yo-yos to the buttoned-up jacket to show your personalized effects better!

(see page 112)

A

B

SUPPLIES
- About 15 buttons in a range of colors that go with the jacket: a mixture of fancy buttons (with a flower design, with spots, fabric effect) and old recycled buttons
- 3 pieces of printed fabric (in colors that go with the jacket)
- Cool cotton mottled red metallic embroidery thread
- Cool cotton mottled yellow-green metallic embroidery thread
- Sewing thread in a color similar to that of the jacket

EQUIPMENT
- Dressmaking scissors
- Tape measure
- Textile felt-tipped pen
- Bristol paper
- Compass
- Iron
- Embroidery needle, pins

Violet-colored mohair scarf

Put this on your shoulders. As light as a feather, it will warm up all your outfits gracefully, casual and more sophisticated alike.

To make the scarf

Make a very loose chain of 73 stitches (see page 15) + 1 stitch to turn. Crochet 1 row in single stitch, then 1 row in single ribbed stitch (see page 15). Continue in garter lace stitch (see the grid on page 113); repeat 6 basic rows 20 times, then crochet once from the 1st to the 5th row. *(A)* You will obtain a rectangle measuring about 16 x 40 in (40 x 100 cm).

Assembly

Assemble the 2 small sides of the rectangle by means of grafting (see page 19). *(B)* Insert the threads on the wrong side.

SUPPLIES

- 1 x 2 oz (50 g) ball very thin violet-colored mohair wool
- Crochet hook no. 4
- Wool needle, pair of scissors

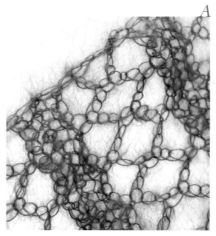

A

B

SUPPLIES
- 64 matching mother-of-pearl pink, red, and violet-colored buttons, 1 to ⅝ in (2.5 cm to 1.3 cm)
- Plum-colored taffeta, 28 x 20 in (70 x 50 cm)
- Woolen fabric, 16 x 16 in (40 x 40 cm)
- Spotted tulle, 16 x 4½ in (40 x 12 cm)
- Printed cotton fabric for the lining, 26 x 20 in (65 x 50 cm)
- Cheesecloth, 16 x 28 in (40 x 70 cm)
- Black, gray, and red felted wool braid, 200 in (5 m)
- 2-tone fuchsia-colored and violet-colored velvet chenille braid, 200 in (5 m)
- Sewing thread in red, plum and black

EQUIPMENT
- Brightly colored seed beads
- 2 leather purse handles
- Bristol paper
- Textile glue spray
- Textile felt-tipped pen
- Tape measure
- Dressmaking scissors
- Pearl needle, pins

Seventies purse

Chic and hippie at the same time, here is a patchwork-effect purse. A floral pin adds to its charm and overall feel.

Purse

1 • Enlarge the pattern for the main part of the purse (see page 114). Lay this model on the wrong side of the taffeta. Trace the outlines with textile felt-tipped pen. Find the seam instructions of the inner squares. Using these, now trace the inner checkerboard of the pattern onto the taffeta. Cut out the shape of the purse, leaving a border of ⅝ in (1.5 cm) all round for the seams.

2 • Draw a 3½ x 3½ in (9 x 9 cm) square on the Bristol paper and cut it out. Draw this cut-out model 6 times in textile felt-tipped pen on the woolen fabric; reproduce it 3 times on the tulle, and cut it evenly. Glue the wrong side of the squares obtained with glue spray and place them on the taffeta checkerboard with the help of the pattern on page 114.

3 • Cut a 9½ in (24 cm) length, a 17½ in (44 cm) length, and a 21¼ in (54 cm) length 4 times from each ball of wool; lay these lengths 2 by 2 on the rows of the checkerboard, crisscrossing them and letting them overlap by ¾ in (2 cm) at each end. *(A)* Pin the wool, then stitch their large sides in running stitch; the tulle and woolen fabric squares will thus be secured by the seam.

4 • Make up a batch of 8 well-mixed buttons (all of different sizes and colors). Sew these 8 buttons onto the empty squares, doubling the red thread. Insert the needle on the wrong side of the fabric and take it out through 1 of the button's holes, then thread 3 or 4 seed beads and insert your needle in the other hole. *(B)* Make a few stitches at the back of the purse, in order to stop the thread. Place the buttons evenly on their front and on their back, in order to vary the effect.

5 • Close the bottom of the purse by overlaying, right side to right side, the A and B guides, then the B and C ones on one side, and on the other side the D, E, and F guides (see the diagram on page 114). Pin these, then insert your needle ⅝ in (1.5 cm) from the edges, stopping the seam ⅝ in (1.5 cm) from the free sides.

A

B

6• Always working right side to right side, pin half of the 2 free sides of the purse (in fuchsia and green, and pink and blue on the drawing on page 114) and insert your needle ⅝ in (1.5 cm) from the edges.

7• Put the purse on the right side and fold the upper borders, wrong side to wrong side, all along. Pin these, taking care to include all the fabric and wool.

8• Draw the purse's pattern in the printed cotton and find the seam instructions once again. Cut out the shape of the purse, leaving a border of ⅝ in (1.5 cm) all round for the seams. Follow steps 5 and 6 once again to assemble the bottom of the lining all along, wrong side to wrong side.

9• Cut out 4 rectangles 1½ x 2½ in (4 x 6 cm) from the taffeta. Fold the perimeter of each by ½ in (1 cm), wrong side to wrong side. Fold them in 2, wrong side to wrong side, flattening the large sides 1 over the other to obtain ribbons of ½ x 2½ in (1 x 6 cm). Pin these, then secure with running stitch using plum-colored thread. Fold the ribbons in 2 and pin them on the edges of the purse, leaving an overhang of ½ in (1 cm). If the handles are not detachable, thread the ribbons through them, then fold them in a loop before pinning them onto the purse.

10• To finish, place the lining inside the embroidered bag, wrong side to wrong side, ensuring that their borders coincide. Pin the upper borders 1 over the other over the

entire perimeter of the purse and secure firmly with running stitch, particularly at the level of the handles.

Floral pin

1• Enlarge the petal pattern (see page 115) and cut it out. Draw this outline 5 times on the wrong side of the toile de Jouy fabric and 5 times on the patchwork fabric in textile felt-tipped pen. Cut out, leaving a border of ½ in (1cm) all round for the seams.

2• Working right side to right side, superimpose the toile de Jouy fabric petals and the patchwork fabric ones. Pin, then sew in backstitch, leaving a small opening. Turn over the petals, fill them with padding, and squeeze them together. Shut the opening with small running stitches.

SUPPLIES

- 5 white raised $5/8$ in (1.4 cm) buttons
- 8 white standard $1/2$ in (9 mm) buttons
- Mother-of-pearl carved buttons: 2 large, 1 in (2.7 cm) (1 mauve and 1 dusky pink); 3 medium size, $3/4$ in (2.3 cm) (1 red, 1 old rose, and 1 blue-gray); 1 small brown-gray button, $3/4$ in (2 cm); 4 iridescent fish eye buttons (blue, red, and lilac)
- Red toile de Jouy fabric, 14 x 4 in (35 x 10 cm)
- Special patchwork fabric with small red and cream-colored flowers, 14 x 4 in (35 x 10 cm)
- Fluorescent yellow, pink, and vermilion tulle, 16 ft (5 m) each
- $1/16$ in (1 mm) wide piece maroon felt
- White braid, $1/8$ in (3 mm) wide, 32 in (80 cm), and yellow braid, 8 in (20 cm)
- Red braid, $1/4$ in (5 mm) wide, 8 in (20 cm), and fluorescent pink, 10 in (25 cm)
- Wool oddments
- Sewing thread in red and white
- Synthetic padding
- Large safety pin, pins

EQUIPMENT

- Textile felt-tipped pen
- Dressmaking scissors
- Tape measure

3• Place the seam in the center of the petal. In matching thread, fold over 1 of the ends of the small white braid and sew it in basting stitch, straddling the seams, starting at 1 of the petals' tips.

4• Join the tips of the 5 petals in a central point and assemble them with small, firm stitches. Sew the white buttons (13 in all) onto the petals in an irregular pattern using red thread.

5• Cut a 6 x $1 1/4$ in (15 x 3 cm) strip out of each color of tulle. Sew a basting stitch on 1 of the large sides and pull on the thread to gather the tulle. Make the flower's center by placing the pink tulle in the middle, the vermilion tulle round, and finally the yellow tulle. Snip a bit with the scissors to make this center stand out, then sew it in the middle of the flower.

6• Stitch the braids and the strand of wool on the back of the flower. To separate them well, make a small stitch in the center of the flower's 2 lower petals.

7• Draw the outline of each corresponding mother-of-pearl button in textile felt-tipped pen on the maroon felt. Cut it out evenly. Insert the braid between a felt circle and a button and sew the latter *(A)*, using the positioning diagram (see page 115). For greater ease, the 2 holes of the buttons should be placed in the same direction as the ribbons. Sew the pin onto a safety pin.

A

Raffia brooch

This project marries natural materials and sparkling paste in a brooch you can casually pin onto your favorite outfits!

To make the brooch

Cut out 1 of the small sides of the fabric rectangle every half in (1 cm), then tear it in order to obtain 15 strips. Crochet as follows (see grids on page 115).

Heart. Roll a strand of raffia into a circle and crochet the 1st row (see page 18). Take up another strand of raffia, leaving about 4 in (10 cm) free at the edge, and crochet the 2nd row. *(A)*

Petals. Use 1 strip of fabric per petal. Crochet the 3rd row by inserting the hook underneath the strand that is behind the single stitches of the 2nd row. Crochet the 4th row by inserting the crochet hook underneath the strand before the single stitches of the 2nd row.

To finish off

Take all the strands (raffia and fabric) through to the wrong side with the crochet hook, then, with a chenille needle, insert the shorter ends. Sew the button onto the center of the heart. Fold the remaining 5 strips of fabric in 2, add a few strands of raffia, and tie everything up at the top with a strand of raffia. Sew this firmly onto the back of the flower. Working wrong side to wrong side, fold the perimeter of the circle of fabric by 1/4 in (5 mm). Secure the circle to the back of the flower with running stitch *(B)*, then sew the brooch back in the center. *(C)* Cut the strands of raffia and the fabric strips into irregular lengths.

Note

Natural raffia is sold in skeins of irregular strands. Choose a few that are long, without worrying too much about the difference in thickness, because this adds to the overall charm of the project.

SUPPLIES

• Natural raffia
• Thin cotton fabric, printed with a floral print on a natural background, a rectangle 6 x 40 in (15 x 100 cm) cut straight; a circle about 2 1/2 in (6 cm)
• Sewing thread in a natural color
• Paste button
• Brooch back
• Crochet hook no. 7
• Tape measure, chenille needle, sewing needle, pair of scissors
• Iron

A

B

C

Fun chain

An assortment of tulle and patchwork fancy buttons in acid colors makes for a very up-to-date piece of jewelry.

SUPPLIES

• About 20 x 2-tone fancy buttons in acid colors: e.g. shoe, motto, heart, etc.
• Patchwork fabric, white with red squares, 44 in (110 cm) wide, 4 in (10 cm); red fabric with white spots, 4 in (10 cm) to make the fabric beads + ³/₄ x 44 in (2 x 110 cm) for the cord
• Piece of fluorescent pink fabric
• Synthetic padding
• Pearl cotton # 5 in bright red
• Fluorescent pink rattail cord, 88 in (2.20 m)
• Sewing thread in red

EQUIPMENT

• Tape measure
• Dressmaking scissors
• Textile felt-tipped pen
• Bristol paper
• Compass
• Embroidery needle, sewing needle

1• Cut 44 in (1.10 m) of rattail cord. Make a ¹/₄ in (5 mm) hollow in the 2 large sides of the ³/₄ x 44 in (2 x 110 cm) red spotted fabric. Put the cord in the center, flatten the large sides, and close with running stitch. *(A)*

2• Sew 1 end of the covered cord onto the end of the other rattail cord, laying them side by side. Knot both cords every 10³/₄ in (27 cm). Join both ends and cut off any excess to equalize them. Secure by sewing.

3• Cut a 1 x ³/₄ in (2.5 x 2 cm) piece of spotted fabric. Fold over all round by ¹/₄ in (5 mm) to obtain a ⁵/₈ x ¹/₂ in (1.5 x 1 cm) rectangle. Roll this up, straddle it onto the join of the cord, and sew it.

4• On the Bristol paper, draw three 2 ¹/₂ and 1¹/₂ in (6.5 and 4 cm) circles which will serve as templates. Draw 2 small circles, 1 medium-size circle, and 1 large circle on the wrong side of the 2 patchwork fabrics and cut them out. Make a ¹/₄ in (5 mm) hollow round the fabric circles and secure with basting stitch. Pull to gather the borders together and pad the inside to form a pearl. *(B)* Pull the threads and secure them with a few stitches.

5• Cut three ³/₄ x 8 in (2 x 20 cm) strips and two 1¹/₄ in x 8 in (3 x 20 cm) strips from the pink tulle. Make a basting stitch in the middle of the strips and pull on the threads to gather them. Secure each "pompon" with a few stitches.

6• Beginning 5¹/₂ in (14 cm) from the join of the cords, sew alternately buttons, fabric pearls, and tulle pompons with pearl cotton, spacing them out between ³/₄ and 1¹/₂ in (2 and 4 cm). *(C)*

A

B

C

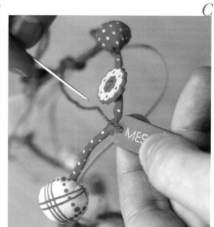

• Pearl cotton # 5, 1 skein black 310
• DMC metallic thread, 1 skein each of copper (Light Effects E301) and gold (Light Effects E3852) and 2 skeins silver (Light Effects E168)
• Copper wire and silver-plated copper wire $1/16$ in (1 mm) in diameter (80 in [200 cm] each reel)
• 8 rings brass wire, $5/8$ in (15 mm) in diameter
• 3 rings zinc-coated steel, $5/8$ in (18 mm) in diameter
• 8 brass wire nuts, $3/8$ in (7 mm) in diameter
• Round sequins, $1/4$ in (6 mm) in diameter (about 160 gold and 90 silver)
• Square sequins, $1/4$ in (5 mm) (30 gold and 30 matt silver)
• 500 tiny steel seed beads
• 8 medium-size iridescent copper seed beads
• 6 in (15 cm) black braid
• 1 matching button
• Thick linen, 36 x 12 in (90 x 30 cm)
• Flat cutting pliers

EQUIPMENT
• Embroidery frame
• Embroidery needles
• Pearl needle
• Sewing thread in black and linen
• Sewing machine
• Pins
• Tape measure
• Thimble
• Scissors
• Water-soluble felt-tipped pen
• Ruler

Stitches used, see page 74
Plan, page 116

Metallic belt and moneybag

Nuts, metallic thread, and a host of clever ideas for this highly fashionable belt or moneybag!

To make the belt and moneybag

1• Following the plan, draw 6 parallel threads along the fabric, 2 in the middle, spaced out at $2^3/4$ in (7 cm) intervals, then 2 at the top and 2 at the bottom, spaced out at $1^1/4$ in (3.5 cm) intervals.

2• Draw 4 threads widthwise: 2 at 32 in (80 cm) and 2 others 1 in (2.5 cm) farther down.

3• In this $2^3/4$ x 32 in (7 x 80 cm) rectangle, build up the vertical lines of each sequence. With the felt-tipped pen, draw the horizontal lines of sequences 4 and 7 as well as the Vs in the sequences 6 (see page 116).

Embroidery
Following the guide, embroider the sequences in pairs from 1 to 7.

1• Feather stitch (silver on the left and copper on the right), then round gold sequins for both.

2• Copper wire on the left, silver-plated copper wire on the right. Roll up the threads in a double spiral with the pliers. Sew them on with the black pearl cotton in couching and embroider all round in basting stitch.

3• Sew on 4 brass wire rings with straight stitch black pearl cotton and place an iridescent copper bead in the center. *(A)*

4• Alternate the 2 colors of square sequins, then secure them with a steel bead. Embroider round in black pearl cotton in chain stitch.

5• Proceed as with sequence no. 2 but with a simple spiral: silver-plated copper wire with silver-plated wire and

A

B

silver thread on the left and copper wire with copper thread on the right. Sew 4 nuts with black pearl cotton. *(B)*

6• Sew the small V in gold thread and the large V in silver thread on the left in satin stitch and the opposite on the right. Surround with steel beads. *(C, following page)*

7• Add a few rows of gold sequins on the left and silver sequins on the right (plan 1), separated by rows of feather stitch in black pearl cotton. Add rings of zinc-coated steel sewn in black pearl cotton.

To assemble the belt
(see plans 2 to 4)

1• Remove the basting thread, then cut the fabric on the pulled outer threads.

2• Fold the black braid in 2 and insert your needle (2). Fold the 1 in (2.5 cm) hem on the wrong side (3), then fold on the middle pulled thread and iron this fold. Then fold on the pulled threads level with the embroidery and crush these folds with your finger.

3• On the wrong side of the fabric, sew the 2 middle folds and the 2 elevations at each end with invisible stitching. Sew on the button. Insert your needle in the braid every ³/₄ in (2 cm) to obtain possible adjustments. *(D)*

Note
You can change the length of the belt by omitting or adding sequences or by varying their lengths as well as the length of the braiding.

- Pearl cotton # 5, 1 skein black 310
- DMC metallic thread, 1 skein gold (Light Effects E3852)
- 20 in (50 cm) brass wire, $\frac{1}{16}$ in (1 mm) in diameter
- 1 x ring zinc-coated steel, $\frac{5}{8}$ in (18 mm) in diameter
- Tiny steel seed beads (about 200)
- 1 x zip fastener, 6 in (15 cm)
- Fairly thick linen, 8 x 16 in (20 x 40 cm)
- Thin fabric for the lining, 8 x 16 in (20 x 40 cm)
- Flat pliers and cutting pliers

EQUIPMENT
- Embroidery frame
- Needles (embroidery, pearl, and sewing)
- Basting thread
- Sewing thread in black and linen and sewing machine
- Pins
- Measuring tape
- Thimble
- Scissors
- Compass

STITCHES USED
- Straight stitch
- Feather stitch
- Basting stitch
- Chain stitch
- Satin stitch
- Sewing on beads
- Placing sequins in a row
- Couching

Guide, page 116

C

D

Round moneybag

Embroidery

1• Using the compass, draw 2 circles $4\frac{1}{4}$ in (11 cm) in diameter on the wrong side of the linen.

2• Place the zinc-coated steel ring in the center of a circle, on the right side of the fabric, and secure it with straight stitch, using black pearl cotton.

3• Sew 2 rounds of sequins, close together, all round in black sewing thread (see page 116).

4• Embroider in feather stitch, using black pearl cotton, $\frac{1}{2}$ in (1 cm) from the edge. Sew 3 beads on the end of each "frond."

5• Make a closed spiral with the brass wire, using the flat pliers to help you. Adjust it in the place between the feather stitch and the sequins. Secure it with the 6 strands of the gold thread or in couching.

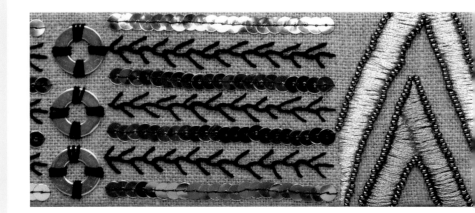

To assemble the moneybag

1• Cut the 2 linen circles ½ in (1 cm) outside the basted stitches, then remove these. Stitch the zip fastener on the outline of each, then open it.

2• Place the circles, right side to right side, and insert your needle in the remaining outline to close the moneybag. Turn the moneybag over delicately so it is once again on the right side so as not spoil the embroidery. Make a lining in the same size, slide it inside the moneybag, and stitch it by hand so it is level with the zip fastener.

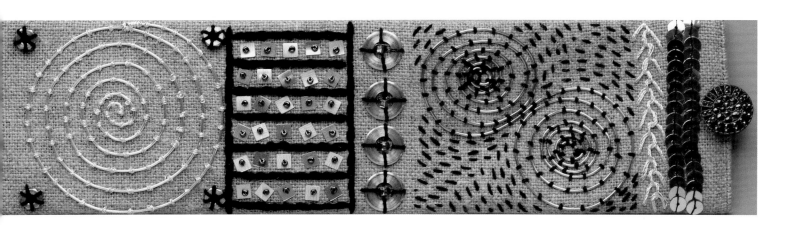

Beads and drawer knobs

Wooden beads and drawer knobs are pyrographed with floral and geometric designs. They can decorate your wrist or the simplest of drawers.

SUPPLIES
• Drawer knobs in beech or pine
• Tracing paper
• Unpolished wooden beads in different sizes

EQUIPMENT
• Pencil
• Pyrography machine
• No. 22 and C23 nibs
• Paintbrush

Drawer knobs

1• Reproduce the floral designs on page 115 in tracing paper on the drawer knobs.

2• With a no. 22 nib, draw the outline of the flowers.

3• Darken the inside or outside of the shapes by pressing firmly.

Beads

1• Thread a bead onto the handle of a paintbrush and keep it steady by pushing it in thoroughly.

2• No. 1 beads: with a no. 22 nib, make small holes in the bead in concentric circles, first on one side, then on the other.

3• No. 2 beads: still using the no. 22 nib, draw petals on top of the bead by bending the handle of the pyrography machine as far as possible to leave a burned trace in the shape of a drop. *(A)* With the same nib, draw small regular strokes or spots all round the bead. *(B)*

4• No. 3 beads: draw flowers on the beads following the previous step, but placing them on the periphery and not close to the holes.

5• No. 4 and no. 5 beads: using a no. C23 nib, draw small circles over all the beads or on the periphery, depending on the beads.

A

B

SUPPLIES

- An assortment of 27 mother-of-pearl and fancy standard buttons, between $^1/_2$ and $^5/_8$ in (1 and 1.5 cm): 5 in various shades of red, 10 in various shades of orange, 12 in various shades of plum
- 1 fancy button, $^3/_4$ in (2 cm), for the flower's heart
- Blue velvet, 16 x 28 in (40 x 70 cm)
- Liberty print fabric, 28 x 44 in (70 x 110 cm)
- Cheesecloth, 16 x 28 in (40 x 70 cm)
- Felt, $^1/_{16}$ in (1 mm) thick, maroon, 4 x 12 in (10 x 30 cm); orange, $4^1/_2$ x 14 in (12 x 36 cm); plum, 6 x $17^1/_2$ in (15 x 45 cm)
- Synthetic flannel: 16 x 28 in (40 x 70 cm)
- 1 stud
- Basting thread
- Sewing thread in blue and red

EQUIPMENT

- Textile glue spray
- Cellulose acetate
- Textile felt-tipped pen
- Dressmaking scissors
- Tape measure
- Sewing machine
- Iron
- Pins

Pouch with flower

With its velvet background edged in Liberty print fabric, this pouch will enclose your most precious secrets.

1• Enlarge the 2 patterns of the pouch (see page 118) and cut them out. Using the glue spray, apply glue to the cheesecloth and stick it on the wrong side of the velvet in order to work the latter more easily.

2• Draw the outline of the patterns on the wrong side of the velvet with textile felt-tipped pen. Cut each piece, leaving a border of $^1/_2$ in (1 cm) all round for the seams. Baste large stitches on the large piece of velvet, following the drawing.

3• Draw the outline of the patterns on the wrong side of the Liberty print fabric and the flannel. Cut each piece, leaving a border of $^1/_2$ in (1 cm) all round for the seams.

4• Cut a 2 in x 14 ft (5 x 430 cm) strip widthwise in the Liberty print fabric. For this, join the strips from 1 end to the other, by the small sides, on the right side of the fabric, by flattening the large sides 1 against the other in such a way as to obtain a ribbon 1 x 14 ft (2.5 x 430 cm) in size. Press the iron over the fold. Also with the iron, make small flat, even folds all along the ribbon. Pin these as you go, then stitch $^1/_4$ in (5 mm) from the edges to secure them.

5• Following the line of basting, pin the gathered ribbon on the right side of the large piece of velvet, taking care to align the edges well. Stitch $^1/_2$ in (1 cm) from the border.

6• Lay the large piece of Liberty print fabric on top and the flannel on the back, right side to right side, and pin. Stitch all round, at $^1/_2$ in (1 cm) from the border, leaving an opening of about 4 in (10 cm). Remove the basting thread, cut at $^1/_4$ in (5 mm)

A

B

C

from the seam, then turn over. Close the opening with running stitch.

7• Overlay the small pieces of velvet and Liberty print fabric (for the pocket), right side to right side, place the flannel on the back, and pin. Stitch all round, leaving an opening once again. Cut at ¼ in (5 mm) from the seam, then turn. Close the opening with running stitch.

8• Pin the small piece of lined velvet (the pocket) to the lower part of the large piece, Liberty print fabric to Liberty print fabric. Join them together by sewing the sides and the lower border in firm running stitches.

9• Using the guide on page 118, fold over the upper part of the pouch to make a flap so the pouch measures 11 x 8½ in (28 x 22 cm).

To make the button flower

1• Reproduce the patterns of the 3 flowers on the cellulose acetate (see page 119), then cut them out. Draw an A shape 3 times on the maroon felt with textile felt-tipped pen. Sew the 5 red buttons with red thread onto the rounded shape of the petals of 1 of the flowers. Glue 1 side of the other 2 flowers and overlay them successively, placing the button flower on top. Repeat this process with the orange felt and a B shape, then with the plum felt and a C shape. Sew the 10 orange buttons with red thread onto 1 of the 3 orange flowers, and the 12 plum-colored buttons on 1 of the 3 plum-colored flowers. (A) If neces-

sary, trim the outline of the flowers.

2• Afterward overlay the 3 flowers, placing the largest one on top and the smallest one on the bottom. Assemble them by sewing in the middle. (B)

3• Sew the flower through all its thicknesses on the flap, at 1½ in (4 cm)

from the edge, with the large fancy button placed in the center of the flower. (C)

4• Sew the stud onto the center of the pouch 1¾ in (4.5 cm) from the edge of the opening. Sew the other part of the stud so it is face to face underneath the flap.

Openwork sandals

Here are some entirely crocheted sandals, inspired by espadrilles and black lace openwork shoes.

To make the shoes

Work with 4 linen and viscose yarns. Make a chain of 24 stitches with crochet hook no. 7 (see page 15) + 1 stitch to turn. Cont with crochet hook no. 5, and crochet in a ring on both sides of the chain in single ribbed stitch (see page 15 and grids on page 118). Make 3 right shoes and 3 left shoes.

To make the shoe vamps

With crochet hook no. 2 and pearl cotton make a chain of 17 stitches + 1 stitch to turn. Crochet 2 rows in single stitch, 34 rows of hoops, the 35th row, then 2 rows in single stitch (see grid on page 118). Crochet a picot edging (see page 18) on each of the large sides (see grid on page 118). Make a 2nd identical vamp.

To assemble the shoes

Bring the yarn through to the wrong side. Reproduce the shape of a crocheted shoe on cardboard or plastic.

Make a 2nd drawing ¼ in (7 mm) inside the first one and cut it out. Cut out 3 further identical shapes. Overlay the 2 crocheted right sandals, slide a shape between them, then assemble them in sections, where you have overcast (see page 118), by sewing with linen and viscose yarn. Place your foot on the right side of the remaining crocheted right sandal. Put a shoe vamp in place and adjust it by folding the small sides under the shoe (it is preferable that this is a little tight because it will loosen when it is worn). Secure the small sides where you have overcast with pearl cotton. *(A)* Place the whole thing on the 2 assembled shoes by inserting a shape, then sew up the sections as previously. *(B)* Make the left shoe in the same way.

Note

The explanations correspond to a European size 38 shoe (American size 7.5), but the width of the shoe vamp can be adjusted when you come to assemble it.

Tips

When you are crocheting these shoes, slip some strands of wool between the increases in the rounded parts to help you find your way. As the work is very dense, take care to take up the 4 threads at every stitch.

A

B

SUPPLIES

• DMC metallic thread, 1 skein each in the following colors: Aquamarine Blue E3849, Lime Pearlescent E966, and Golden Dawn E135

• 12 different-size seashells

• 6 small seashell pendants

• 8¹/₂ ft (260 cm) sky-blue ribbon

• Bright turquoise fabric (shown here is moiré) 34 x 16 in (85 x 40 cm)

• Fabric for the lining, 21¹/₄ x 11 in (53 x 28 cm)

EQUIPMENT

• Embroidery hoop or frame
• Sewing needle
• Sewing thread in turquoise
• Sewing machine
• Pins
• Carbon paper for fabric
• Measuring tape
• Thimble
• Scissors
• Pencil   • Ruler
• Mini-drill

STITCHES USED

• Couching
• Straight stitch

Guide and design page 120

Seashell purse

Seashells adorn this pretty purse with iridescent stitches, creating a pearly effect worthy of a pouch in which to keep all your treasures.

Embroidery

1• Draw a rectangle measuring 28 x 10 in (70 x 25 cm) on the wrong side of the turquoise fabric. Following the guide, draw the fold at the bottom of the purse EF, then the AB, CD, and GH lines. Baste the lines you have drawn.

2• Trace the design on carbon paper on the right side of a CDFE square. Check its position in the square.

3• Fit the fabric into the embroidery frame and embroider the lines in Couching in the colors indicated. Use all 6 strands of the metallic thread on the fabric, and 2 strands of the same color for the stitching. *(A)*

4• Make 2 or 3 small holes in the seashells. Arrange them on the embroidery as shown in the photograph, and secure them with several satin stitches (made working from the outside to the inside of the seashell) with 2 strands of metallic thread of your choice. *(B)* Do not stitch the small seashell pendants yet.

5• Take the work out of the hoop or frame. Cut the 28 x 10 in (70 x 25 cm) fabric to ⁵/₈ in (1.5 cm).

To make the purse

1• Fold the rectangle right side to right side on the bottom fold and pin, letting the D, B, A, and C points coincide. Stitch the sides on the tracings, leaving an opening of 1 in (2.5 cm) on each of them, between D and H on 1 side and between C and G on the other side.

2• Open up these seams with your fingernail and cut them at an angle at the bottom of the purse.

A

B

C

3• Round each 1 in (2.5 cm) opening, stitch ⅛ or ¼ in (3 or 4 mm) on the opened-out seams.

4• Fold the top of the purse on the AB lines, then stitch 2 in (5 cm) lower down (on the CD lines) all round the purse. Make a last insertion of your needle 1 in (2.5 cm) farther up (the spotted area on the guide) just above the openings to create the hem.

5• Take out the basting stitches. Sew the seashell pendants along the edges of the embroidery, on the seams.

To finish off

1• Fold the fabric rectangle for the lining in 2, right side to right side. Stitch the sides ⅝ in (1.5 cm) from the edges, open up the seams, then fold ⅝ in (1.5 cm) at the top, on the side of the seams. Insert the lining in the purse and secure it by making small stitches on the CD seam.

2• Cut the sky-blue ribbon into 2 equal 52 in (130 cm) lengths. Slide 1 ribbon in the hem using a safety pin so it goes all the way through. Slide the other ribbon in, starting from the opposite opening. Tie the ends. Pull the ribbons on each side to close the purse. *(C)*

Lily brooch

Wear this spectacular and elegant flower with spirit as a jacket decoration!

1• Wind up the strands of green wool in your hands lengthwise with warm soapy water to create the stem. Make a thicker bulge on 1 of the ends to create the flower's heart.

2• On the foam support, overlay a few crossed layers of green wool to make a rough leaf shape. Then stitch the wool with the needle to flatten it (that is, needle-felt it without using water) and shape it (see page 24).

3• Once the leaf is done, join it to the stem with a felting needle.

4• Wet-felt a piece of white wool (see page 22) and, once it is dry, cut out the shape of the lily's corolla (see pattern on page 119).

5• Felt the edges once again in your hands using warm soapy water (to dry-cut them would give a stiffer, less effective result).

6• Wind up the white corolla you have obtained at the top of the green stem. Pinch it at the bottom to finish shaping the flower, and insert a felting needle to join the edges of the lily to the bottom to keep its shape, and to secure it to the stem. *(A)*

Extra idea...

Use 2 shades of green merino wool to animate the flower's stem and the leaf.

SUPPLIES
• Green (5 g) and white (10 g) merino wool

EQUIPMENT
• Towel
• Bubble wrap
• Synthetic tulle
• Soap
• Sponge
• Felting needle with a large point
• Foam support
• Dressmaking scissors

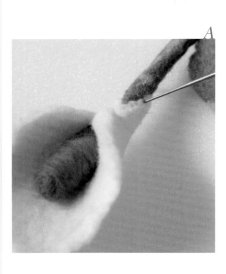

A

Embroidered hat decoration

Using various shades of thread and in different colors, this embroidery project is made entirely in French knot. It makes a beautiful camouflage in the countryside, and gives a spectacular, luminous effect in the city.

SUPPLIES
• DMC cotton thread, 3 skeins in each of the following colors: 4040, 4050, 4060, and 4070
• DMC matt twisted thread, 2 skeins in each of the following colors: 2142, 2495, 2715; and 1 skein of 2144
• Linen or wool beret

EQUIPMENT
• Embroidery needles with large and medium eyes
• Sewing thread and needle
• Air-erasable textile felt-tipped pen (optional) or pins
• Sewing machine (optional)
• Thimble
• Scissors

STITCH USED
• French knot

Before you begin
If your beret is made of wool and is unlined, you can embroider directly on it. If it is made of linen and is lined, however, you will have to unpick the edges and remove the lining.

1• Depending on what your beret is made of, draw the areas to be embroidered in air-erasable felt-tipped pen or mark them out with pins. Baste the outline of these areas before the felt-tipped pen marks are erased (or take out the pins before you start embroidering).

2• Cover the areas to be embroidered with French knot, making up a harmonious variation of shades by using different-colored threads and single-color matt twisted threads. You do not have to use all the colors for each area.

3• The size of French knot will vary depending on the number of threads used and will intensify the shaded effect; start by embroidering 1 end of the area by using 2 matt twisted threads and ordinary sewing threads (use 6 strands twice for the latter). Continue with just 1 thread of each kind (that is to say, 6 strands for the ordinary sewing thread).

4• When you start embroidering an area in a particular color, make stitches that are close together, then gradually space them out more, in order to place stitches in the following color. This will create the shaded effect. Continue in this way until you have covered a given area completely.

5• Once you have finished embroidering, replace the lining inside the beret as necessary and machine-stitch the edges all round the beret.

Note
Change needle size depending on the number of threads used.

Cake apron

If you melt at the sight of a small cake or cream puff, this good enough to eat apron is for you: it enables you to cook without putting on weight!

To make the transfers
Enlarge the cake pictures and reproduce them on transfer paper. Cut them out without a surrounding border.

To make the apron
1• Draw the apron and pocket patterns (see page 121) on the cross-ruled pattern paper to enlarge them and reproduce them on the back of both pieces of linen. Cut out each piece on the drawing (the 1/2 in [1 cm] seams are not included).

2• Cut two 2³/₄ x 20 in (7 x 50 cm) strips in each color of linen. Join the natural linen strips to the pink ones, right side against right side. Stitch lengthwise and widthwise once every 1/2 in (1 cm). Turn the strips over and iron.

3• Pin the ends of each strip on the top of the natural linen apron piece, right side to right side, at ⁵/₈ in (1.5 cm) from each angle (see guide on page 121).

4• Join the 2 pieces of the apron together right side to right side and stitch 1/2 in (1 cm) from the edge, leaving an 8 in (20 cm) opening at the bottom.

5• Remove the pins, notch the rounded parts, then turn the apron over and iron. Close the opening with invisible stitches, then insert your needle and make a straight stitch 1/2 in (1 cm) from the edge over the entire periphery of the apron.

6• Join the 2 pockets right side to right side and stitch the sides and the rounded part, leaving the top open.

A

B

Notch the rounded parts, turn the apron over so it is on the right side once again, and iron.

7● Mark out a ¹/₂ (1 cm) hollow (toward the inside) above the pocket and sew it in invisible stitches. Sew the pocket onto the apron with invisible stitches.

8● Place the transfers in position (see page 39): the large plate on the front of the apron, the chocolate cream puff on the pocket, the small plates at the end of the ties and on the back (see guide on page 121).

9● With the thermo-swelling paint, draw the outline of the cream on the cream puff. Let dry for 24 hours, then iron on the wrong side to make the painting swell up. *(A)*

10● To close the apron behind, stitch on some studs 2¹/₂ in (6 cm) apart (see guide on page 121). *(B)*

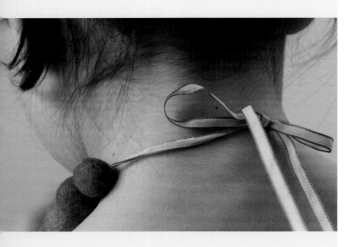

Hot pink bead necklace

A series of small balls of red, pink, and maroon felt, a small matching leaf, a pretty ribbon...and the necklace is made!

SUPPLIES

- Merino wool in different shades of red, maroon, fuchsia, and old rose (1½ oz [40 g] in total)
- Blue-gray ribbon with raspberry-colored border, ¼ in (5 mm) wide, 34 in (85 cm)

EQUIPMENT

- Soap
- Large wool needle
- Pliers
- Felting needle with a medium point
- Foam support

1• To make each ball, take a small amount of merino wool in your chosen color and roll it in the palm of your hand with warm soapy water for 15 minutes. Repeat the process for each bead, varying the colors to create a pretty effect of different shades of red.

2• Finish all the balls and let dry.

3• Thread the ribbon into the wool needle and insert it in each ball. Use pliers to get a better grip on the needle and to be able to "thread" the felted wool beads. *(A)*

4. On the foam support, make 2 leaves by piercing a mixture of scarlet and pink wool with the felting needle (see page 24).

5• Afterward stitch the 2 leaves together, place them between 2 balls, knot them by crossing 1 over the other, and sew up everything with the felting needle. *(B)*

6• Tie an attractive bow in the ribbon to close the necklace.

A

B

Leaf purses

Very simple but stylish purses suitable for a walk in the woods.

SUPPLIES
- Color photocopies of enlarged dried leaves, A4 format
- Textile transfer paper, A4 format
- Thick white cotton
- Cotton thread in white
- White grosgrain ribbon, 1¼ in (3 cm) wide

EQUIPMENT
- Computer, scanner, and color printer
- Scissors and dressmaking scissors
- Tape measure
- Iron
- Pins
- Sewing machine

1• Scan your photocopy and print the design on a piece of textile transfer paper.

2• For the purse shown in the foreground in the photograph, cut out with scissors level with the printed designs.

3• Remove the protective layer and lay the printed side of the design on top of a piece of cotton larger than the A4 leaf (add ½ in [10 mm] for the left border, the right border, and the bottom, and 1¼ in [30 mm] for the upper border). *(A)*

4• Set your iron to the highest temperature and select the steam option. Place the protective sheet with the transfer paper between the design to be printed and the iron. Iron all over the design, pressing down firmly and avoiding backward and forward movements. Let the fabric cool and gently remove the protective sheet. *(B and C)*

5• In the cotton fabric, cut out a rectangle of the same size as that on which you have transferred your design and oversew the circumference of both pieces of fabric.

6• Join the pieces of fabric together, right side to the right side, by machine-stitching ½ or ⅝ in (11 or 12 mm) from the edges on the 2 large sides and the bottom of the purse.

7• Turn the purse over, make a 1¼ in (30 mm) hollow on the upper border, and pin. Cut two 12 in (30 cm) lengths in the grosgrain ribbon for the handles and pin to the inside of the purse as shown on page 120.

8• Stitch both thicknesses of fabric and the grosgrain ribbon together ¼ in (5 mm) from the upper edge.

A

B

C

A bouquet of flower decorations

Each one more alluring than the other, here are flowers to decorate or trim hats, purses, jackets, and other fashion or home accessories!

Flowers

1• Lay a towel on the table and a piece of bubble wrap on top. On top of these lay some strands of wool to make a piece 4½ x 4½ in or 4 x 4 in (12 x 12 cm or 10 x 10 cm). Build up 4 layers by crossing the direction of each of these (they should always be perpendicular in relation to the others).

2• Cover with the tulle, then moisten with warm soapy water (see page 22).

3• Lay another piece of bubble wrap on top and rub with the sponge for 20 minutes.

4• Roll up the whole thing—towel, bubble wrap, and wool—both ways for 10 minutes, then remove the felted wool and flatten it to the required size. Let dry.

5• Cut out a circle in the wool with scissors.

6• Also with scissors, cut out the flower's petals *(A)*, removing any excess felt. *(B)*

7• Rub for a further 5 minutes between your hands with warm soapy water to equalize the petals.

8• Rinse the flower in fresh water.

9• Make the center of the flower by rolling up a strand of wool on itself until it forms a ball. Soak it in warm soapy water, take it out, and roll it firmly in your hands until the center is formed. Let dry.

10• Place the ball in the center of the flower and sew it in place with the large felting needle until it holds well below and on the sides.

SUPPLIES
• White (10 g) and green (5 g) merino wool

EQUIPMENT
• Towel
• Bubble wrap
• Synthetic tulle
• Soap
• Sponge
• Felting needle with a large point
• Foam support
• Dressmaking scissors

A

B

Extra idea...
Add a few uneven green strands of wool on the final layer of the white flower to animate the petals.

Lime-green flowers

1• Cut out a star (see pattern on page 113) in felt with a cutter. *(A)*

2• Fold each petal toward the inside and sew them onto the center with a few stitches. *(B)*

3• Finally, sew a mother-of-pearl button in the middle of the flower to create the center and to hide the stitching of the petals. *(C)*

SUPPLIES
• Lime-green felt, $\frac{1}{16}$ in (2 mm) thick
• White mother-of-pearl buttons, ø $\frac{5}{8}$ in (14 mm)
• Sewing thread in pale lime-green

EQUIPMENT
• Cutter
• Sewing needle

A

B

C

String bag

A ribbon string bag lined with blue taffeta will be the ideal companion for an afternoon's shopping, and would also be suitable for formal occasions.

To make the string bag

Roll up the yarn in a ring, then crochet a medallion (see pages 18 and 122).

Background. Croch the 1st row to the 6th row: you will obt 36 sc.

Main part. Croch the 7th row (you will obt 36 rings of 4 ch each), then the 8th row.

9th to 13th row: as the 8th row.

14th to 17th row: as the 8th row but with 3 sl st at the beg, and rings of 5 ch.

18th to 36th row: as the 14th row but with rings of 6 ch.

Borders. [1 sl st in each of the 3 first ch, 1 ch, 1 sc] in the first ring of the 36th row, *[2 ch, 1 sc in each of the foll 9 rings = 28 sts. Croch 6 rows in ribbed st (see page 15) on these 28 sts. Cut the yarn*. Pass 8 rings, 1 sl st in the foll ring, rep once from * to *.

Handles. 1st row: work as the grid = 92 sts.

Cont as follows; at each row, beg with 1 ch, and end with 1 sl st in the first sc of the row.

2nd and 5th rows: 92 sc.

3rd row: 4 sc, *pass 1 sc, 6 sc*, rep 3 times from * to *, 12 sc, °pass 1 sc, 5 sc°, rep 5 times from ° to °, pass 1 sc, 11 sc = 81 sc.

4th row: 3 sc, *pass 1 sc, 4 sc*, rep 4 times from * to *, 11 sc, °pass 1 sc, 5 sc°, rep 4 times from ° to °, pass 1 sc, 11 sc = 70 sc.

6th row: 1 sc, *2 sc in 1 sc, 4 sc*, rep 3 times from * to *, 2 sc in 1 sc, 12 sc, rep 5 times from * to *, 2 sc in 1 sc, 10 sc = 81 sc.

7th row: 4 sc, *2 sc in 1 sc, 5 sc*, rep 3 times from * to *, 11 sc, °2 sc in 1 sc, 4 sc°, rep 5 times from ° to°, 2 sc in 1 sc, 11 sc = 92 sc. Croch the 2nd handle in the same way.

To finish off

Pull the yarn through to the wrong side. Sew the small taffeta sides together with a French seam (see page 122). Insert a double thread of gathers ¼ in (5 mm) from the upper edge to adjust the perimeter of the fabric so it is the same as the bag. Insert the fabric in the bag. Align the gathered edge underneath the 3rd row of the edges and stitch them in running stitch. Fold the first 3 rows of the edges over the fabric, and stitch them in running stitch (see sketch 1 on page 122). Fold the handles in 2, then stitch them at the bottom onto the fabric in running stitch and close them (see sketch 2 on page 122). Gather the bottom of the fabric ½ or ¾ in (1 or 2 cm) from the edge, then sew it onto the center of the crocheted background. Wrong side to wrong side, fold over the perimeter of the fabric circle so it is the same size as the crocheted background. Baste this hollow, then sew the circle at the bottom of the bag in running stitch.

Supplies

- Brightly colored ornamental buttons in old rose, 6 of ⁵/₈ in (1.5 cm) and 6 of ¹/₂ in (1.2 cm)
- Matt floral buttons, in pale pink, 2 of ⁵/₈ in (1.5 cm) and 2 of ¹/₂ in (1.2 cm)
- Patchwork fabric, white with small pink flowers, 44 in (110 cm) wide, 4 in (10 cm)
- White satin ribbon with pink spots, ¹/₂ in (1 cm) wide, 28 in (70 cm) (A)
- White woven ribbon with red spots, ¹/₄ in (5 mm) wide, 24 in (60 cm) (B)
- White woven ribbon with pink spots, ¹/₄ in (5 mm) wide, 24 in (60 cm) (C)
- Pink woven ribbon with white spots, ¹/₄ in (5 mm) wide, 32 in (80 cm) (D)
- Pearl cotton # 5 in pale pink
- Sewing thread in pink

Equipment

- Textile glue spray
- Neoprene glue
- Dressmaking scissors
- Tape measure
- Textile felt-tipped pen
- Sewing needle and embroidery needle

Floral decorations for summer pumps

Ribbon and button decorations go well on this pair of summer pumps, but would work equally well on slippers.

1• Cut the following lengths at an angle in the ribbon to make 2 large and 4 small flowers. Large flower: 3 times 2¹/₂ in (6 cm) in the A ribbon, 2 times 2¹/₂ in (6 cm) in the B and C ribbons. Small flower: 2 times 1¹/₄ in (3.5 cm) in the A ribbon and 2 times 1¹/₄ in (3.5 cm) in the B and C ribbons.

2• Arrange the ribbon pieces in a star shape and secure them with a few stitches in the center. *(A)*

3• In the center of the 6 flowers, sew the 6 large ornamental buttons with pearl cotton. *(B)* Sew the remaining buttons in pearl cotton as a trompe-l'oeil effect (see page 21).

4• Apply a little Neoprene™ glue to the back of the matt buttons and the ribbon flowers and stick them onto each pump as shown in the photograph; each shoe should have 1 large and 2 small ribbon flowers, 3 small ornamental buttons, 1 large flower button, and 2 small flower buttons. *(C)*

5• Cut the D ribbon in 2 and sew it in running stitch along the edge of each pump.

6• Remove the soles from both pumps and draw their outline with textile felt-tipped pen on the wrong side of the patchwork fabric. Cut the outline evenly. Using the glue spray, attach these fabric shapes and place the soles inside the pumps.

A

B

C

Milky Way

On this purse you can make a comet from a CD, some foil, a few sequins, and beads, and be transported to another galaxy.

SUPPLIES
- DMC pearl cotton # 5, 1 skein green 907
- CD 4¹/₂ in (12 cm) in diameter
- 4 silver sequins with holes (1 at 1¹/₄ in [35 mm] in diameter and 3 smaller ones)
- Silver straw beads
- Foil
- Khaki purse with flap

EQUIPMENT
- Embroidery needle
- Sewing needle and sewing thread (in gray and red)
- Pins
- Tape measure
- Thimble
- Scissors
- Water-soluble felt-tipped pen

STITCHES USED
- Buttonhole stitch
- French knot

Diagrams 1 to 5, page 122

1• Place the CD on the flap of the purse. Sew it on with large stitches, from the central hole toward the edges, using the red sewing thread. You will afterward remove this basting. *(A)*

2• With just one 48 in (120 cm) piece of green pearl cotton, make 6 very long, taut satin stitches about 4¹/₄ in (10.5 cm) in the flap of the purse, level with the edges of the CD (diagram 1, page 122). Mark out the places where you should insert the pearl cotton with pins.

3• Embroider round the CD with green pearl cotton in buttonhole stitch. *(B)* Use the taut green threads for this; as you stitch they will loosen and form the embroidered circle which will hold the CD. The needle should be inserted in the fabric so it is level with the CD and be taken out ¹/₁₆ in (1 mm) farther down (diagrams 2 and 3, page 122). Keep the same tension for stitches of equal height. Embroider the hollowed-out center of the CD in French knot.

4• Sew the sequins onto the purse. Embroider them, following the technique of the CD, starting with a 6-point thread star (diagram 4). Adjust the size of the buttonhole stitch here.

5• Draw lines in erasable felt-tipped pen to represent the comet's tail and sew the straw beads on top with gray thread (diagram 5).

6• Tear off different-size pieces of foil and roll these up tightly into balls. Flatten them slightly and sew them on in gray sewing thread in radiating stitches, always working from the outside toward the center. *(C)*

A

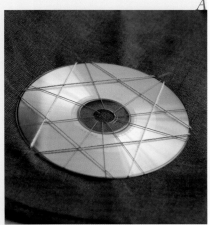

B

C

Propeller hat

For little rascals everywhere, an amusing hat decorated with a knotted helix, the top of which seems to go into a spin.

SUPPLIES

• Light mauve felt, ¹/₁₆ in (2 mm) thick, 4 pieces measuring 6 x 12¹/₃ in (15 x 31 cm)
• Purple felt, ¹/₁₆ in (2 mm) thick, 4 pieces measuring 6 x 12¹/₃ in (15 x 31 cm) and 1 measuring 8 x 4 in (20 x 10 cm) for the helix
• Sewing thread in light mauve

EQUIPMENT

• Dressmaking scissors
• Cutter
• Paper
• Ballpoint pen
• Pins
• Sewing needle
• Sewing machine

1• Measure the circumference of the child's head. Divide this number by 4; it will correspond to the exact dimensions of the base of the hat.

2• Reproduce the pattern of 1 side of the hat and the half-helix (see page 123) and cut these out. Using this as a model, draw 4 times in ballpoint pen on the hat design on the mauve felt, adding ¹/₄ in (4 mm) on the large sides for the seams. Cut out the 4 sides of the hat. Repeat the process with the purple felt.

3• Overlay the 2 colors of felt for each of the hat's sides, mauve on top, and pin. Machine-stitch the 4 sides of the hat, ¹/₄ in (4 mm) from the edges, by piercing the 4 thicknesses together. *(A)*

4• To shape the top of the hat, pinch and flatten the right-side edge on itself at the top of a side, ¹/₂ in (1 cm) wide and about ³/₄ in (2 cm) in height. Keep this pinched shape by sewing it up with a few stitches. Repeat the process for the other 3 points of the hat.

5• Using the double helix model, draw the design in ballpoint pen 2 times on the last piece of purple felt. Cut the 2 half-helixes and slit 1 of them in the center with the cutter. Put the other through the slit *(B)*, then tie them together to finish the helix. *(C)* Sew the center of the helix onto the hat.

A

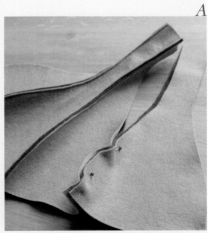

B

C

Giraffe decoration

Giraffes are always popular with small children and this design, reproduced on a baby outfit, is no exception.

Transfer

1• Photograph or photocopy a giraffe toy of your choice. Reproduce it to the desired scale on the transfer paper and cut out the image with or without a border, depending on the type of paper used.

2• Transfer the design (see page 38) onto the front of the outfit, centering it well.

To finish off the outfit

1• Embroider a detail on the photograph— the eyes, for example— in black in satin stitch (see page 13), with in the center a white stitch embroidered in satin stitch. Thread 2 strands of sewing cotton in different shades (here 2 shades of gray) and embroider in satin stitch (see page 13) 6- to 8-point different-size stars

on the front and cuffs of the outfit. *(A)*

2• Remove the original ribbon from the outfit and cut it so it is level. Cut the colored ribbon in 2. Mark out a double hollow of ¼ in (5 mm) on one end of each piece of ribbon before sewing them together. *(B)*

SUPPLIES
• Cotton thread in light gray, medium gray, black, and white
• Ribbon, 16 in (40 cm), in gray that resembles the photograph, ⅜ in (7 mm) wide
• Embroidery needles and sewing needles

EQUIPMENT
• Photograph of child's toy
• Transfer paper for light fabric
• Iron
• Scissors
• White baby's outfit with ribbons

A

B

Mauve slippers

A romantic pair of slippers created as if by magic with two colors of felt and a very simple pattern!

1• Reproduce the pattern of the soles (see page 123), and draw this in textile felt-tipped pen on each piece of white felt. Cut out the soles with the cutter.

2• On each piece of mauve felt, reproduce and draw 2 times the pattern of half the slipper (see page 123). Cut these out with the cutter. *(A)*

3• Pin and machine-stitch together the front and back of each slipper, edge to edge, wrong side to wrong side, ¼ in (4 mm) from the edges.

4• Pin the underneath of the slippers onto the soles, wrong side to wrong side, *(B)* then sew them together in blanket stitch with the double-threaded embroidery thread.

SUPPLIES
• Mauve felt, ¹/₁₆ in (2 mm) thick, 2 rectangles measuring 14 x 8¹/₂ in (35 x 22 cm)
• White felt, ¼ in (5 mm) thick, 2 rectangles measuring 8 x 4 in (20 x 10 cm)
• Sewing thread in mauve
• Embroidery pearl cotton in mauve

EQUIPMENT
• Textile felt-tipped pen or ballpoint pen
• Cutter
• Pins
• Sewing needle
• Sewing machine

A

B

SUPPLIES

• Check cotton in colors that match the drawing
• Assorted sewing threads
• Sewing machine and sewing needle
• Rattail cord in lime-green, 48 in (120 cm), and orange, 8 in (20 cm)
• Satin ribbon in pink, fuchsia, and lime-green, $^1/_{16}$ in (2 mm) wide: 8 in (20 cm)
• 2 large pink beads
• 1 heart-shape mother-of-pearl button

EQUIPMENT

• Child's drawings
• Transfer paper for light fabric
• Iron
• Scissors
• White cotton

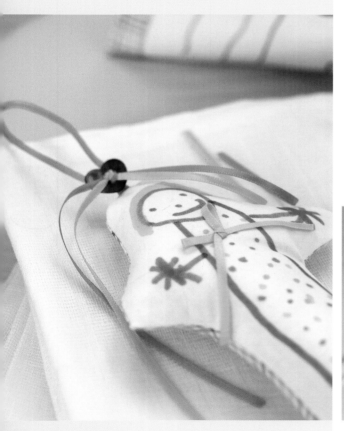

Doll and purse transfers

On this purse that will hold many treasures and this good-luck doll, a child's drawings take pride of place.

Transfer for the purse

1• Reproduce the drawing at the bottom of the transfer paper, leaving a $^3/_4$ in (2 cm) margin on the sides and bottom of the drawing.

2• Transfer the entire sheet of transfer paper (A4) onto white cotton (see page 38).

Transfer for the doll

1• Reproduce the drawing of a character about 6 in (15 cm) in size on the transfer paper.

2• Cut out the drawing, leaving a 2 in (5 cm) margin all round, and transfer it onto white cotton.

To make the purse

1• Cut out the transferred fabric to A4 format, then cut a 12 x 12 in (30 x 30 cm) rectangle from the check fabric.

A

2• Join the check fabric and the transferred fabric together height-wise, right side to right side, and stitch $^1/_2$ in (1 cm) from the edge. Flatten the tube thus obtained, centering the transferred fabric, and stitch the bottom of the purse $^1/_2$ in (1 cm) from the edge (see diagram 1, page 114). Turn the purse over.

3• Cut two $2^1/_2$ x $10^1/_4$ in (6 x 25.5 cm) strips of check fabric. Join them together right side to right side by their small sides and stitch $^1/_2$ in (1 cm) from the edge, leaving a $^5/_8$ in (1.5 cm) opening $^3/_4$ in (2 cm) from the bottom for the ribbon to go through (diagram 2).

4• Thread the ring you have thus obtained on the top of the purse, right side to right side, placing the bottom of the ring on the edge of the purse, and stitch $^1/_2$ in (1 cm) from the border of the purse (diagram 3).

5• Flatten the ring and mark out a $^1/_2$ in (1 cm) hollow on its unstitched border. Fold the ring inside the purse and sew it in invisible stitches $^1/_2$ in (1 cm) from the edge of the purse, that is to say, at the level of the seam (diagrams 4 and 5).

6• Cut the lime-green cord in 2. Using a safety pin, thread one cord all the way through an opening in the hem at the top of the purse, and bring it out again through the starting hole. Thread on a bead, tie the tips of the cord, and hide this knot with the bead. *(A)*

7• Repeat the process with the other cord, this time through the hem of the other opening.

To make the doll

1• Cut out the transferred image, leaving a 1¼ in (3 cm) margin round the drawing.

2• Fold the orange cord in 2 and glue its tips at the top of the character, on the right side of the fabric on which you have transferred the image.

3• Afterward join the fabric on which you have transferred the image and the check fabric, right side to right side, and pin together. Stitch, leaving the bottom open.

4• Remove the pins, cut any excess check fabric, then notch the corners and the rounded parts.

5• Turn the fabrics on the right side and stuff the doll with padding. Close the bottom by sewing invisible stitches.

6• Tie a bow with the green ribbon and sew it onto the doll. Tie bows in the pink ribbons round the orange cord after you have sewn on the heart-shape button.

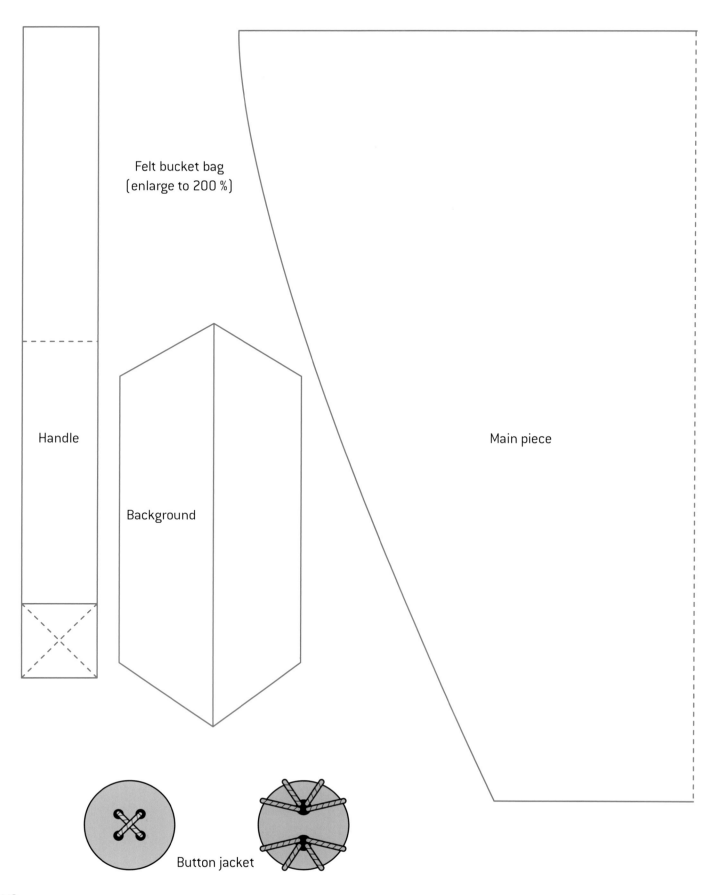

Felt bucket bag
(enlarge to 200 %)

Handle

Background

Main piece

Button jacket

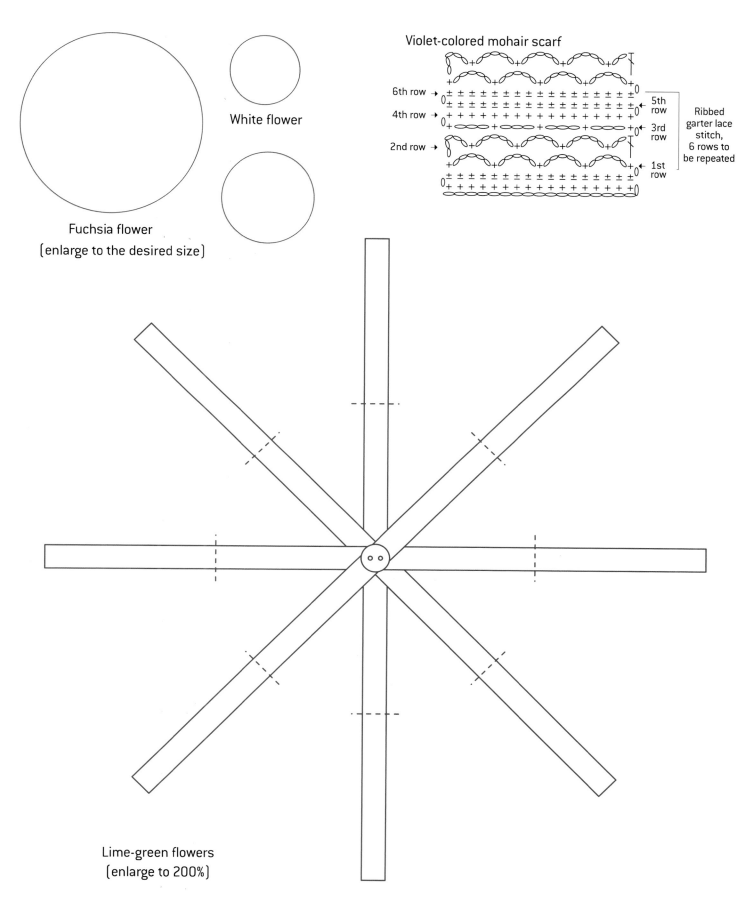

White flower

Fuchsia flower
(enlarge to the desired size)

Violet-colored mohair scarf

6th row →
4th row →
2nd row →

5th row ←
3rd row ←
1st row ←

Ribbed
garter lace
stitch,
6 rows to
be repeated

Lime-green flowers
(enlarge to 200%)

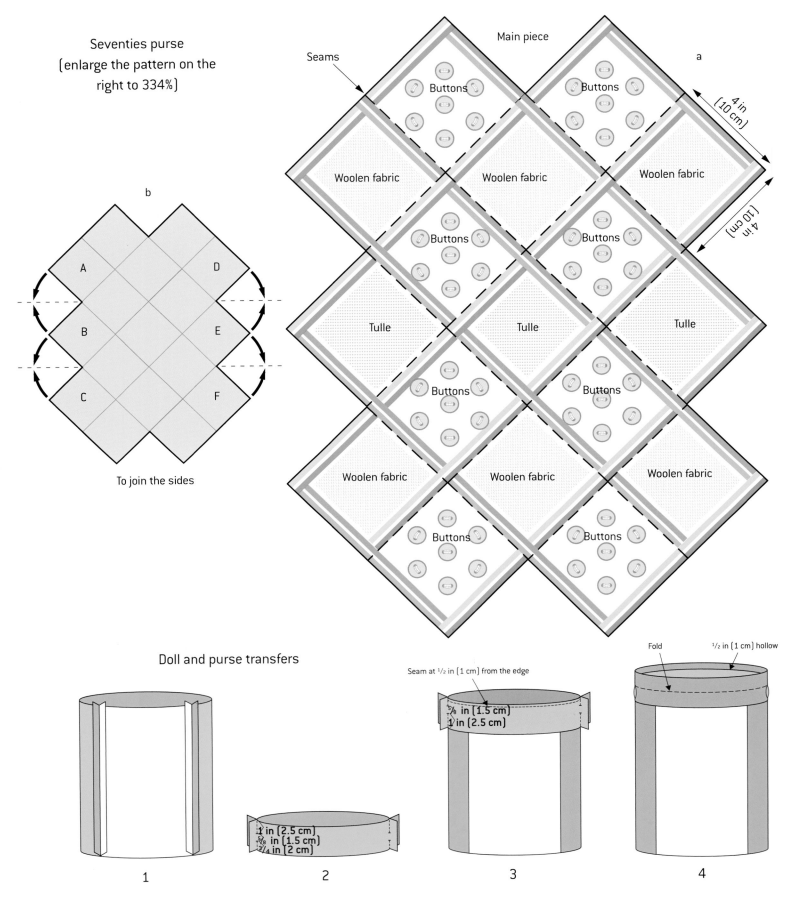

Seventies purse
(enlarge the pattern on the right to 334%)

Main piece

Seams

a

4 in (10 cm)

4 in (10 cm)

Buttons

Woolen fabric   Woolen fabric   Woolen fabric

Buttons   Buttons

Tulle   Tulle   Tulle

Buttons   Buttons

Woolen fabric   Woolen fabric   Woolen fabric

Buttons   Buttons

b

A	D
B	E
C	F

To join the sides

Doll and purse transfers

1

2

1 in (2.5 cm)
5/8 in (1.5 cm)
3/4 in (2 cm)

3

Seam at 1/2 in (1 cm) from the edge

5/8 in (1.5 cm)
1 in (2.5 cm)

4

Fold   1/2 in (1 cm) hollow

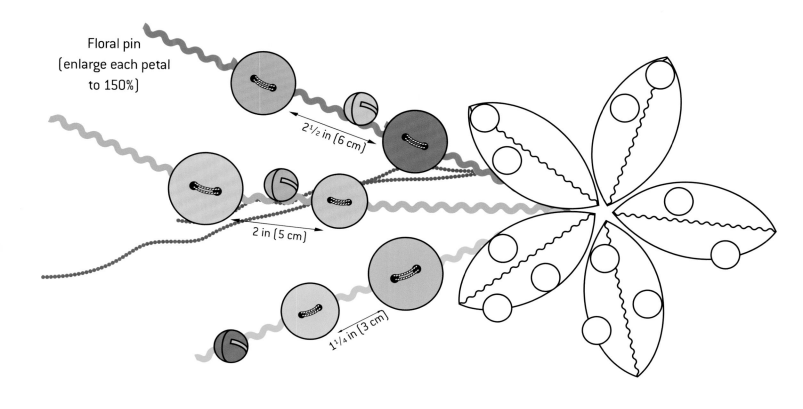

Floral pin
(enlarge each petal
to 150%)

2¹⁄₂ in (6 cm)

2 in (5 cm)

1¹⁄₄ in (3 cm)

Raffia brooch

For every row,
the first 2 stitches
are shown in blue,
and the last 2 in pink.

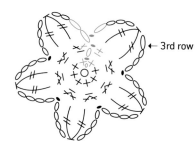 ← 3rd row

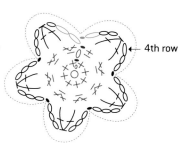 ← 4th row

Hand-sewn hem

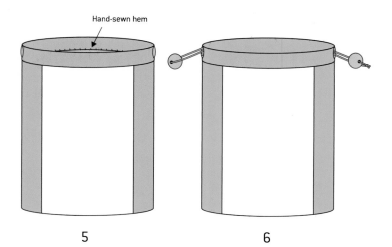

5

6

Drawer knobs

Metallic belt and moneybag

Placing the sequins in a row

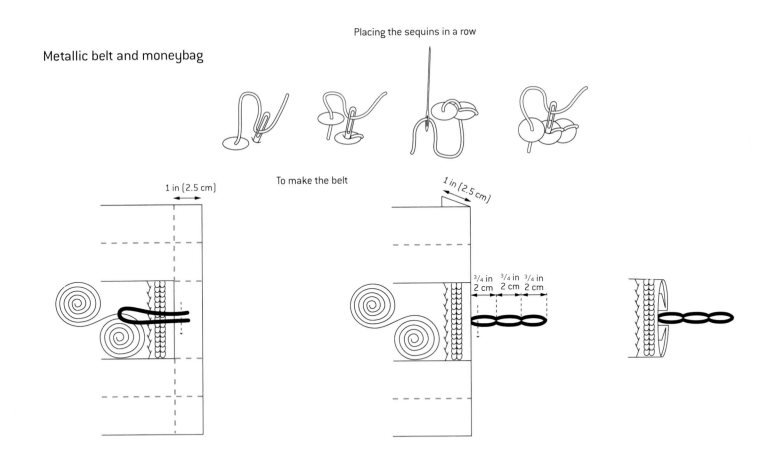

To make the belt

1 in (2.5 cm)

1 in (2.5 cm)

³/₄ in 2 cm   ³/₄ in 2 cm   ³/₄ in 2 cm

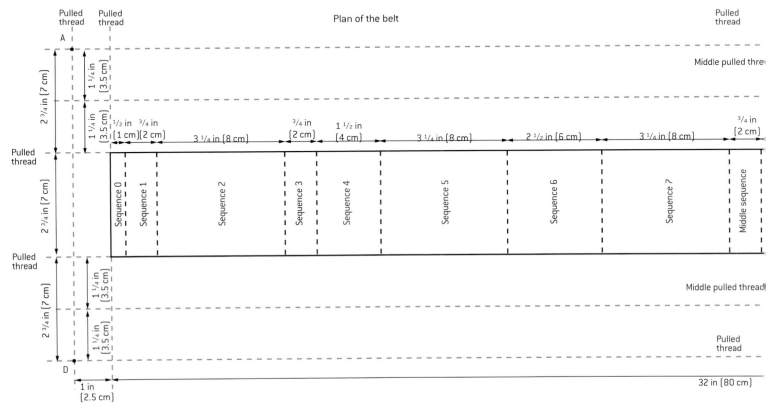

Diagrams of the stitches

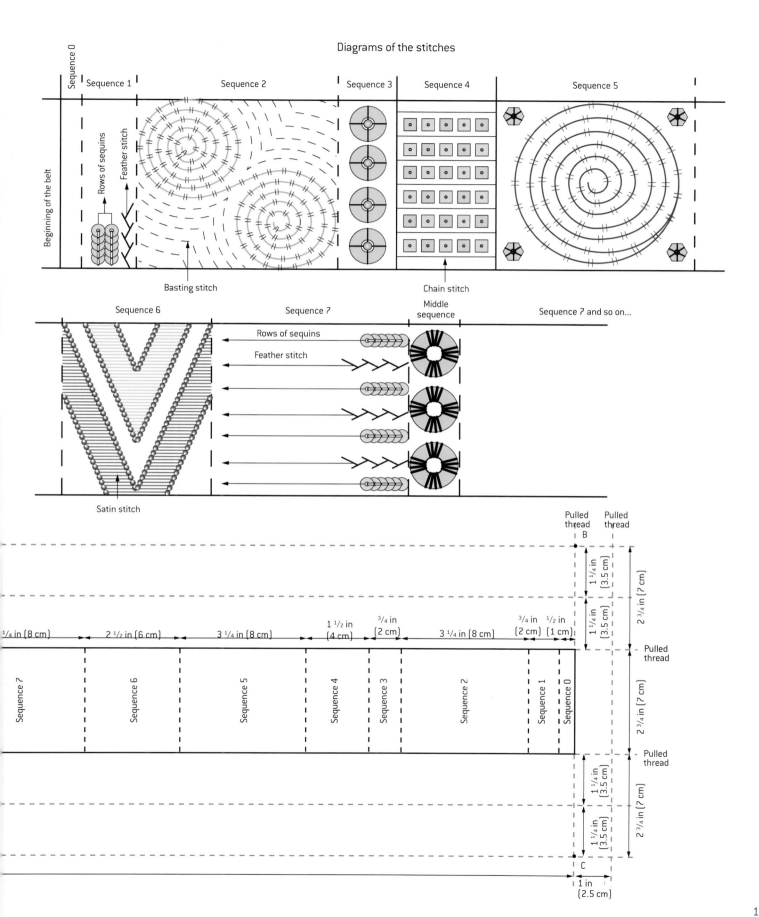

Sequence 0

Sequence 1

Sequence 2

Sequence 3

Sequence 4

Sequence 5

Beginning of the belt

Rows of sequins

Feather stitch

Basting stitch

Chain stitch

Sequence 6

Sequence 7

Middle sequence

Sequence 7 and so on...

Rows of sequins

Feather stitch

Satin stitch

Pulled thread

Pulled thread

B

1 1/4 in (3.5 cm)

2 3/4 in (7 cm)

1 1/4 in (3.5 cm)

1 1/2 in (4 cm)

3/4 in (2 cm)

3/4 in (2 cm)

1/2 in (1 cm)

Pulled thread

1/4 in (8 cm)

2 1/2 in (6 cm)

3 1/4 in (8 cm)

3 1/4 in (8 cm)

2 3/4 in (7 cm)

Sequence 7

Sequence 6

Sequence 5

Sequence 4

Sequence 3

Sequence 2

Sequence 1

Sequence 0

Pulled thread

1 1/4 in (3.5 cm)

2 3/4 in (7 cm)

1 1/4 in (3.5 cm)

C

1 in (2.5 cm)

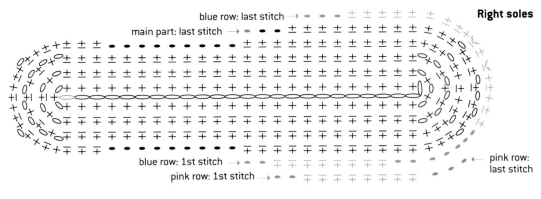

Right soles

blue row: last stitch →

main part: last stitch →

blue row: 1st stitch →

pink row: 1st stitch →

pink row: last stitch

Openwork sandals

• **Soles.** The first stitch of the chain is marked in red. After you have crochet on both sides of the chain, cut the yarn, then crochet the rows of the tip in the order indicated by the colors: blue, pink, and, for the left sole, green.

pink row: last stitch →

main part: last stitch →

Left soles

pink row: 1st stitch

blue row: last stitch

green row: last stitch

blue row: 1st stitch →

green row: 1st stitch →

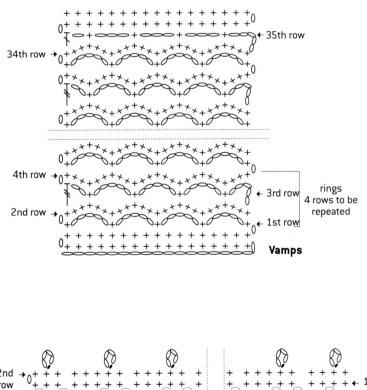

35th row

34th row →

4th row →

2nd row →

3rd row

1st row

rings 4 rows to be repeated

Vamps

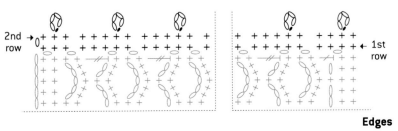

2nd row →

1st row

Edges

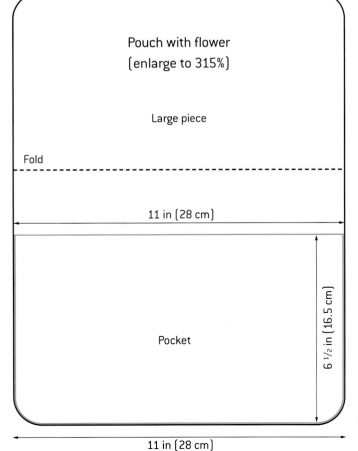

Pouch with flower
(enlarge to 315%)

Large piece

Fold

11 in (28 cm)

Pocket

14 ¾ in (37.5 cm)

6 ½ in (16.5 cm)

11 in (28 cm)

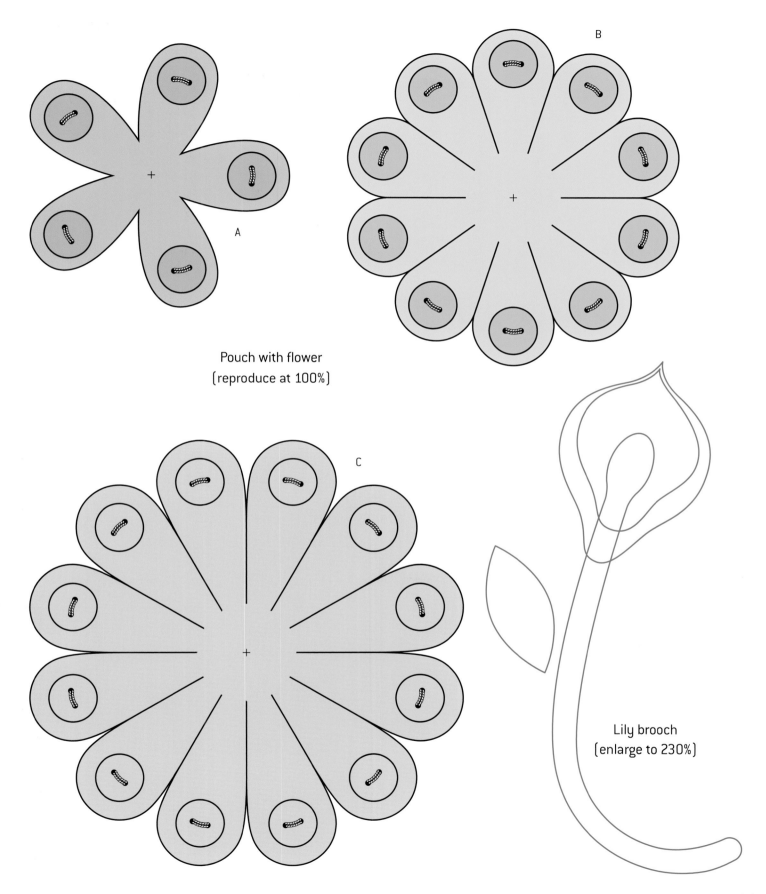

Pouch with flower
(reproduce at 100%)

A

B

C

Lily brooch
(enlarge to 230%)

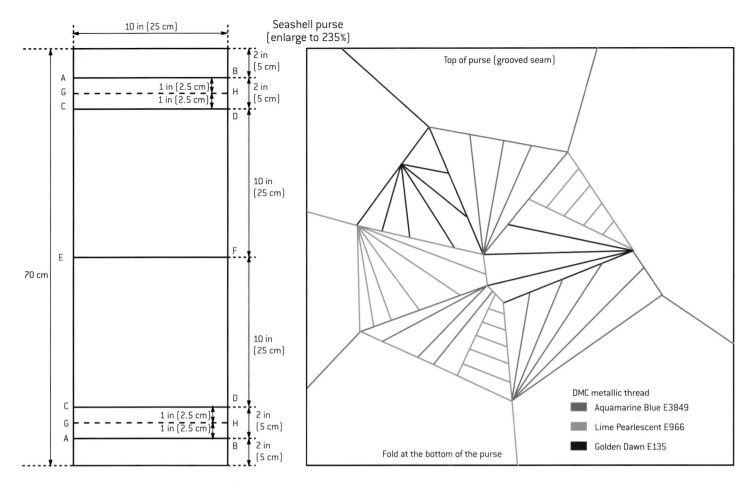

Seashell purse
(enlarge to 235%)

10 in (25 cm)

70 cm

2 in (5 cm)

A — B
1 in (2.5 cm)
G — H   2 in (5 cm)
1 in (2.5 cm)
C — D

10 in (25 cm)

E — F

10 in (25 cm)

C — D
1 in (2.5 cm)
G — H   2 in (5 cm)
1 in (2.5 cm)
A — B
2 in (5 cm)

Top of purse (grooved seam)

Fold at the bottom of the purse

DMC metallic thread

Aquamarine Blue E3849

Lime Pearlescent E966

Golden Dawn E135

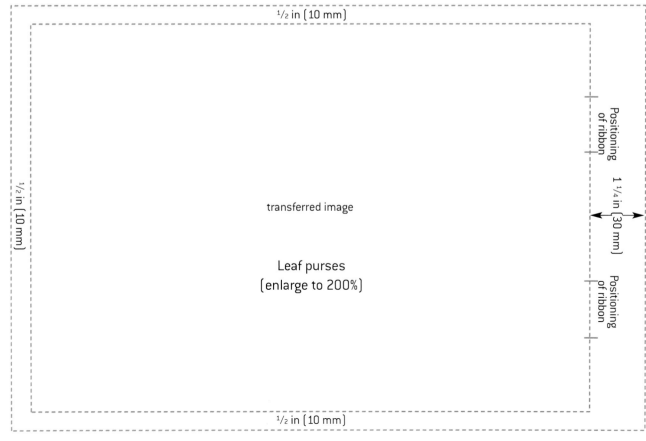

¹/₂ in (10 mm)

¹/₂ in (10 mm)

transferred image

Leaf purses
(enlarge to 200%)

¹/₂ in (10 mm)

Positioning of ribbon

1 ¹/₄ in (30 mm)

Positioning of ribbon

Cake apron

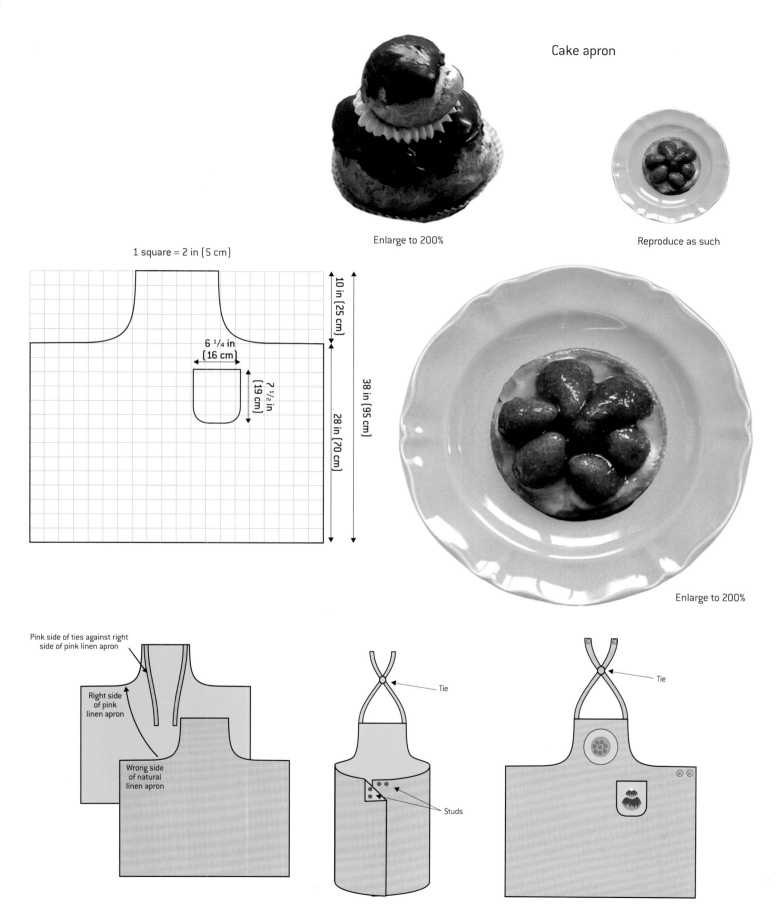

Enlarge to 200%

Reproduce as such

1 square = 2 in (5 cm)

10 in (25 cm)

6 ¼ in (16 cm)

7 ½ in (19 cm)

38 in (95 cm)

28 in (70 cm)

Enlarge to 200%

Pink side of ties against right side of pink linen apron

Right side of pink linen apron

Wrong side of natural linen apron

Tie

Studs

Tie

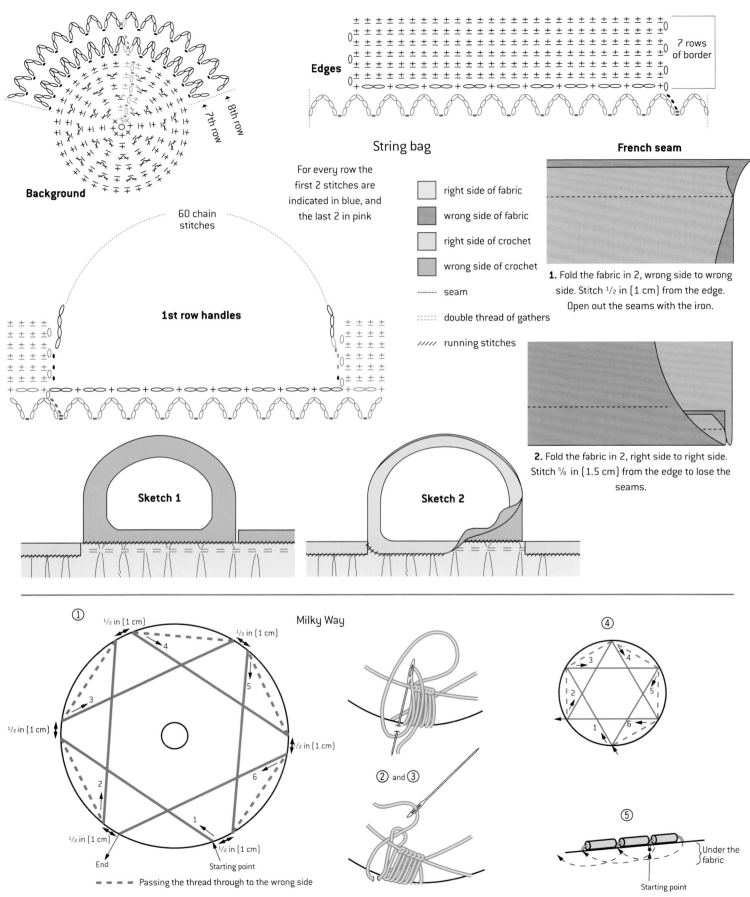

Background

7th row
8th row

Edges

7 rows of border

String bag

For every row the first 2 stitches are indicated in blue, and the last 2 in pink

60 chain stitches

1st row handles

	right side of fabric
	wrong side of fabric
	right side of crochet
	wrong side of crochet
-------	seam
┈┈┈┈	double thread of gathers
/////	running stitches

Sketch 1

Sketch 2

French seam

1. Fold the fabric in 2, wrong side to wrong side. Stitch ¹/₂ in (1 cm) from the edge. Open out the seams with the iron.

2. Fold the fabric in 2, right side to right side. Stitch ⁵/₈ in (1.5 cm) from the edge to lose the seams.

Milky Way

① ¹/₂ in (1 cm)   ¹/₂ in (1 cm)
¹/₂ in (1 cm)
4
3
5
¹/₂ in (1 cm)
¹/₂ in (1 cm)
2
6
¹/₂ in (1 cm)
1
¹/₂ in (1 cm)
End
Starting point

② and ③

④
3 4
2 5
1 6

⑤
Under the fabric
Starting point

- - - Passing the thread through to the wrong side

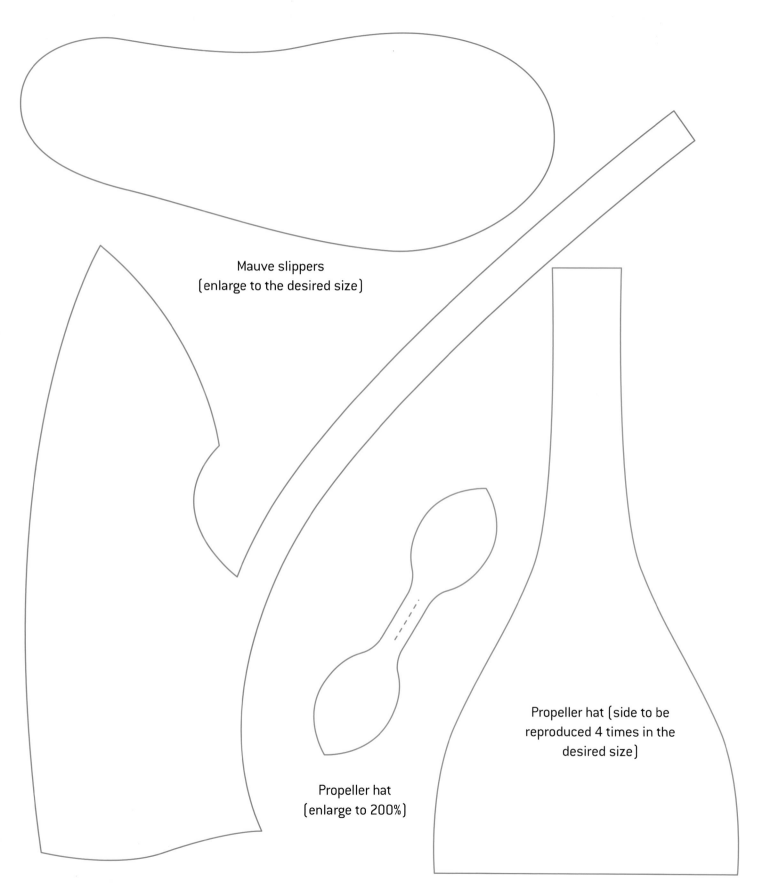

Mauve slippers
(enlarge to the desired size)

Propeller hat
(enlarge to 200%)

Propeller hat (side to be
reproduced 4 times in the
desired size)

Interior
design
projects

Floral frame

A simple unpolished wood frame becomes very decorative when it is covered in Japanese designs. Two small layers of paint and the project is done!

1• Reproduce the floral design given on page 184 and transfer it carefully to the frame.

2• Draw circles round the flowers with the small cutter.

3• Pyrograph the floral designs with nib no. 21, ensuring that the wood is well grooved.

4• With nib no. 22, make small, fairly deep holes round the circumference and the diagonal lines of the circles, and in the center of the flowers.

5• Apply a layer of acrylic paint with the paintbrush all over the frame, taking care to cover the holes and the pyrographed lines. Let dry. *(A)*

6• Apply a second layer of acrylic paint in a different color with the foam roller and let dry. *(B)* Ensure you make even strokes with the roller and do not overload it with paint; the pyrographed designs should not be filled with the second color.

SUPPLIES
• Unpolished wood frame
• Tracing paper
• Small cutter, about 1¼ in (3 cm) in diameter
• Acrylic paint in 2 colors

EQUIPMENT
• Pencil
• Pyrograph machine
• Nos. 21 and 22 nibs
• Paintbrush
• Small foam roller

A

B

Lined beanbag

An interplay of lines and points in warm colors makes a comfortable beanbag that invites you to indulge in pleasurable idleness.

SUPPLIES
• Orange-brick cotton, 56 x 28 in (140 x 70 cm)
• 1 x spool linen cord about 114 feet (35 m), 1/8 in (3 mm) in diameter
• 4 x skeins cotton matt twisted thread for tapestry in brick color
• Matching sewing thread
• 1 package synthetic padding

EQUIPMENT
• Measuring tape & dressmaking chalk
• Scissors
• Pins with heads
• Embroidery needle
• Sewing machine

1• Cut 2 squares 20 in (50 cm) across in the fabric, and 4 rectangles measuring 20 x 8 in (50 x 20 cm). Refer to the sketch on page 184 for the correct positioning of the shapes.

2• Cut 48 lengths of cord 20 in (50 cm) long, and 36 lengths 8 in (20 cm) long. Arrange them on the pieces of fabric, spacing them out by 2 in (5 cm) to form a checkerboard design; while you are doing this, create a weaving effect by passing each strand over its neighbor, then the next one, and so on.

3• Pin the cord to the fabric. *(A)*

4• Secure each intersection with a stitch made with the embroidery needle and the doubled tapestry thread. To keep the thread in place, begin and end sewing by making a double knot on the wrong side of the fabric. Remove all the pins. *(B)*

5• Pin the pieces of fabric, right side to right side. Machine-stitch each side of the beanbag, leaving 8 in (20 cm) open on 1 side. Remove all the pins except the pins on the opening.

6• Turn the beanbag over, stuff it with padding, and close the opening by hand with an invisible seam. *(C)*

A

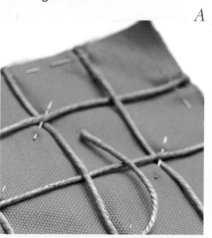

B

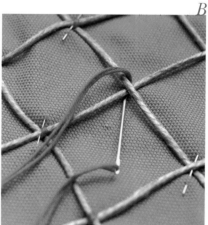

C

Decorated round vase

Filling all areas, a multitude of small stylized flowers take over the surface of round vases.

1• Thoroughly clean the vase with a cloth soaked in white spirit to eliminate all traces of grease.

2• Draw flowers with a marker pen, taking into account the suggested designs (see page 184). Start by arranging 2 or 3 large ones. Take care to fill all the gaps with a series of decorative strokes or stars. The idea is to give an impression of opulence. *(A)*

3• Engrave, following the drawn lines. When you first go over them, press lightly so as not to let the engraver slip. You can afterward go over them more firmly. *(B)*

4• Wipe regularly with the cloth to get rid of glass dust.

5• To clean away the last traces of the marker pen, wipe the engraving with a cotton cloth soaked in solvent.

Tip

If you decide to position your designs on a particular area of the vase, begin by drawing the outline of the chosen area. When you have finished working you can erase what you have traced. Take care that you press your designs precisely on this line.

SUPPLIES
• Round or oval orange vase
• White spirit
• Soft cloth
• Solvent
• Cotton cloth

EQUIPMENT
• Fine marker pen
• Electric engraver
• Thin diamond burr

A

B

Special jigsaw puzzle

Use these jigsaw frames, which can be combined endlessly, to hold your most precious family portraits.

1 • Enlarge the jigsaw puzzle pattern (see page 184) and cut it out as a model. Remove the central part with the cutter.

2 • Draw the puzzle shape in textile felt-tipped pen, using the model as guide, on the 2 pieces of felt as many times as is necessary, depending on the size of your photograph holder. Cut carefully along the line you have drawn. *(A)* Remove the central part of the puzzle pieces with embroidery scissors.

3 • Glue the underside of the pink felt and lay the orange felt on top. *(B)* Let dry.

4 • Sew 1 button in the center of the jigsaw puzzle pieces as indicated in the photograph, varying the shapes and colors.

5 • Make a ³/₄ in (2 cm) cut with embroidery scissors in the center of the puzzle pieces that are to be buttoned to another puzzle piece.

6 • On the 2¹/₂ x 2¹/₂ in (6 x 6 cm) square of fuchsia-colored felt, apply a thin layer of glue on 3 sides only and stick these to the back of the puzzle pieces with their centers removed. Let dry. Put 1 photograph in the side that is not glued.

Tip

Add as many puzzle pieces as you want and mix them into whatever shape you wish (lengthwise, widthwise, squarewise, etc).

SUPPLIES

For each puzzle piece:
• 2 ball knobs or buttons with a design (e.g. flower, star) in an acid color, between ¹/₂ and ⁵/₈ in (1 and 1.2 cm)
• 1 square pink felt, ¹/₄ in (5 mm) thick, 4 in (10 cm) along each side
• 1 square orange felt, ¹/₄ in (5 mm) thick, 4 in (10 cm) along each side
• 1 square fuchsia-colored felt, ¹/₄ in (5 mm) thick, 2 ¹/₂ in (6 cm) along each side
• Matching sewing threads

EQUIPMENT

• White textile glue
• Textile felt-tipped pen
• Embroidery scissors
• Cutter
• Tape measure
• Sewing needle

A

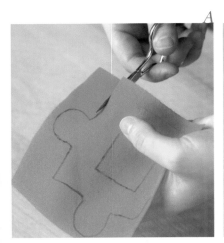

B

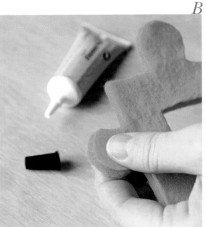

Theo and Leah

To each his seat! Why not create these personalized stools for each member of the family?

SUPPLIES
- Wooden stool
- Tracing paper
- Pencil
- Medium-size painting brush
- Clear matt varnish

EQUIPMENT
- Children's photographs
- Adhesive photograph paper
- Scissors
- Cloth

To prepare the transfer

Enlarge your photograph and reproduce it on adhesive paper.

To finish the stool

1• Draw the round part of the stool on tracing paper, then cut it following the lines you have traced.

2• Lay the tracing on the printed photograph to determine the centering. Once you have done this, place the rounded drawing on the printed photograph, then carefully cut it out. Afterward cut any excess paper from the photograph so only the face is left. *(A)*

3• Remove the protective backing from the adhesive paper and fix the photograph in place on the stool. Ensure it sticks well by pressing down with the cloth.

4• Apply 1 or 2 thin layers of varnish over the seat to protect it. *(B)*

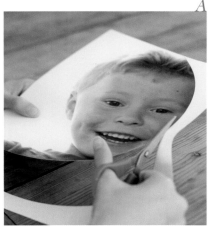

A

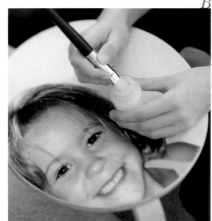

B

Taffeta decorations

A technique that is not widespread but is a very easy way to decorate cushions and drapes, and even to give new life to an outdated skirt.

SUPPLIES

- Taffeta
- Glass
- Egg cup
- Sewing thread to match the taffeta
- Satin string
- Grommet pliers
- White or colored cotton sheet
- Velvet in the same color as the taffeta
- Polyester fiber to stuff the cushions

EQUIPMENT

- Pencil
- Ruler
- Scissors
- Pyrograph machine
- No. B24 nib
- Pins
- Needle
- Sewing machine

1• **Cushion no. 1**: Cut a piece of taffeta to the required size for your cushion and add ⅝ in (15 mm) for the seams. Then make a check pattern on the fabric, drawing even lines in pencil.

2• **Cushion no. 2**: With the glass and the egg cup or any similar cylindrical object, draw circles on a piece of taffeta the same size as the cushion (+ ⅝ in [15 mm] for the seams). *(A)*

3• **Drape**: As for cushion no. 2, draw circles on a piece of taffeta cut to the same size as the window for which it is intended (+ ⅝ in [15 mm] for the seams).

4• **Drape and cushions**: With the pyrograph machine set on the lowest temperature, pierce the pieces of taffeta where the lines join up for cushion no. 1 and, for cushion no. 2 and the drape, on the lines of the circles, spacing the holes regularly, about ⅛ in (3 mm) apart. *(B)*

5• **Drape**: Make a ⅝ in (15 mm) hem on the 4 sides of the drape, having oversewn the entire circumference of the fabric piece. Hang it from the satin string with grommet pliers.

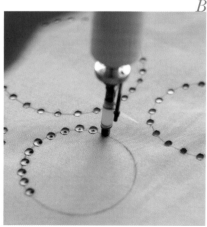

6• **Cushions**: Cut a piece of cotton sheet the same size as the taffeta piece and pin it on the wrong side of the taffeta by placing the pins on the sheet side. Cut 2 rectangles in the velvet of the same size as the taffeta but with a lesser width ($^2/_3$). With your sewing machine, make a $^1/_2$ in (10 mm) turnover in 1 of the small sides of 1 of the velvet rectangles; this will be a border for the opening of the cushion.

7• Position the pieces of taffeta and velvet right side to right side. Put the taffeta down first, the right side facing upward; then the hemmed piece of velvet, aligning its unhemmed sides with those of the taffeta; and, finally, the second piece of velvet, making it straddle the first. Pin and machine-stitch the entire circumference of the cushion $^5/_8$ in (15 mm) from the edges.

8• Remove the pins, turn the cushion over, and stuff it with polyester fiber. Hand-stitch the opening to close.

Art Deco mirrors

From a 1930s frieze here is a game of dominoes engraved on mirrors that can be displayed as a series for a very Art Deco effect.

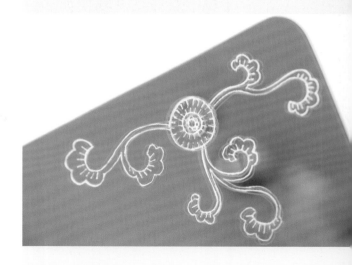

1930s frieze

1• Clean 1 mirror with a cotton cloth soaked in white spirit then, with the ruler, draw a line with marker pen 1 in (2.5 cm) from the edge. You will thus obtain an inner square. *(A)*

2• Afterward draw a circle on each corner in marker pen (see page 185). With the ruler, divide each side into sequences (here, 1 measuring 1¹/₂ in [4 cm], then 4 measuring 1¹/₄ in [3 cm], and, finally, the last measuring 1¹/₂ in [4 cm]). End the drawing by tracing a circle in the center of each of the rectangles thus obtained.

3• Put masking tape all along the inner square. Follow it to engrave these lines. Remove the masking tape and engrave the other designs. *(B)*

4• Finally, wipe the mirror with a cotton cloth soaked in solvent.

Dominoes

1• Using the ruler, trace rectangles measuring 1 x ³/₄ in (2.5 x 2 cm) on 2 edges of 1 of the mirrors in marker pen.

2• Engrave these traced lines, then create the tips of the dominoes (see page 185).

Floral design

1• Trace the floral design on page 185. Reproduce this traced design on the reverse of the mirror.

2• Using the diamond burr fitted in the engraver, reproduce the traced design. For greater visibility of the design, you can make a new engraving on the right side of the mirror by following the tracing that has already appeared.

3• Once you have finished engraving, wipe the entire surface of the mirror with a cotton cloth soaked in solvent.

Note

By engraving on the reverse of the mirror, you obtain a very interesting shadowy effect.

SUPPLIES
• Square 8 x 8 in (20 x 20 cm) mirrors
• White spirit
• Masking tape
• Tracing paper
• Solvent
• Cotton cloth

EQUIPMENT
• Marker pen
• Flat ruler
• Pencil
• Electric engraver
• Thin diamond burr

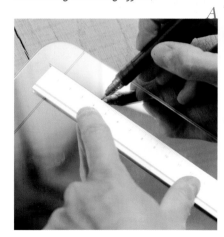

A

B

Letters for pouffe

A pouffe, some cutout letters that are then applied in attractive shades of felt-tipped pen, and the project is ready! This can be adapted using different colors.

SUPPLIES
- Pouffe or foam cube
- Purple felt, 13 x 12 in (33 x 30 cm) for the letter A; 9 x 11 in (23 x 28 cm) for the letter O
- Double-sided adhesive interfacing, 2 pieces the same size as the felt letters
- Thick raw linen, 49 x 33 in (124 x 84 cm)
- Sewing thread in natural color

EQUIPMENT
- Cutter
- Sewing machine
- Iron

1• Measure 1 of the square sides of the pouffe which is to be covered and cut 5 linen squares the same size (add a margin of ½ in [1 cm] all round for the seams). Start the cover by machine-stitching the star squares—4 squares round the central square. Sew, right side to right side, the 2 sides of the squares laid side by side to make a bottomless cube (see page 186).

2• Enlarge 2 letters—here the letters A and O—on a computer or photocopying machine, then reproduce them on each piece of felt. (You can also enlarge letters cut out from magazines.) With the iron, apply the rectangle of interfacing that corresponds to the back of each piece of felt (on the "virgin" side).

3• Following their outlines, cut out the letters with the cutter. *(A)*

4• Place the cover on the pouffe or foam cube. Position the purple felt letter in its place, then iron it, on the right side this time, to fix it to the linen cover. *(B)* Repeat the process for the other letter. To make more of a graphic statement you can straddle each letter on the sides of the pouffe! *(C)*

A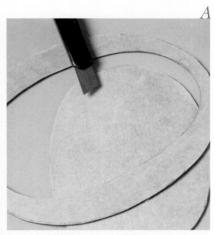

B

C

Drape tieback

A few exotic seeds make for a very elegant drape tieback.

Like a piece of jewelry

SUPPLIES
- About 30 *Hymenea courbaril* seeds
- 3¹/₂ oz (100 g) dried black or black-eyed peas
- Waxed cotton cord
- Thick wire
- Clear matt varnish
- Black thread

EQUIPMENT
- Handheld drill
- Scissors
- Cutting pliers
- Pliers
- Paintbrushes
- Sewing needle

1• Pierce a hole in the *Hymenea courbaril* seeds lengthwise and a hole in the black or black-eyed peas through their thickness.

2• Cut the cord into 3 different-size pieces, reckoning on the thickness of your drape. Thread the *Hymenea courbaril* seeds in a random fashion onto the 3 cords, taking care to keep back 8 for the loop and fastener.

3• The loop is made up of 3 concentric pea rings joined together here and there by the *Hymenea courbaril* seeds. Cut a piece of thick wire to the desired size for the first ring, plus 4 in (10 cm). Thread the peas, then close the ring by twisting the 2 ends of the wire with pliers; keep any leftover wire to secure the rings to each other and cut this at the end of the work.

Make the 2 other rings in the same way, their size being the same as that of the first ring. *(A)*

4• Cut a piece of wire long enough to join the 3 rings together. Thread on a *Hymenea courbaril* seed and position it flat over the 3 rows of peas. Keep it in place by twisting the wire behind the work, taking care not to crush the peas. Repeat the process and space out the 3 *Hymenea courbaril* seeds. *(B)*

5• For the fastener, thread 5 *Hymenea courbaril* seeds onto a piece of thick wire and, using pliers, reinsert the excess wire on each side in the seeds. Slid inside the loop, this fastener will secure the drape.

6• Varnish the different elements of the loop and the fastener; the resin contained in the varnish will help to make them rigid. Apply several layers if necessary. Finally, using a fine paintbrush, varnish the *Hymenea courbaril* seeds on the cords 1 at a time.

A

B

7• Lay the 3 cords flat in front of you, 1 on top of the other; lay your pea loop on the left and the *Hymenea courbaril* seed fastener on the right. Sew the 3 cords onto these elements with needle and thread.

Tips

The size of drill bit used for the Hymenea courbaril seeds will depend on the size of your cord; do not make too large a hole because the seeds must not slip on the cord once the loop is finished. For the black-eyed peas choose a fine drill bit.

A belt for your drapes

1• Lay the entada seeds flat, then drill 2 holes 1 next to the other lengthwise and through the thickness of the seeds; if the drill bit is not long enough, make another 2 holes exactly opposite the first ones. Hold the *Hymenea courbaril* seeds in the pliers and pierce them lengthwise, crossing them equally.

2• Fold the cord in 2 equal lengths. Put a piece of wire, like a U-shape staple, in the fold of the cord; this will act as a needle. Thread 3 *Hymenea courbaril* seeds on the doubled-up thread and make them slide farther down on the cord. Thread a fourth *Hymenea courbaril* seed but only go past the wire staple: the cord should just reach the seeds' exit point. *(A)* Remove the staple. Leave this aside and turn to the 2 cords at the other end.

3• Fold 1 of these cords into the staple and thread the entada seeds onto it. *(B)* Repeat the process with the second cord, in the second hole of the seeds. Push the seeds toward the threaded *Hymenea courbaril* seeds, then hold the cords at the ends and stretch them to adjust the doubled-up end.

4• With the staple, and working this time with both cords together, thread the 4 remaining *Hymenea courbaril* seeds. Position the last so it is opposite, the cord being on the same level as the hole's exit.

5• Lay your loop flat in front of you, stretch it well, and slide the seeds onto the cord so they are symmetrical. Discreetly glue the cords where each seed falls, put the seeds back into their place, and let dry. Finally, carefully varnish the seeds.

SUPPLIES
- 6 entada seeds
- 8 *Hymenea courbaril* seeds
- 48 in (1.20 m) waxed cotton cord
- Piece of wire
- Clear superglue
- Clear matt varnish

EQUIPMENT
- Handheld drill
- Pliers
- Paintbrush

A

B

Dried leaf frieze

To cheer up your sitting room walls and give them an undergrowth feel, try glueing on a profusion of oak leaves.

SUPPLIES
- Dried oak leaves
- Superglue
- Soft cloths
- White silk paper

EQUIPMENT
- Flat paintbrush
- Ruler
- Pencil
- Scissors

1• Glue the oak leaves at regular intervals to make either a frieze or a covering for the entire surface of the wall. For the latter, apply a layer of superglue to the back of each leaf and stick it to the wall by pressing firmly with a soft cloth. Remove any excess glue with another cloth. *(A)*

2• With the ruler and pencil, draw rectangles measuring about $3^{1}/_{4}$ x 5 $^{1}/_{2}$ in (8 x 14 cm) in the silk paper. Cut them out with scissors.

3• Apply a thin layer of superglue on 1 of the sides of a silk paper rectangle and place this on the wall, centering it carefully on an oak leaf. Work the silk leaves 1 at a time because once it is glued, the paper becomes very fragile. *(B)*

4• Gently pat the silk paper rectangles on the wall with a soft cloth and let dry. *(C)*

A

B

C

Memory board

Cord and string join forces to make an ideal support for family photographs and postcards.

SUPPLIES

- Brightly colored fabric with horizontal stripes, 55 x 20 in (140 x 50 cm)
- Hardboard, 24 x 16 in (60 x 40 cm)
- Glue spray
- 14 small brass eyelets, $\frac{1}{8}$ in (3.5 mm) in diameter
- Linen string, $\frac{1}{16}$ in (2 mm) in diameter
- Cotton cord, $\frac{1}{4}$ in (4 mm) in diameter
- Linen cord, $\frac{1}{4}$ in (4 mm) in diameter
- Sewing thread to match the fabric
- Fishing net or string shopping bag
- Small and medium-size wooden pegs

EQUIPMENT

- Dressmaking scissors
- Dressmaking chalk
- Grommet pliers
- Ruler
- Needle

1 • Cut 2 rectangles of fabric measuring 28 x 20 in (70 x 50 cm). Glue 1 of these rectangles to 1 side of the hardboard; fold the fabric overlap on the other side and glue it.

2 • Following the sketch on page 186, work out the position of all the eyelets at the top of the memory board, including those on the fastenings. Put in place with eyelet pliers. *(A)*

3 • For the fastenings, prepare a 12 in (30 cm) length of $\frac{1}{16}$ in (2 mm) linen string, fold it in 2, and make a Flemish or figure of eight knot (see page 40) on the loop side. Thread 2 strands in the top eyelets and tie them to the back of the memory board so they are invisible. Repeat the process for the second fastening.

4 • Cut off 28 in (70 cm) of cotton cord and 28 in (70 cm) of linen cord.

A

Make 3 overhand knots, taking both cords together.

5 • Cut 28 in (70 cm) of linen cord and make 4 overhand knots. The final length should be 20 in (50 cm).

6 • Finally, cut 2 x 40 in (1 m) lengths of cotton cord. On each of these make 8 monkey's fist knots. The final length should be 20 in (50 cm). Tie these 2 cords together, interweaving the $\frac{1}{16}$ in (2 mm) linen string in the loops. Finish by making a double knot and cut the linen string flush with the knot.

7 • Thread the lengths you prepared in steps 4 to 6 through the eyelets and make a double knot behind the memory board to make them invisible.

8 • Secure the string at the bottom of the memory board with a few stitches behind. Thread 20 in (50 cm) linen cord at the top of the string to reinforce it and sew the cord behind the memory board.

9 • Glue the second fabric rectangle behind the memory board, making a hollow of 2 in (5 cm) on each side.

10 • Peg the photographs onto the board.

Woolen flowers

Add a note of softness to your decor all year round with imaginary flowers made of mohair wool.

SUPPLIES
- White and green mohair wool
- White brass wire
- Imitation flower pistils

EQUIPMENT
- Knitting needles 10 ½ (3/3.5)
- Wool needle

1 • Begin by knitting the flower petals in both colors, bearing in mind that you will need 5 petals for each flower. Cast on 3 stitches, knit in stocking stitch, then in the 4th row increase by 1 stitch on each side as well as at the 8th row, at the 12th row, then at the 16th row (11 sts in all). On the 20th row, decrease by 2 stitches on each side, then, on the 22nd and 23rd rows, by 1 stitch on each side. Flatten the 3 remaining stitches. Let 4 in (10 cm) wool hang loose. *(A)*

2• Sew a row of white brass wire in chain stitch round each petal with a wool needle. *(B)*

3• With the wool needle, sew together the 5 flower petals on the bottom to make a flower. *(C)*

4• Slide the pistils into the center of the flower, then crisscross the strands of wool that are free of the petals to secure them; finish by tying a knot on the reverse of the flower. Change the petals' direction with the brass wire.

You can multiply the number of flowers and vary their uses. Put them on a cushion with a safety pin sewn behind the flower, or round a carafe, rolling up a strand of wool round the neck, and so on.

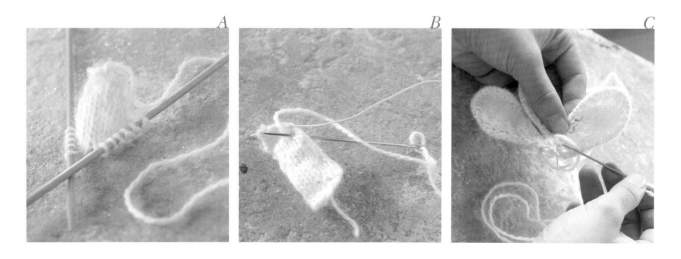

A B C

SUPPLIES

For the "rosebuds"

• 1 x 2 oz (50 g) ball cotton thread for crochet hook no. 2½–3 in pale green

• 1 x 2 oz (50 g) ball microfiber cotton thread for crochet hook no. 2½–3 in medium green and pink

For the "leaves"

• 1 x 2 oz (50 g) ball cotton thread for crochet hook no. 2½–3 in pale green

• 1 x 2 oz (50 g) ball microfiber cotton thread for crochet hook no. 2½–3 in medium green

• 1 x 2 oz (50 g) ball pure wool for crochet hook no. 3½, moss green

For the 2 cushions

• Pearl gray fabric, 18 x 18 in (45 x 45 cm), and cream-colored fabric, 18 x 18 in (45 x 45 cm) (for a cushion)

• Basting threads, threads to match the crochet threads (or clear nylon thread)

• Cushion, 16 x 16 in (40 x 40 cm)

• Crochet hooks no. 2½ and no. 3

• Wool needle, sewing needle, pins with heads, pair of scissors

• Sewing machine (optional)

• Iron and ironing board

Country cushions

Rosebuds and leaves: designs with a timeless charm worked in a modern harmony of delicate shades.

"Rosebud" cushion

With crochet hook no. 2 ½, crochet 14 rosebuds, 14 pale green calyxes, and 14 medium green stems/sepals (see the stitches on pages 15 to 17 and the grids on page 187); leave some loose threads on the ends at about 8 in (20 cm) for later assembly.

Place a calyx at the base of a rosebud and secure the chain on the bottom with a small stitch. Superimpose a stem/sepals, and fix in the same way. Make 14 rosebuds in this way.

"Leaf" cushion

Crochet 9 pale green leaves, 7 medium green leaves, and 6 moss green leaves (see the stitches on pages 9 to 11 and the grid on page 187); make a chain and crochet the 1st row of slip stitch with crochet hook no. 3, then continue with crochet hook no. 2½.

To assemble the cushions

Pull the yarns through to the wrong side. Lightly iron the designs on the wrong side. Arrange the designs on a square of fabric (gray for the rosebuds and cream-colored for the leaves). Pin and baste them, then sew their outline in small invisible stitches in matching threads or clear nylon thread.

Overlay the whole thing on the "virgin" square of fabric, right side to right side. Stitch the 4 sides 1 in (2.5 cm) from the edges, leaving an opening of about 10 in (25 cm) on 1 of them. Turn the work over to the right side. Put the cushion inside the cover, then close the opening with small invisible stitches.

Springtime frame

Display your photos ina frame of colors borrowed from nature with a thousand shiny beads.

1• Paint the top and bottom of the frame with gold paint. Let dry.

2• Using the guides on page 186, draw an assortment of large and small leaves on the felt. Cut them out and embroider them with beads to suggest the veins of a leaf. (A)

3• Place the leaves and butterflies in 2 opposite corners of the frame. Glue them in place and let dry. (B)

Extra idea...

Many different kinds of small imitation flowers, insects, and birds are available in stores which could personalize your creation further.

SUPPLIES

- 1 photograph frame in unpolished wood
- Gold pearl acrylic paint Pébéo Déco no. 40
- Green felt
- 1 tube tubular-shape pale green glass beads , 1 tube opaque pale green glass beads, 1 tube translucent lime-green glass beads, 1 tube dark green glass beads
- Embroidery needle suitable for sewing beads
- 2 imitation butterflies
- Paste

EQUIPMENT

- Paintbrush no. 14
- Embroidery needle suitable for sewing beads
- Fine felt-tipped pen, scissors, thimble

A

B

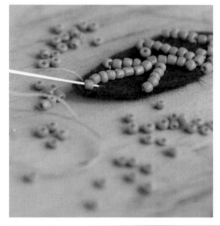

* Freestanding bedside table, cupboard, or meat safe
* Waterproof fiberboard $^7/_8$ in (19 mm) thick
* 1 x pine batten $1^1/_2$ in (40 mm) wide and $^3/_4$ in (20 mm) thick
* Wood glue
* $1^1/_4$ in (30 mm) lost head nails
* Wood paint
* Pebbles, $^1/_2$ in to $^3/_4$ in (10 to 20 mm) diameter
* Tile adhesive
* Waterproof coating
* Grout
* 4 wood screws, $1^1/_2$ x $1^1/_4$ in (4 x 35 mm)

EQUIPMENT

* Tape measure
* Pencil
* Jigsaw
* Hammer
* Sandpaper
* Paintbrushes
* $^1/_4$ in (4 mm) glue spatula
* Small bowl or pan
* Cat tongue trowel (or filling knife)
* Sponge, soft cloths
* Electric drill (or screwdriver)

Cream bedside table

Decorated with cream-colored pebbles, an old meat safe can be changed and have a new life...

1 • Saw the waterproof fiberboard so it is the same size as the top of the bedside table if you plan to take away this top; if you are keeping it allow $^3/_4$ in to $1^1/_4$ in (2 to 3 cm) extra. In the case of the latter, the waterproof fiberboard will be screwed onto the old top.

2 • Saw the batten to the necessary length to cover the perimeters of the fiberboard. Afterward glue and nail the resulting sticks round the top, leaving the upper part of the pebbles' thickness to overlap. Sand the sticks' ridges and paint the whole thing. *(A)*

3 • Wash and dry the pebbles. Having thoroughly dusted the table top, apply tile adhesive all over it with a glue spatula. *(B)*

4 • Stick on the pebbles, leaving very little space between them. If they are not all of the same thickness, tap them gently with a piece of batten once you have laid them in place so they are level. The glue will remain soft for a moment, so you can make whatever adjustments are necessary. *(C)*

5 • To make the grouting easier and avoid blobs of grout on the pebbles, apply a layer of waterproof coating with a paintbrush on top of the pebbles that are already in place, without overlapping onto the glue.

6 • If the door is recessed in such a way as to make it possible for you to put pebbles on the front, decorate it in the same way as the top, laying it flat in order to work more comfortably.

A

B

C

7• Mix the grout in the small bowl, following the manufacturer's instructions. Using the cat tongue trowel, fill in the spaces between the pebbles, letting the excess overflow.

8• When the grout begins to harden, clean the pebbles and the area round them with a wet sponge, rinsing it in clear water and wringing it out after each wipe. Repeat the process several times, taking care not to cross the grouted joints; if a joint should by mistake be too hollow, wet and grout it once again with grout that is still soft. Finish the polishing with the cloth. *(D)*

9• Once it is completely dry (after at least 24 hours), apply a layer of waterproof coating on the top and door of the bedside table, to avoid stains and make them easier to maintain.

10• Center the top on the bedside table and screw it underneath, ensuring the screws are not too long. Finally, put the door on once again.

Tips

If your piece of furniture is made of polished wood, sand it down and paint it in the same colors as the pebbles. You can, as here, use sheets of ready-assembled pebbles, 12 x 12 in (30 x 30 cm), which you can cut out with scissors or with a cutter. In this case, take very great care with the edges and joins; if necessary, invert some pebbles for a more precise result.

D

E

Note

To avoid having joints that are too large on the sides, along the molding, it is possible to "cut" the pebbles. Lay a pebble on a hard surface (like concrete) and strike a blow with a straight hammer; the pebble will split quite cleanly in this way. Be careful not to hit it flat, though, unless you need small pieces of pebble. (*E*)

Decorations for pouffe

Circles and spirals freely decorate this single-color pouffe cover. This idea can be adapted to other pieces of furniture, to breathe a little bit of originality into your home!

SUPPLIES

• 2 x 2 oz (50 g) balls matt cotton thread for crochet hook no. 2 ½–3 in natural color

• Crochet hooks no. 2½ and no. 3

• Square pouffe, 16 in (40 cm) on the sides, with removable fabric cover

• Basting and sewing threads in natural color

• Measuring tape, wool needle, sewing needle, pins with heads, pair of scissors

• Sewing machine (optional)

• Iron and thick flannel

Spirals

With crochet hook no. 3, make a chain of 58 stitches (see page 10). With crochet hook no. 2½ work in the following way: pass the 1st chain, 2 single crochets (see page 10) in each of the following 6 chain, *1 single crochet in the next chain, 2 single crochets in the next single crochet, repeat 3 times from * to *, **1 single crochet in each of the next 2 chains, 2 single crochets in the next single crochet**, repeat 3 times from ** to **, ° 1 single crochet in each of the next 3 chains, 2 single crochets in the next single crochet °, repeat 3 times from ° to °, °° 1 single crochet in each of the next 4 chains, 2 single crochets in the next single crochet °°, repeat 2 times from °° to °°. Make 20 spirals in this way.

Circles

With crochet hook no. 2½, make 20 small and 20 large circles (see page 18, stitches on page 15, and grids on page 188).

To make the decorations

Pull the yarn through to the wrong side. Lightly iron the designs on the wrong side. Pin the designs onto the cover, then baste them. Secure the outlines of each of these with straight stitch (see page 19), or machine-stitch them. Steam-iron the cover on the wrong side under the flannel. Iron 1 side after the other, waiting for each side to dry before ironing the next.

Love those spots!

This cushion cover has a certain fun-loving quality and celebrates color with pearly, multicolored buttons!

Supplies

- 29 mother-of-pearl buttons measuring 1 in (2.5 cm) in a mixture of red, purple, blue, and orange
- 29 sequins measuring 3/4 in (2.2 cm) in sky-blue, green, and navy blue
- 29 sequins measuring 1/4 in (6 mm) in orange and pink
- 29 seed beads in bright yellow
- Velvet with thin sides, 28 x 18 in (70 x 45 cm)
- White cotton, 20 3/4 x 8 in (52 x 20 cm)
- Turquoise cotton, 24 1/2 x 12 3/4 in (62 x 32 cm)
- Sewing thread in red
- Basting thread

Equipment

- Bristol paper
- Carbon paper for embroidery
- Textile felt-tipped pen
- Tape measure
- Dressmaking scissors
- Compass
- Sewing machine
- Sewing needle suitable for sewing beads, pins

1• With textile felt-tipped pen, draw a rectangle measuring 20 x 4 1/2 in (50 x 12 cm) on the wrong side of the velvet. Baste it all along and cut it, leaving a 1/2 in (1 cm) border for the seams.

2• Enlarge the drawing indicating the position of the buttons (see page 187). Pin the inked side to the right side of the velvet on the carbon paper and trace the word "LOVE" that you will later write with the buttons.

3• Sew on the buttons, varying the colors. Pierce through 1 of the buttonholes again and thread a large sequin through, then a small one, and, finally, a seed bead. Pierce through the sequins once again, then through the second buttonhole. *(A)*

4• Draw a rectangle measuring 20 x 7 in (50 x 18 cm) on the right side of the white cloth. Lay the large upper side of the white cloth on the lower large side of the velvet, right side to right side, and pierce 1/2 in (1 cm) from the margins. Open up the seams with the iron.

5• Draw a 3 1/2 in (9 cm) circle on the Bristol paper with a compass and cut it out. Using this as a model, draw 23 circles in textile felt-tipped pen on the wrong side of the remaining velvet. Cut out each circle. Draw a 1 3/4 in (4.5) circle on the Bristol paper and cut it out. Make a basting stitch over the entire circumference of each velvet circle 1/4 in (5 mm) from the edge, without tying it, and leaving the thread to overrun at each end. Put the small Bristol paper round in the middle of a circle and pull the ends of the thread. *(B)* The velvet will close round the Bristol paper. Flatten the folds with the iron, then remove the Bristol paper. Repeat the process

A

B

until you have created the 22 other large circles.

6• Pin 18 velvet circles on the white cloth using the drawing as a positioning guide (straddle the 5 others on both sides of the cushion cover, to be sewn later). Sew these in running stitch.

7• Make the back of the cushion cover.

On the wrong side of the blue cloth, draw then cut out 2 pieces measuring 12^1/$_2$ x 12^3/$_4$ in (31 x 32 cm). Make a hollow first of ^{3}/$_8$ in (8 mm) and then 1 of ^{3}/$_4$ in (1.2 cm) on 1 of the small sides of each piece, wrong side to wrong side (each piece will then measure 11^1/$_2$ x 12^3/$_4$ in [29 x 32 cm]). Machine-stitch this hem. Right side to right side, straddle the 2 pieces over 2^1/$_2$ in (6 cm), hemmed sides in the center, to make up a rectan-

gle measuring 20^3/$_4$ x 12^3/$_4$ in (52 x 32 cm). Pin and pierce the large sides ^{1}/$_2$ in (1 cm) from the edges. Align the 4 sides of the front and back of the cushion cover, right side to right side, pin these and pierce ^{1}/$_2$ in (1 cm) from the edges. Turn the cover over.

8• Sew the last 5 velvet circles in running stitch and straddle them between the back and front of the cover.

Vase with felt

Red felt circles surround a shot glass to make a very elegant vase.

SUPPLIES
• Red felt, ¹/₄ in (5 mm) thick, 15 ¹/₂ x 20 in (40 x 50 cm)
• White felt, ¹/₁₆ in (2 mm) thick, 4 x 8 in (10 x 20 cm)
• Shot glass

EQUIPMENT
• Compass
• Sheet of Bristol paper
• Scissors
• Fine textile felt-tipped pen
• Cutter (or stylus knife)
• Textile glue

1• Draw a 4 in (10 cm) circle on the Bristol paper and cut it out. Draw the outline of this model with textile felt-tipped pen 16 times on the red felt and 2 or 3 times on the white felt. Cut out the circles with the cutter.

2• Also with the cutter, cut out rounds the same size as the shot glass in the center of the felt circles, using the glass as model. *(A)* Vary the central arrangement of the holes in the rounds slightly, in order to give greater

A

movement to your vase. Leave 3 whole red rounds to make the bottom of the vase.

3• Stack up the first 3 circles a bit to suggest movement and join them together by applying a few drops of textile glue between them. Lay the first emptied-out round on top, then the shot glass in position. Slide the other felt circles onto the glass and secure them by applying a few drops of textile glue between them.

4• Contrast occasionally with a white, thinner circle (here the 6th and the 13th).

Paper blind

Here is a clever but easy idea to create. The blind can be made in any range of colors you wish.

SUPPLIES

• Thin bonding paper, 3 A3 sheets in turquoise, 1 A3 sheet in mauve
• 1 x roll tracing paper, 2 sheets measuring 24 x 50 in (60 x 125 cm)
• 2 adjustable window rods, with tips and self-adhesive hooks
• Saran wrap
• Adhesive tape
• Glue stick
• Wallpaper paste

EQUIPMENT

• Pencil
• Rule
• Cutter
• Cutting mat
• Glass pot
• Silk bristle paintbrush

Note

Adapt the size of the traced sheets and the number of strips depending on the desired finished size. The simplest solution lies in having a safety margin, then in cutting out the blind once the papers have shrunk during drying.

1• Draw strips measuring 16¹⁄₂ in (42 cm) on the thin papers as follows: turquoise, 12 strips ³⁄₄ in (2 cm) wide, 9 strips 1 ¹⁄₄ in (3 cm) wide, 3 strips 1¹⁄₂ in (4 cm) wide, and 2 strips 2 in (5 cm) wide; mauve, 3 strips ³⁄₄ in (2 cm) wide, 3 strips 1 ¹⁄₄ in (3 cm) wide, and 3 strips 1 in (2.5 cm) wide. Cut these out with the cutter on the cutting mat, guiding the blade against the rule.

2• With the glue stick, join the strips of the same color and width together 3 by 3, slightly overlapping their ends; you will obtain 9 turquoise strips and 3 mauve strips about 50 in (125 cm) in length.

3• Place Saran wrap on your work counter and secure it in place with adhesive tape so you have a surface measuring about 60 x 34 in (150 x 85 cm) to work on.

4• Cut out the tracing into 2 sheets measuring 50 x 24 in (125 x 60 cm). Thin down the wallpaper paste in the pot. Apply it to the Saran wrap on the work counter, then place the 2 tracings on top, glueing them to each other. Let dry so they have the time to shrink.

5• Also with the wallpaper paste, put the mauve and turquoise strips on the tracing; space these out as you wish, but ensure they are parallel with each other. *(A)* Let dry for 24 hours.

6• Wrong side to wrong side, fold over the 2 sides of the tracing at about 1¹⁄₄ in (3 cm) and secure them with glue from the glue stick. *(B)* Slide the rods under the flaps thus created, and thread the tips onto the ends. Hang the blind with self-adhesive hooks.

A

B

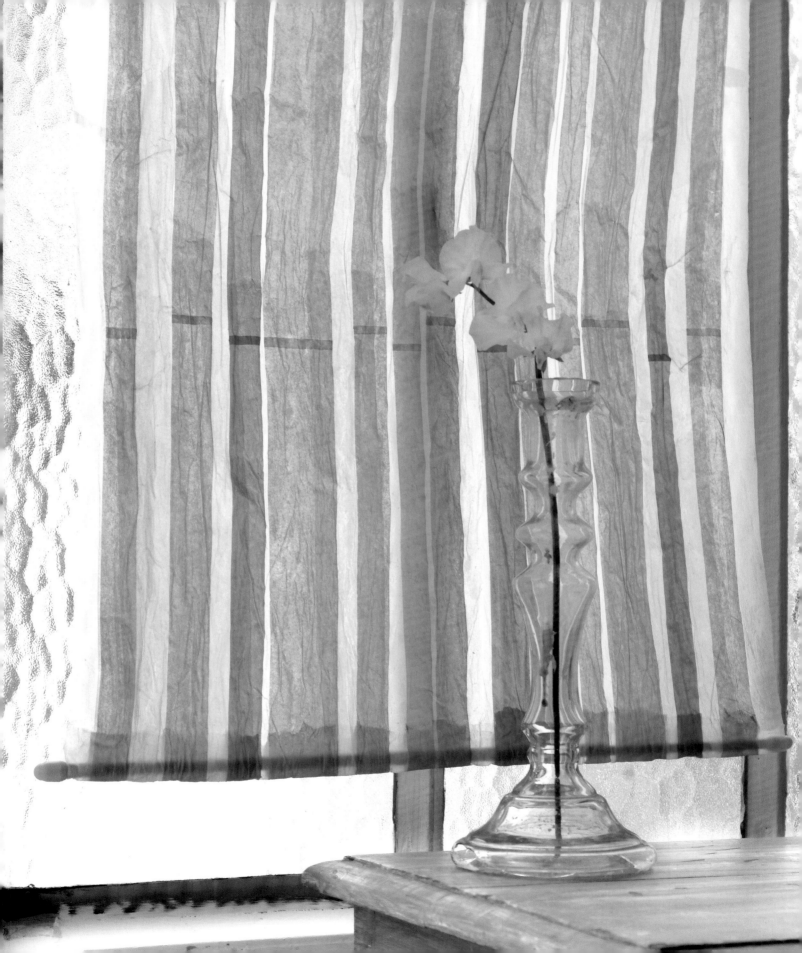

Trompe-l'oeil cushion

The embroidered buttons at the center of this linen cover cleverly imitate the printed fabric used for this precious cushion.

SUPPLIES

• 138 transparent plastic pearly 2-hole buttons, ³⁄₈ in (9 mm)
• 1 white 4-hole button, ¹⁄₂ in (13 mm)
• Linen fabric, 12¹⁄₂ x 15¹⁄₂ in (32 x 39 cm)
• Flower-patterned fabric in green, 2 pieces measuring 6¹⁄₄ x 15¹⁄₂ in (16 x 39 cm), 2 pieces measuring 13¹⁄₂ x 15¹⁄₂ in (34 x 39 cm), and 6 strips measuring 12 x 5 in (30 x 13 cm) (for the pompons)
• Cheesecloth, 12¹⁄₂ x 15¹⁄₂ in (32 x 39 cm)
• Pearl cotton # 5 in pink, red, and green
• Sewing thread to match the fabrics
• Basting threads

EQUIPMENT

• Dressmaking scissors
• Tape measure
• Textile felt-tipped pen
• Carbon paper for embroidery
• Textile glue spray
• Sewing machine
• Sewing needle, pins

1 • Spray the cheesecloth and lay on the back of the linen fabric. On the right side, in the center, draw a rectangle measuring 12 x 14 ¹⁄₂ in (30 x 37 cm). Baste this.

2 • Enlarge the drawing, indicating the position of the buttons (see page 188). Pin the inked side of the carbon paper to the right side of the linen and the drawing. Mark the red, green, and pink axes of the designs.

3 • Starting from the center of the design, sew on the 2-hole buttons with matching pearl cotton. Bring out your needle underneath the linen fabric, through 1 of the holes, going underneath the button, then pierce the second hole and pierce again next to the button in the axis of the holes. *(A)* At the centre of the rose-shape decoration, sew the 4-hole button on in red pearl cotton, in the

A

same way, in a star (see the photograph opposite).

4 • On both sides of the linen fabric, on the small sides, sew on the pieces of 6 ¹⁄₄ x 15 ¹⁄₂ in (16 x 39 cm) patterned fabric, piercing ¹⁄₂ in (1 cm) from the edges.

5 • On each piece of 13 ¹⁄₂ x 15 ¹⁄₂ in (34 x 39 cm) patterned fabric, on the large sides, wrong side to wrong side, make a ¹⁄₄ in (5 mm) hollow, then a hollow of ¹⁄₂ in (1 cm), and pierce. Right side to right side, lay the pieces on top of each other, the hemmed side in the middle, and straddle them by 2 in (5 cm) on the front of the cushion. Pin and pierce the 4 sides ¹⁄₂ in (1 cm) from the edges. Turn the cover over.

6 • From a 12 x 5 in (30 x 13 cm) strip of printed fabric, cut off ribbons measuring ³⁄₈ x 5 in (7 mm x 13 cm). Stack these and secure them by rolling about ³⁄₈ (7 mm) pearl cotton. Make a further 5 pompons, varying the color of the pearl cotton. Sew these on the sides of the cushion: 2 on the outer edges and 1 in the middle of 1 of the small sides of the cover.

Eastern mirror

Linen cord and arabesques harmonize on this mirror, which is brightened up with an exotic touch.

SUPPLIES
• Stiff cardboard, 18 x 18 in (45 x 45 cm)
• Acrylic paint in maroon
• 1 x reel linen cord, ⅛ in (3 mm) in diameter
• 1 x square mirror, 12 in (30 cm) each side

EQUIPMENT
• Ruler
• Pencil
• Cutter
• Flat paintbrush
• Glue gun
• Scissors

1• Draw and cut out a square measuring 10 in (25 cm) on the sides (see page 188) in the center of the cardboard. Paint the borders of the frame you have obtained and let dry.

2• Roll up the linen cord round the frame, beginning and ending with a dab of glue behind the frame. Stick the diagonal lines in each corner with a line of glue. *(A)*

3• Cut off 8 pieces of cord measuring 6 in (15 cm) for the arabesques.

4• Load the glue gun once again and let it heat for 3 to 4 minutes. Draw the arabesques in the corners with a thin line of glue, then stick the pieces of cord onto the arabesques. *(B)*

5• To make the mirror's fastening, cut 14 in (35 cm) of cord and secure it with a double knot at the back of the frame, at the base of the diagonal lines.

6• Cut 4 lengths of cord measuring 18 in (45 cm).

7• Place the mirror on the back of the frame. Attach the cords that will trim the frame by a double knot to fix the mirror in place. *(C)*

Tip

Glue in various stages: load the glue gun only for as long as it takes to stick on the beginning of the cord (step 2). Afterward make the frame's trimming, loading the gun once again for a few minutes to stick on each diagonal line, then the end of the cord. Finally, draw the arabesques.

A

B

C

SUPPLIES

For a net drape measuring 63 x 80 in
(1.60 x 2 m)
• White organdie, 63 in (160 cm)
wide, 110 in (280 cm)
• White A4 paper
• Cotton thread in white
• Dried leaves
• Retaining ring pliers

EQUIPMENT

• Measuring tape and dressmaking
chalk
• Pencil
• Sewing scissors
• Scissors
• Sewing machine
• Ruler
• Pinking scissors
• Pins

Organdie net drape

*The see-through quality of autumn leaves and the light-
ness of the organdie are joined to create a filtered light.*

1 • Cut out a rectangle measuring 80
x 63 in (2 x 1.60 m) in the organdie
and oversew the 4 sides in a wide,
tight Bosnian stitch.

2 • Choose the dried leaves you wish
to place on the net drape, lay each of
them on a sheet of A4 paper, and
draw a model of its "pouch" by tracing
a rectangle all round it. Leave a border of about ¹/₂ in (1 cm). Make a
note on the paper model of the name
of the leaf or number the 2 elements
so as to match them up when you
come to slip each leaf in its pouch.

3 • Draw the models on the remaining organdie and cut out the rectangles with pinking scissors.

4 • Pin the organdie rectangles on
the large net drape and arrange
them in a harmonious way.
Machine-stitch them in a wide, tight
Bosnian stitch (overcast stitch), by
piercing the left-hand and right-hand
borders as well as the bottom of the
pouch.

5 • Slide the leaves into their
organdie pouches and hang the net
drape with a drape rod using retaining ring pliers.

Elegant quilted cushion

To adorn sofas or bedspreads, here are two cushion covers in watery and fernlike colors.

SUPPLIES

For a 20 x 20 in (50 x 50 cm) cushion
- Taffeta, 53 ¹/₂ x 21 ¹/₂ in (134 x 54 cm)
- Green khaki velvet, 13 ¹/₂ x 13 ¹/₂ in (34 x 34 cm)
- Turquoise ribbon, 27 in (68 cm)
- Peacock blue ribbon, 27 in (68 cm)
- Basting thread, cream-colored thread
- 16 olive-green beads, 13 turquoise glass beads, 20 faceted green glass beads
- 1 tube turquoise seed beads
- 2 handfuls opaque tubular-shape turquoise glass beads

EQUIPMENT

- Sewing needle no. 9
- Pins with heads
- Scissors, pencil, fine felt-tipped pen, thimble, tape measure, ruler, iron, sewing machine

Velvet and taffeta cushion cover

1• Make a ³/₄ in (2 cm) hem on the 2 small sides of the taffeta rectangle (see page 189), iron, then tack with basting thread. Sew over this on the machine, then remove the basting thread.

2• Oversew the 2 large sides of the rectangle in Bosnian stitch with the sewing machine. Lay the rectangle down flat lengthwise. Flatten the left side on 10¹/₂ in (26 cm) and iron. Divide the remaining part in 2, 1 for the front and 1 for the back.

3• Leave a margin of ³/₄ in (2 cm) all round the velvet square for assembly. Starting from this ³/₄ in (2 cm), draw 5 horizontal lines and 5 vertical lines with fine felt-tipped pen, spaced out at 2 in (5 cm) intervals. You will obtain 36 squares. Draw 2 diagonal lines that will link the 4 squares in the middle in fine felt-tipped pen. Machine-stitch over the drawing.

4• Fold the ³/₄ in (2 cm) border toward the inside and iron. Position the velvet square on top of the cover and center it carefully. Tack with basting thread. Machine-stitch over the tacking.

5• Sew all round the square, where the lines meet and, alternating them, 1 olive-green bead and 1 flower. Sew 4 olive-green beads onto the corners of the central square cut on the diagonal. Sew a flower where the diagonal

lines meet. Finally, sew 1 green faceted bead where the lines meet. *(A and B)*

6• Fold the 2 parts of the cover, the front and the back, right side to right side. Tack the 2 open sides opposite, at ³/₄ in (2 cm) from the edge. Machine-stitch over the tacking, taking up all 3 thicknesses of fabric (front, back, and flap). Remove the basting thread.

7• Turn the cushion cover to the right side once again, machine-stitch 13¹/₂ in (34 cm) ribbons along the opening, 5 in (13 cm) from each side, taking care to mix the colors to create a positive—negative effect on each knot.

A

B

Taffeta cushion cover

1• Start by making a ³/₄ in (2 cm) hem on the 2 small sides of the taffeta rectangle (see pattern on page 189). Iron, then tack with basting thread. Machine-stitch over the tacking, then remove the basting thread.

2• Follow step 2 of the previous cushion cover instructions.

3• Lightly draw 9 vertical lines, spaced out at 2 in (5 cm) intervals, in pencil on 1 of the squares (this will become the underside of the cushion). Machine-stitch over them, taking care not to sew the 10 ¹/₂ in (26 cm) flap.

4• On the other part of the cover, lightly draw 4 vertical and 4 horizontal lines, spaced out at 4 in (10 cm) intervals. You will obtain 25 squares measuring 4 x 4 in (10 x 10 cm).

5• Lightly draw the diagonal lines of the squares. Machine-stitch all the lines.

6• Hand sew a turquoise bead on each corner of the squares and a faceted green bead where the diagonal lines meet.

7• Afterward follow steps 6 and 7 of the previous cushion cover instructions.

SUPPLIES
For a 20 x 20 in (50 x 50 cm) cushion
• Taffeta, 51 x 21 ¹/₂ in (130 x 54 cm)
• Basting thread, brown thread
• 16 turquoise glass beads, 25 green faceted glass beads
• Turquoise ribbon, 27 in (68 cm)
• Peacock blue ribbon, 27 in (68 cm)

EQUIPMENT
• Sewing needle no. 9
• Pins with heads
• Scissors, pencil, thimble, measuring tape, ruler, iron, sewing machine

Small colored vases

These vases sport clover leaves and wild grasses. By multiplying these, you will create enchanting decorations.

SUPPLIES
- Colored glass goblets
- White spirit
- Cotton cloth
- Tracing paper
- Adhesive tape
- Soft cloth

EQUIPMENT
- Fine felt-tipped pen
- Scissors
- Electric engraver
- Fine and large diamond burrs

1• Thoroughly clean the goblets with a cloth soaked in white spirit to eliminate all traces of grease. *(A)*

2• Trace your chosen designs (see page 188). Cut them out, leaving a border of ¼ in (5 mm) all round. Place them inside the goblets, then stick them carefully on the glass with adhesive tape. *(B)*

3• Engrave the outlines that are visible through transparency. When you have gone over the outlines once with the engraver, press lightly so the engraver does not slip. Pass the engraver over the outlines once again, more firmly this time. Fill in the designs if necessary with the large diamond burr. *(C)*

4• Wipe the surface regularly with the cloth to get rid of glass dust.

Tips
You can draw the simpler designs by hand directly on the glass, using a fine marker pen. To engrave, you will only have to go over the drawn lines. Wipe the last traces away with solvent.

A

B

C

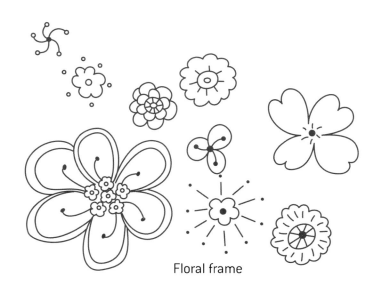

Floral frame

Decorated round vase

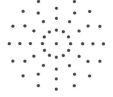

Special jigsaw puzzle (enlarge to 120%)

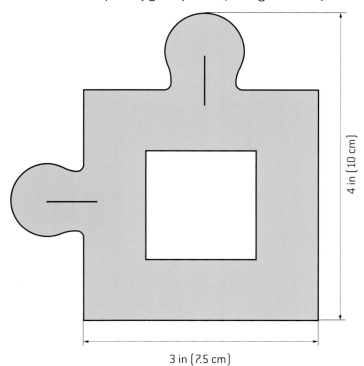

4 in (10 cm)

3 in (7.5 cm)

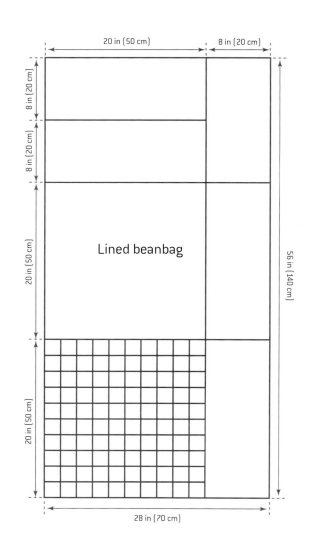

20 in (50 cm)

8 in (20 cm)

8 in (20 cm)

8 in (20 cm)

20 in (50 cm)

Lined beanbag

56 in (140 cm)

20 in (50 cm)

28 in (70 cm)

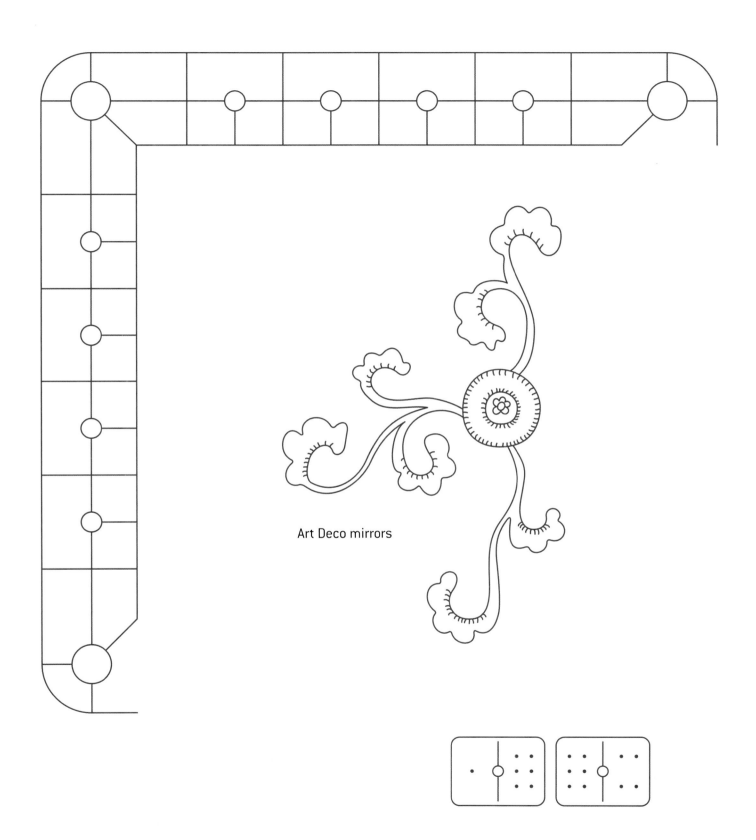

Art Deco mirrors

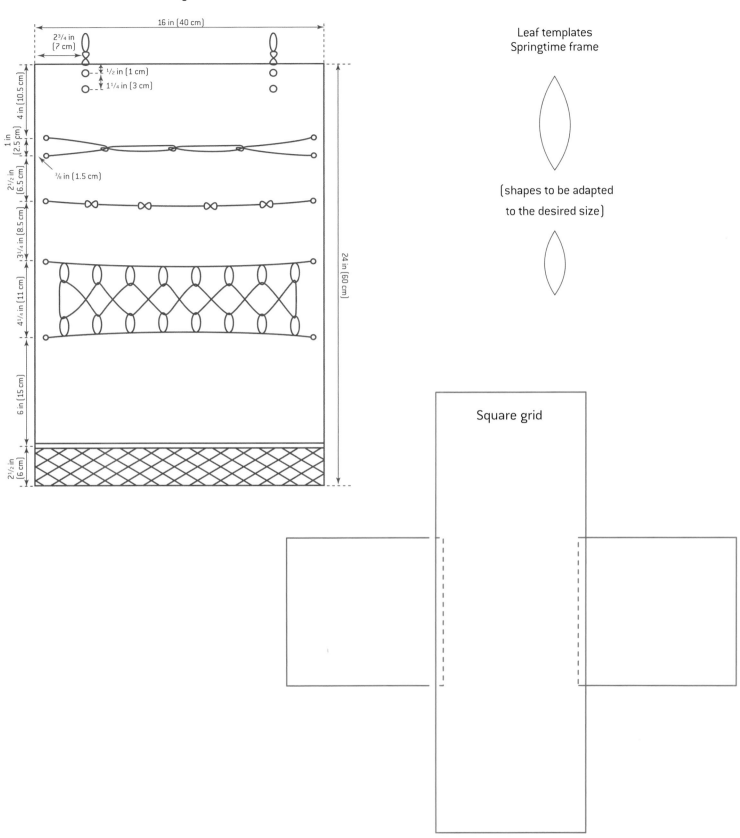

Memory board

16 in (40 cm)

2³/₄ in (7 cm)

¹/₂ in (1 cm)

1¹/₄ in (3 cm)

4 in (10.5 cm)

1 in (2.5 cm)

³/₈ in (1.5 cm)

2¹/₂ in (6.5 cm)

3¹/₄ in (8.5 cm)

4¹/₄ in (11 cm)

6 in (15 cm)

2¹/₂ in (6 cm)

24 in (60 cm)

Leaf templates
Springtime frame

(shapes to be adapted
to the desired size)

Square grid

Country cushions

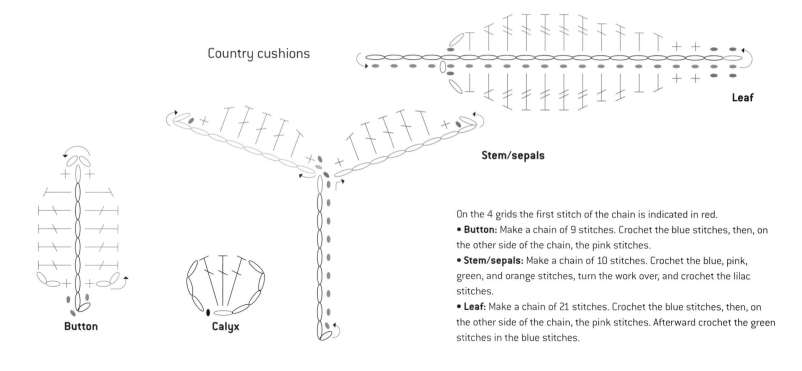

Leaf

Stem/sepals

Button

Calyx

On the 4 grids the first stitch of the chain is indicated in red.
- **Button:** Make a chain of 9 stitches. Crochet the blue stitches, then, on the other side of the chain, the pink stitches.
- **Stem/sepals:** Make a chain of 10 stitches. Crochet the blue, pink, green, and orange stitches, turn the work over, and crochet the lilac stitches.
- **Leaf:** Make a chain of 21 stitches. Crochet the blue stitches, then, on the other side of the chain, the pink stitches. Afterward crochet the green stitches in the blue stitches.

Love those spots! (enlarge to 280%)

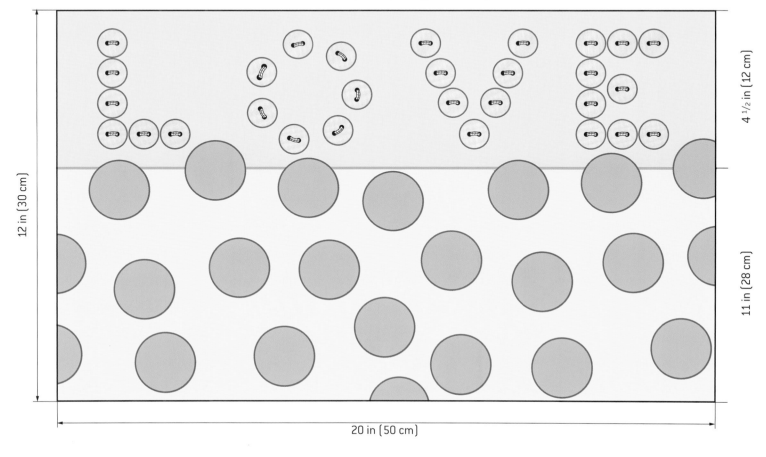

4 ¹/₂ in (12 cm)

12 in (30 cm)

11 in (28 cm)

20 in (50 cm)

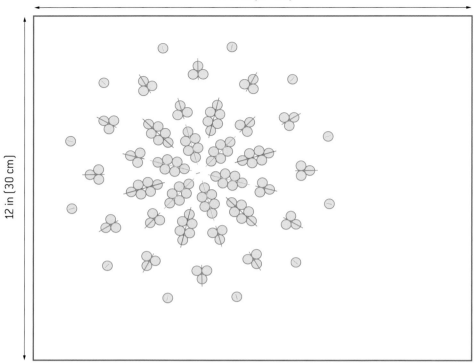

14½ in (37 cm)

12 in (30 cm)

Trompe-l'oeil cushion
(enlarge to 315%)

———— red pearl cotton

———— green pearl cotton

———— pink pearl cotton

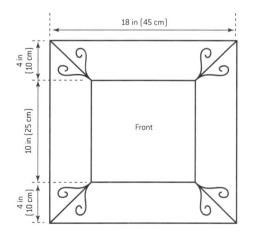

18 in (45 cm)

4 in (10 cm)

10 in (25 cm)

4 in (10 cm)

Front

Eastern mirror

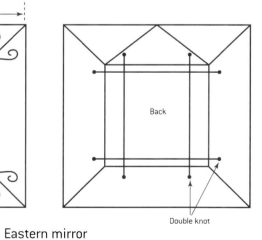

Back

Double knot

Small colored vases

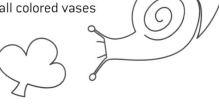

Decorations for pouffe

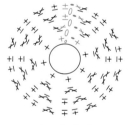

Small circle

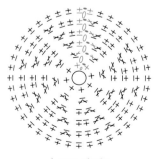

Large circle

For each row, the first 2 stitches are indicated
in blue, the last 2 in pink.

Taffeta cushion cover

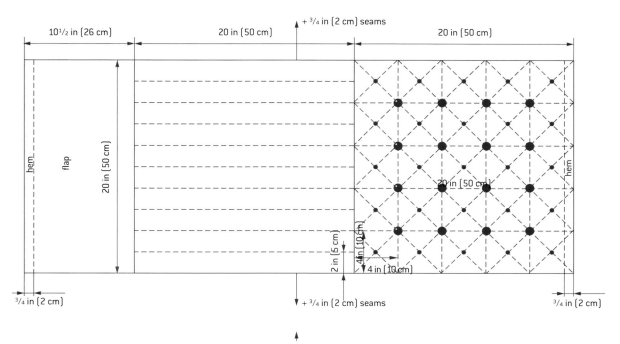

Velvet and taffeta cushion cover

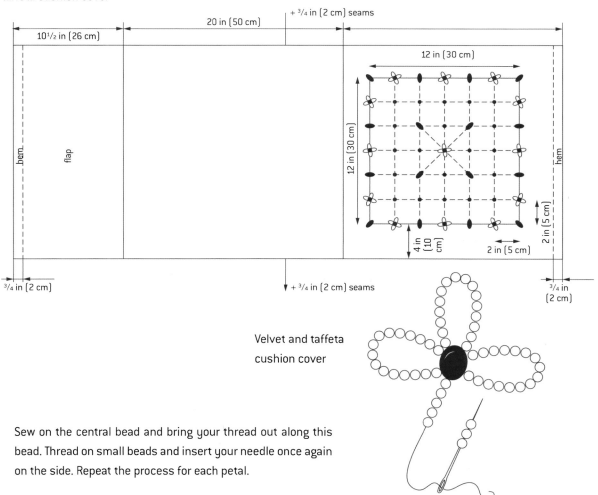

Velvet and taffeta
cushion cover

Sew on the central bead and bring your thread out along this
bead. Thread on small beads and insert your needle once again
on the side. Repeat the process for each petal.

Beautiful
lighting

Square candleholder

Japanese-inspired designs pyrographed in beechwood: a simple way to decorate an elegant candleholder.

1• Reproduce the floral design given on page 236 and transfer it to the sides of the candleholder. *(A)*

2• Go over the drawn lines in pencil if necessary for greater legibility.

3• Pyrograph the candleholder with the no. 21 nib, following the pencil-drawn lines. Beech being a fairly hard wood, regulate the temperature of your pyrograph machine so it is at its highest setting and press the nib down firmly on the candleholder. *(B)*

A

B

Garland paper lamp

Reminiscent of the clearings where fairies and elves dance, this slender leaf-shape garland will cast a gentle light on the interior of your home.

1• Draw 20 simple leaf shapes measuring about 3¼ in (8 cm) in length on Saran wrap. Draw veining in the center of each of them. Stick the wrong side of the Saran wrap on the work counter with adhesive tape.

2• Tear the papers into small strips about ¼ in (5 mm) wide and ¾ to 1½ in (2 to 4 cm) long.

3• Cut 20 plastic ties 4½ in (12 cm) in length.

4• Thin down the glue in the pot. Stick 1 of the drawn leaves onto the Saran wrap. Cover the central veining with strips of paper, then glue a tie on top; align it on the point in such a way that it passes the side of the stem. Glue on some more strips of paper in order to hide the plastic tie and to draw side veinings. *(A)* Make 19 other leaves in the same way, using a single type of paper for each of them. Let dry for 1 or 2 days.

5• Gently detach the leaves from the Saran wrap. Varnish them on both sides. Let dry.

6• Fix the leaves on the electric garland by rolling up the ties round lamp holders. *(B)* Bend these to animate the whole.

SUPPLIES
• Almond green and apple green silk paper
• Green-colored wrapping paper
• Bright green single-color wrapping paper
• White plastic ties (for freezer packages)
• Electric 20-bulb garland with a transparent cable
• Saran wrap
• Adhesive tape
• Wallpaper paste
• Washable matt varnish

EQUIPMENT
• Felt-tipped pen
• Pair of scissors
• Glass pot
• Flexible silk bristle paintbrush

A

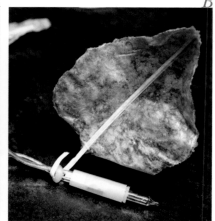

B

SUPPLIES

• Lamp with stand and lampshade
• 1 x reel thin linen string (1.5 mm in diameter)
• Fabric paints in khaki and lime-green

EQUIPMENT

• Glue gun
• Scissors
• Flat paintbrush

String lamp

A string-clad lamp soberly decorated with straight lines gives off a sense of calm and harmony.

1 • Load the glue gun and let it heat for 3 to 4 minutes. Put a thin trail of glue on the base of lampshade or at the foot of the lamp. Press the first row of linen string to stick it down. Glue the following rows in the same way, taking care to avoid excess glue; each row must be glued but not necessarily along all its length. Roll up the linen string over the entire lampshade, including the foot, pressing each row of string firmly against the preceding one. *(A)*

2 • Draw a large khaki strip round the lampshade and the base of the lamp with a paintbrush, then paint a thin lime-green strip. *(B)*

Tips

For safety reasons, take care not to glue the string too close to the lamp holder when you are decorating the base of the lamp. The end result will be more subtle with a filtered lighting effect, so preferably choose a 20 watt bulb.

Variation

You can decorate the lampshade only, matching the strips of color to the base of the lamp or to your interior.

A

B

Magic chandelier lamp

This classic chandelier seems as though it has just come out of a fairy tale, thanks to a few snow-covered twigs and frosted pearls.

Supplies
- 1 x 5-branch metal chandelier lamp
- Birchwood twigs
- 1 reel wire
- 10 iridescent drop-shape glass pearls + 10 very small ones
- Snow spray

Equipment
- Pruning shears
- Cutting pliers

1 • For steps 2 to 4, cut out twigs the same length as the base of the lamp or as the branch of the chandelier that is to be decorated.

2 • Begin with the central base of the chandelier lamp. Make a bundle of twigs that is sufficiently voluminous to surround the base, then attach them with wire, first on the base, then in the middle, and, finally, at the top. Proceed in the same way for the central branch. *(A)*

3 • For the other bases, choose the more supple twigs. Tie a bundle at the top of each base with several circles of wire, then bend the bundles toward the bottom of the bases; tie once again with 2 or 3 circles of wire.

4 • Proceed in the same way for the branches of the chandelier lamp; first attach the bundle to the bottom of the branch, then afterward bend the twigs toward the top of the branch. Let the twigs stick out for a more magical effect. *(B)*

5 • Thread each glass pearl onto a bit of wire, then slide this between the twigs that are interspersed throughout the chandelier lamp. *(C)* Reserve the smaller pearls for the free twigs at the top of the chandelier lamp. End by spraying a thin coating of snow over.

A

B

C

Crocheted fern lamp

With backlighting that is reminiscent of undergrowth, graceful black cotton fern leaves marry poetry and modernity. This idea can be used on all kinds of lamp-shades, drapes, or screens.

SUPPLIES
- 1 x 2 oz (50 g) ball matt cotton for crochet hook no. 2¹/₂–3 in black
- Crochet hook no. 3
- Luminous screen in natural-colored fabric, 24 x 37¹/₂ in (60 x 95 cm)
- Basting thread, sewing thread in black
- Wool needle, sewing needle, pins with heads, pair of scissors
- Sewing machine (optional)
- Iron and ironing board

To make the crocheted fern lamp

Thread the yarn onto the crochet hook as if for a chain (see page 15), then crochet following the grid on page 237. Make 7 ferns in this way (see explanation of picot edging pattern on page 18).

Shaping the crocheted fern lamp

Pull the yarn through to the wrong side. Place the ferns on the ironing board, on the wrong side. Pin them in such a way as to spread out the designs. Steam-iron them without laying the iron on them. Let dry before removing the pins.

Assembly

In order to be able to work without taking up the 2 thicknesses of fabric, put the screen on the ironing board. Arrange the ferns front side upward. Pin them, then baste the central vein and the leaves of each. Make a stitch with the sewing thread in the middle of each central vein then, progressing from the latter toward the outside, in the middle of each leaf. Do not pierce the picots of the leaves.

Tip

To preserve the composition, stick the designs on by stitching through the middle of the stem and leaves. Proceed vein by vein and stop the yarns after each one.

Hydrangea lamp

Real hydrangea petals dance in the artificial lighting: spring is keeping us waiting!

SUPPLIES

- Adhesive backed vinyl sheet
- 2 lampshade frames measuring 8 in (20 cm) in diameter (1 simple, the other ring-shape)
- Bedside lamp frame (for the small lampshade)
- Tracing paper or photocopying machine
- Dried hydrangea petals
- Silk paper or white organdie
- Soft cloth
- Double-sided adhesive tape, 1/2 in (1 cm) wide
- Duct tape, 1 1/4 in (3 cm) wide

EQUIPMENT

- Tape measure
- Metal ruler
- Pencil
- Scissors

1 • Cut out a plastic film the same size as the base (adding 1/2 in (1 cm) at the circumference) and lay it flat down on your work counter. For the small lampshade, draw the shape on page 236 on the adhesive backed vinyl sheet.

2 • Peel off the adhesive backing and lay the hydrangea petals on it evenly. Then lay a sheet of silk paper on top, avoiding marking the folds. Pat with the cloth so the paper adheres all over and cut off excess paper all round. *(A and B)*

3 • Close the **small lampshade** with the double-sided adhesive tape, letting the edges overlap about 1/2 in (1 cm). *(C)*

4 • Measure the length of duct tape you will need to go round the **large lampshade** and add a margin of 1/4 in (5 mm). Cut off 3 equal lengths. Fold the duct tape in 2 widthwise all along its length, the cloth side toward the inside.

5 • Close the lampshade securely as in step 3, bending the adhesive backed vinyl sheet on the simple circle (at the top) and the ring-shape circle (below). Apply duct tape to the top of the lampshade, aligning the fold on the edge of the cylinder. Flatten the duct tape toward the inside. Stick it down all over the circumference of the lampshade, keeping the circle between the adhesive backed vinyl sheet and the tape. If necessary, notch the tape on the inner side to avoid folds.

6 • Begin the previous process again for the bottom of the lampshade. Cut the third piece of duct tape in 2, where the fold is. Apply the tape to the lampshade at the desired height.

A

B

C

Cylindrical tartan lamps

Different-texture strips crisscross one another as in tartan fabric; this idea can be easily and freely adapted to create superb transparent effects.

1 • Cover the external side of the cardboard cylinder with Saran wrap stuck on with adhesive tape.

2 • Draw and cut out 6 strips ¾ in (2 cm) wide and 4 in (10 cm) wide in the nonwoven fabric. From the silk paper, draw and cut out 6 strips identical to those in the nonwoven fabric, and 3 or 4 strips of the same width but with a length equal to the cylinder's circumference.

3 • Thin down the glue in the pot. Stick the cylinder down at a height of 4 in (10 cm). Arrange the strips of nonwoven fabric all round, vertically, evenly spaced out, then insert the small silk paper strips; apply the strips from top to bottom and coat each of them with glue before laying the next down. Glue the large silk

paper strips so they are perpendicular to the others. *(A)* Let dry for 1 or 2 days.

4 • To unmold, fold the inner lining of each cylinder on itself and gently remove the paper lamp.

5 • Put the small glasses in each of the lamps, then place a candle inside each.

Variation

Make a series of coordinated lamps by varying the height of the cylinders, the color of the strips, or the rhythm of the crisscross lines.

A

SUPPLIES
• Nonwoven mauve fabric
• White silk paper
• Small thick glasses
• Tealights
• Saran wrap
• Adhesive tape
• Wallpaper paste

EQUIPMENT
• Cardboard cylinders (crackers package, an inner tube of household wipes, etc)
• Pencil
• Small ruler
• Pair of scissors
• Glass pot
• Flexible silk bristle paintbrush

Pale blue pleated lamp

A circle of felt is gathered with your sewing machine to make a lampshade which delicately filters the light.

SUPPLIES
- Pale blue felt $1/16$ in (2 mm) thick, 20 x 20 in (50 x 50 cm)
- Sewing thread in pale blue
- Lampshade frame (upper $1^1/2$ in [4 cm]; lower $3^1/2$ in [9 cm])
- Lampshade pedestal, 8 in (20 cm) high

EQUIPMENT
- Textile felt-tipped pen
- Compass
- Cutter
- Pins
- Sewing needle
- Sewing machine

1 • Draw an 18 in (45 cm) circle on the blue felt and cut it with the cutter.

2 • Draw a second circle, 4 in (10 cm) in diameter at the center of the first circle and cut it out using the cutter.

3 • Fold the circle in 2 and make the lampshade gathers by folding every $1^1/2$ to 2 in (4 to 5 cm), as for darts. To do this, start at $3/8$ to $1/4$ in (3 to 5 mm) on the upper edge to arrive at $3/4$ or 1 in (2 or 2.5 cm) at the bottom. Secure each fold with pins before machine-stitching. *(A)*

4 • Repeat for the entire circumference of the lampshade—16 folds in all here.

5 • Emphasize the irregularity of the gathers by sewing certain folds on ($1^1/4$ in [3 cm]), starting at the bottom, *(B)* or by making a new fold, toward the inside this time, between 2 machine-stitched folds. To do this, secure it with a few stitches.

6 • Fit the lampshade onto the frame on the pedestal.

Tip
Ensure that the gathered lampshade is adapted to the size of your lamp frame.

A

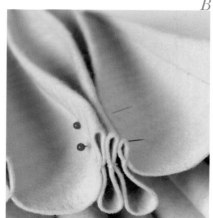

B

Button candleholder

A lamp made up of all sorts of things, from twisted wire to mother-of-pearl buttons.

SUPPLIES
• 40 mother-of-pearl buttons measuring ⅝ in (7 mm), 33 in moss green and 7 in blue
• Thin silver wire (25 mm thick)

EQUIPMENT
• Jewelry pliers
• Wooden spikes

1 • Cut 31 in (80 cm) wire with pliers. Fold it in 2. In the fold, place a wooden spike and make it turn on itself to twist the wire and double it. *(A)*

2 • Thread 9 buttons onto the twisted wire, spacing them out at ¾ in (2 cm) intervals (leave ½ in [1 cm] free at the beginning of the thread). Thread the twisted wire through just 1 hole of a last button and thread the beginning of the thread through the second hole to form a circle. Place the pearly side of the button toward the inside of the circle (see drawing on page 238). Pull on the thread so as always to have ¾ in (2 cm) between each pair of buttons. Twist both threads together and cut at ¼ in (5 mm). Flatten out the thread on the button.

3 • Repeat the process so you obtain 4 other circles of 10 buttons, taking care to vary their color.

4 • Cut 24 in (60 cm) of wire, fold it in 2, and thread the loop thus obtained through 1 of the buttons on the first ring, between the button and the twisted wire (see drawing b on page 238). Twist the 2 ends of the thread together by hand, at a length of ¾ in (2 cm). As before, pass the thread through a button of the second ring. Repeat until you have joined the 4 rings together. Twist the 2 threads by a further ¾ in (2 cm) and cut. Repeat the assembly for the 9 remaining rings to finish the lamp. *(B)*

5 • Flatten the twisted ends on the front side of the last button (inside). Swing the pearly side of the buttons at the top of the lamp toward the outside to create the effect of a corolla. Slip a glass pot inside.

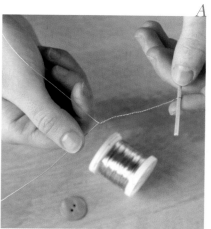

Tutti frutti candles

Caught in transparent gel or poured into traditional candles, seeds punctuate the light, adding surprising touches of color here and there.

SUPPLIES
- 1 package paraffin wax flakes
- Candlewick
- Fairly large transparent glasses
- Few pink peppercorns
- 1 handful black or black-eyed peas
- 1 handful orange lentils

EQUIPMENT
- Large saucepan
- Small saucepan

Paraffin candle

1• Paraffin wax pellets are a ready-to-use product. Fill a large saucepan with water, plunge the closed package of paraffin pellets inside, and heat up to liquefy the flakes. Grasp the package carefully and shake it in order to mix the product thoroughly.

2• Fill half a glass with paraffin, place the wick in the center, and pour a few pink peppercorns into the liquid. Fill the glass up to the top, leaving the wick to stick out by ¹/₂ in (1 cm). Let harden.

3• For the orange lentils and the black or black-eyed peas, fill up the first third of the glasses, position the wick in the middle, and let the candle harden for a few minutes. Keep the package of paraffin warm in the saucepan.

4• Spread an even thickness of seeds over the first layer of the candle, taking care that you do not move the wick, then finish filling up the glasses, leaving the wicks to stick out by ¹/₂ in (1 cm). Let harden slightly, then reintroduce black peas in one of the glasses and orange lentils in the other. Let harden on a flat and stable surface.

5• The following day, heat a small saucepan of water and plunge the glasses in turn into it in order to unmold the candles easily. *(A)*

Tip

You can add candle coloring and/or perfume if you wish.

Gel candle

Supplies
- 1 pot candle gel, candle wicks
- Fairly large transparent glasses
- 1 handful orange lentils
- 2 shea seeds
- 5 or 6 *Hymenea courbaril* seeds
- 1 handful black or black-eyed peas

Equipment
- Large saucepan
- Wooden spatula

1• Fill a saucepan with water, place the opened package of gel inside, and heat so that the gel liquefies. As soon as it begins to soften, mix it with a small spatula until it is of a liquid consistency.

2• Lower the heat, carefully remove the package from the saucepan, and pour the gel into glasses until almost full. Plunge the package into the hot water once again to keep the gel liquid. Put a wick inside each candle, centering it well. Do not twist the wick and ensure no air bubbles are made when you plunge it into the gel.

3• Let the candle cool and harden; when the gel has thickened, drop in the seeds individually: sprinkle over the lentils, lay the shea grains on top, and let the *Hymenea courbaril* seeds

and the peas drop. They should not fall directly into the bottom of the glass; if this does occurs, be ready to introduce some others instead.

4• Check with the spatula that the gel in the saucepan remains quite liquid and finish filling up the glasses full of seeds, letting the wicks stick out by $1/2$ in (1 cm). Let harden on a flat and stable surface. This second layer of gel will heat up the first; it is thus normal for the seeds to sink slowly.

Tip

You can add candle coloring and/or perfume to the gel if you wish. You will find this in the same department of the store.

CAREFUL!

When heating up the gel, do not leave it unattended, and ensure that no water seeps into the package. Preferably use a hotplate.

Glass and pebble lamp

Pebbles are here "coiled" on a glass, their soft and rounded shapes filtering the light.

SUPPLIES
- Large, smooth glass mustard pot
- About 14 small pebbles (up to 1½ to 2 in [40 to 50 mm] in diameter)
- Acetone
- 2-part adhesive
- Broken pieces of colored glass
- Masking tape (or elastic band)
- Sand
- Tealights

EQUIPMENT
- Cloth
- Piece of cardboard
- Spatula

1• Eliminate all traces of grease from the pebbles and the glass by wiping with a cloth soaked in acetone, either in fresh air or a well-ventilated room.

2• Prepare the glue (see page 42), then stick the pebbles round the glass, avoiding any excess glue. Start by sticking them on to the bottom of the glass, then move toward the top. Afterward glue the broken pieces of colored glass between the pebbles. *(A and B)*

3• Use masking tape or an elastic band to keep the pebbles firmly in place as they dry. Let dry thoroughly. then fill the glass with sand and place the candle on your lamp.

Tip

If, as here, you plan to decorate your lamp with broken pieces of colored glass, make sure they do not have any sharp edges. If they do, blunt them with a grindstone.

A

B

Lace-effect lamps

As is always the case with lace, delicacy is the key word... Whether you opt for friezes or individually placed designs, elegance is ever present.

Supplies
- Blue glasses
- White spirit and soft cloth
- Tracing paper
- Adhesive tape

Equipment
- Pencil
- Measuring tape
- Photocopying machine
- Scissors
- Electric engraver
- Thin diamond burr

1• Carefully clean the glasses with the cloth soaked in white spirit to get rid of all traces of grease.

2• Trace your chosen design (see page 237). Cut it out, leaving a small (5 mm) margin all round. Make little nicks that will enable the paper to mold better into the shape of the glass. Place the design inside the glass, then stick it on with adhesive tape, flattening it well against the surface of the glass. *(A and B)*

3• Afterward engrave the outlines that appear through transparency. When you engrave the outlines the first time, press only lightly to avoid slipping. Afterward go over more firmly. *(C)*

4• Wipe regularly with the cloth to get rid of glass dust. Once you have finished engraving, clean the glass thoroughly in warm soapy water.

Note

For the lace frieze (see page 237), you must first of all measure the circumference of the glass, then reduce or enlarge the design on the photocopying machine until you obtain the exact length you have measured.

A

B

C

Pearl candleholder

These lamps, that combine glass and the translucence of pearls, will brighten up your mellow summer nights.

"White flower" candleholder

1 • Glue the white vinyl flowers all round and on the entire surface of the glass pot. Let dry.

2 • Dab a little glue on the center of each flower and apply a gold bead. Glue the iridescent beads on the neck of the glass pot. Let dry.

Extra idea...

To create a supplementary effect, you can vary the size, color, and shape of the beads.

Net candleholder

1 • Cut a piece of net equal in size to the circumference of the glass, plus a little extra, and shape it into a cylinder so that it takes the shape of the glass. *(A)*

2 • Stick a pearl on each stitch of the net with brass wire. Use flat-nose pliers to twist the thread and an old pair of scissors (or pliers) to cut off the excess. *(B)*

3 • Finally, fit the embroidered net cylinder on the glass.

SUPPLIES & EQUIPMENT

"White flower" candleholder
- 1 glass pot
- 1 package white vinyl flowers
- Superglue
- 1 tube gold beads
- 26 iridescent beads

Net candleholder
- 1 cylindrical glass
- Gold-colored netting
- Brass wire
- 2 tubes Plexiglas iridescent pearls
- Flat-nose pliers
- Old scissors or cutting pliers

A

B

Button lamp

A lampshade decorated in linen and set off by rows of pearly buttons and exotic buttons.

SUPPLIES

• 1 lampshade of your choice in a light-colored fabric
• About 20 mirror-faceted buttons, ³/₄ in (2 cm)
• About 50 eau-de-nil pearl buttons, ³/₄ to ⁵/₈ in (1.3 to 1.5 cm)
• About 30 fancy buttons in a range of green shades—from lime-green to bronze-green, ¹/₂ to 1¹/₄ in (1 to 3 cm)
• Patterned linen fabric with a blue-green background (measurements will depend on the size of the lampshade)
• Bias binding to match the linen
• Fusible interfacing, 28 x 24 in (70 x 60 cm)
• Pink and red felt, ¹/₁₆ in (2 mm) thick, 8 in (20 cm) each
• Pearl cotton # 5 in maroon
• Basting thread

EQUIPMENT

• Textile glue spray
• White fabric glue
• Compass to take the felt-tipped pen
• Brown paper
• Bristol paper
• Adhesive tape
• Textile felt-tipped pen
• Tape measure
• Dressmaking scissors
• Iron
• Embroidery needle, sewing needle

1• Roll up the lampshade in the brown paper and secure it with pieces of adhesive tape. Mark the position of the metallic circles on the paper by sliding the tip of the pencil over the upper circle and beneath the lower circle. Mark the height of the lampshade with a vertical line, using the lamp's vertical height. Remove the brown paper and carefully cut out the pattern. Put it over the lampshade to check your measurements.

2• Stick the fusible interfacing to the wrong side of the linen using the iron. Draw the outline of the lampshade pattern in textile felt-tipped pen on the fusible interfacing, placing the middle of the pattern in the direction of the grain (see drawing on page 239). Do not cut this out.

3• Following the drawing, baste on the right side of the linen in order to show the limits of the pattern. On the wrong side, mark the central point of the circles with a cross. Draw 3 semi-circles in textile felt-tipped pen, using a compass: 1 at ¹/₂ in (1.2 cm) from the upper edge, and the 2 other spaced evenly (see drawing b on page 239). These drawn lines will enable you to arrange the buttons attractively, diminishing their number as and when required. Cut the linen, leaving a ⁵/₈ in (1.5 cm) margin where the rounded parts are, and a ¹/₂ in (1 cm) margin on the sides.

4• On the Bristol paper, draw a circle measuring 1 in (2.5 cm) in diameter and cut it out. Place this shape on the red and pink felt to obtain about 60 circles. If the right side of the felts you have chosen have a different shade from the wrong side, vary the direction of their application.

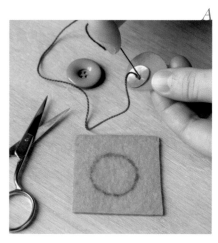
A

B

5• Sew 1 faceted button on the upper part of 13 felt circles. *(A)* Using the drawn part of the first semicircle (on the wrong side), sew these circles on the right side, spacing them out at regular intervals and alternating their colors. Center them on the drawing and sew them on the top of the lampshade. Be careful: arrange them so the space between the first and last circle and the edge of the pattern is equal to half the measurement from 1 circle to the next.

6• Sew a faceted button and a pearly button on the upper part of 18 felt circles, on the right side or the wrong side. Sew them in the same way on the second drawing, alternating the buttons.

7• Sew a pearly button on 12 felt circles. Sew them in the same way on the third drawing, alternating them with buttons without felt. *(B)*

8• The lines will now be visible on the right side, so jumble up the rhythm a bit by sewing on felt circles trimmed with a mother-of-pearl button here and there on each line. Sew the green fancy buttons irregularly on the linen fabric. *(C)*

9• Stick the ¹/₂ in (1 cm) margin with white fabric glue to the back of one of the lampshade's sides and fold it wrong side to wrong side following the drawing. Glue the wrong side of the linen structure with the glue spray and position it on the lampshade, making sure the sides coincide, the hollow being placed on the top.

10• Shape the excess fabric into a triangle at the level of the lampshade's circles. Stick the excess fabric onto the inside of the lampshade with white fabric glue and flatten it. Cut a length of bias binding, fold it, stick it down, and place it on the notched hollows to camouflage them.

C

Duo of candleholders

The brightness of pearl cotton associated with glass enhances the subtle light given off by the candles.

SUPPLIES
• 1 x 2 oz (50 g) reel pearl cotton for crochet hook no. 2 in each of the following colors: pink, purple, orange
• 2 candleholders measuring about 2 in (5 cm) in diameter x height of 2³/₄ in (6.5 cm)
• Crochet hook no. 2
• Wool needle, pair of scissors
• Foil
• Starch, powder or spray

To make the candleholder covers

Thread the pink yarn into a ring, then crochet a medallion as follows (see page 18 and grid on page 238).

Background: crochet from the 1st to 7th row = 48 rib stitches (see page 15).

Inside: 8th to 19th row: crochet 2 times the 6 rows in a fancy stitch. Crochet the 20th row in orange thread. Crochet 2nd identical piece, but starting with the purple thread.

To finish off

Pull the yarns through to the wrong side. Wrap each candleholder with a strip of foil. Soak the pieces in starch (or put them in position, then spray starch on them). Let dry, remove the foil, and put the candleholder covers back in place.

Note

On the 11th row, pierce the single crochets exactly inside the chain stitches of the previous row.

Tip

This project can easily be adapted for a larger candleholder. Work a greater number of stitches (in multiples of 6), and add rows until you obtain the required diameter and height.

Flying butterflies

Personalize an openwork wall lamp with two colored insects that create lively and unexpected animation.

1• Measure the height and circumference of your frame and wet-felt a strip of white wool a little larger than this, following the instructions for wet felting on page 22. Here, the strip of felted wool measures 13½ x 6¼ in (34 x 16 cm).

2• Reckon on a 3½ in (9 cm) bend, corresponding to a half side at the back, and make a first vertical line of 3 holes with the punch (the 1st and 3rd holes will be ⅝ in (1.5 cm) from the edges). Make a second vertical line of 2 holes at a distance of 1¼ in (3 cm) from the previous line, the holes being 2 in (5 cm) away from the edges. Make 8 lines in total, alternating 3-hole lines and 2-hole lines.

3• Sew the piece of felt you have thus decorated on the hoops in front of the frame with needle and thread. *(A)* Assemble the flaps at the back with backstitch.

4• Felt the turquoise and mauve butterflies with a needle on the foam frame (see page 24). First shape the wings with a medium-size needle, then the turquoise and purple bodies with a fine needle. Afterward join the 2 pieces of each butterfly by stitching them to amalgamate the wool. *(B)*

5• Sew the butterflies onto the lamp on the reverse with a few discreet stitches at the level of the body.

SUPPLIES
• White merino wool, 50 g (2 oz)
• Small amount turquoise merino wool (5 g), purple merino wool (3 g), and mauve merino wool (5 g)
• White sewing thread
• White metal frame

EQUIPMENT
• Bubble wrap
• Synthetic tulle
• Soap
• Punch
• Sewing needle
• Pins
• Felting needle with a fine point
• Felting needle with a medium-size point
• Foam frame

A

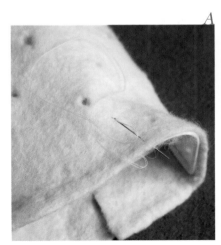

B

Seed light

Like a fashionable dress, this hanging light mixes exoticism with high design.

SUPPLIES

SUPPLIES
- About 20 entada seeds
- Very fine wire
- Round light frame
- Thin braid, 40 in (1 m)
- Clear superglue
- Clear matt varnish

EQUIPMENT
- Drill
- Cutting pliers
- Small peg
- Paintbrush

1• With a drill and a fine drill bit, pierce 20 seeds in 4 places for the first 2 rows, and 10 seeds in a single place for the last row. *(A)*

2• Cut the pieces of thin wire to a length of about 1½ in (4 cm).

3• Start by fixing the seeds individually onto the light. To do this, slip a piece of wire into 1 of the seed's holes and fold the wire on the lamp, forming a loop about ¼ in (5 mm) long, then twist the 2 ends of the wire. Afterward roll up the excess wire (about ¾ in [2 cm]) on the light. Repeat the process with another seed and, once this is in place, join it to the first with a piece of wire bent to a U-shape staple. Twist the fastening inside the light and leave the excess wire; these lengths will be cut at the end of the work.

4• Make the first row in this way, then hang a few seeds on the second row, clasping the wire fastenings tightly. The last row hangs from the second but the seeds are not joined together, they hang freely.

5• Carefully glue 1 end of a ¾ in (2 cm) length of braid, then attach it to the light and roll up the braid on top of it, passing between the wire fastenings and taking care to cross the braid slightly on itself each time you go round; keep it in place by dabbing a bit of glue on every 2 in (5 cm). Finally, glue the end of the braid at ¾ in (2 cm) and press it firmly against the light for a few moments with a peg, to make it adhere.

6• Once you have finished the light, check the condition and overall appearance of the seeds; tighten or loosen some fastenings as required in order to harmonize the work. Cut off the excess wire.

7• Hang the light and varnish the seeds. Let dry.

Tips

Entada seeds have an overall square shape with rounded edges. Imagine there is a cross drawn on each seed and pierce at the ends. The holes will not always be exactly opposite each other, so always leave a space between the seeds when you apply them to the light; the end result will thus be more flexible and delicate.

A

Rose net

Small vividly colored roses decorate this net candle-holder.

SUPPLIES

• DMC Retors matt cotton, 1 skein in each of the following colors: blackcurrant 2916, raspberry 2109, mandarin 2946, orange 2740, and golden yellow 2741
• Red netting with hexagonal holes, 4 x 20 in (10 x 50 cm)

EQUIPMENT

• Blunt needle
• Sewing thread in red for firm hems
• Flannel
• Measuring tape
• Thimble
• Scissors
• Cutting pliers

STITCHES USED

• Bullion stitch
• Buttonhole stitch

Diagrams 1 to 4, page 238
Guide page 238

1• To embroider without scratches, cover the cut edges of the netting with flannel surrounded by fabric, then sew everything up with large stitches. *(A)*

2• Prepare 18 in (45 cm) pieces of Retors matt cotton and work color by color, starting with blackcurrant at the bottom of the netting (see guide).

3• To begin a design, leave 3¼ in (8 cm) of thread (diagram 1) and turn round the axes by going once over the top and once below (diagram 2). Keep the design between the thumb and index finger of your free hand to contain it within the netting. Do not tighten the threads too much; the design should be enlarged very slightly each time you go over it until it forms a small, almost flat circle and not a ball. The tension of the thread should not be too loose or too tight. *(B)* Go over it 28 times. At the last time, tie the 2 ends of the thread on the wrong side, reassemble them, and cut them evenly.

4• Embroider 5 staggered rows of 9 designs in this way.

5• With the pliers, cut the netting at the edge of the twisted sections (see guide), having removed the flannel to obtain a length of netting measuring about 14 in (35 cm).

6• Form a cylinder, put the twisted ends so they face one another, then surround them with red sewing thread. Tighten and tie firmly (diagram 3).

7• Continue to surround them by stitching in buttonhole stitch in which you keep the starting thread (diagram 4). Finally, bring the thread through to the wrong side of the stitch with a fine needle and cut it. *(C)*

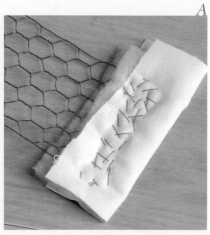

A

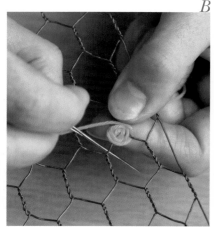

B

C

Pink candleholder

Decorated with a voluptuous tulip-colored curve, here is a rounded candleholder for charmed evenings.

1• Cover the outer part of the stemmed glass with Saran wrap and stick this on with adhesive tape.

2• Tear the tracing paper into strips 1/8–1/4 in (3–4 mm) wide and 1/2 in (1 cm) longer than the main part of the glass (without counting the stem).

3• Thin down the glue in the pot. Glue the stemmed glass with the paintbrush, then cover it with strips of tracing paper; apply these from top to bottom, overlapping them slightly. Glue each of these before laying down the next. *(A)* Surround the top of the stem with strips of tracing paper at a height of 1/2 in (1 cm). *(B)* Let dry for 1 or 2 days.

4• Cut the tracing paper lengthwise with the cutter and remove the stemmed glass.

5• Close the candleholder by sticking adhesive tape inside. Hide the join by glueing 1 or 2 strips of tracing paper on the outside. *(C)* Let dry. Remove the adhesive tape.

6• Place the small glass inside the candleholder, then put a tealight inside.

SUPPLIES
• Thick raspberry-colored tracing paper
• Small thick glass
• Tealight
• Saran wrap
• Adhesive tape
• Wallpaper paste

EQUIPMENT
• Slightly curved stemmed glass
• Glass pot
• Flexible silk bristle paintbrush
• Cutter

A

B

C

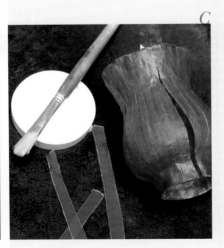

Assorted candleholders

Seeds offer many opportunities for you to create surprising seasonal candleholders.

SUPPLIES
• About 20 star anise
• Glass pot
• Tealight

EQUIPMENT
• Glue gun
• Cocktail stick

Star anise candleholder

The glass pot serves as a mold here. Use this shape to stick on the seeds between themselves, without ever glueing them to the pot which you will remove when you have finished working.

1• Load the glue gun and let it heat up. Choose a few unblemished star anise and remove the peduncle (at the center of the star anise).

2• To make the first row, you will have to detach a small "petal" from each star anise in order to have an almost horizontal base; reserve the detached petals. Place the star anise next to each other round the pot, dabbing a bit of glue on the petals that touch each other. The glue should be as invisible as possible. *(A)*

3• Continue applying the star anise up to the top of the pot. Each petal that touches another should be glued. The reserved ones from the first row could be used to fill the gaps that are a little too large.

4• Let dry for 5 minutes, then gently remove the pot. Put a little warm glue on the nozzle of the glue gun with the tip of a cocktail stick and make the candleholder stiff by reglueing, always on the inside, all the petals that touch another. Remove the trails of glue by pulling on them.

5• Finally, add a last row of star anise that are slightly bent toward the inside of the candleholder.

6• Place the tealight in the center. Once it is lit, it will heat up the star anise and thus release their fragrance.

A

Tip

The glue that comes out of the glue gun is liquid, very hot, and dries quickly; you should always use this tool carefully.

Hymenea courbaril and orange lentil candleholder

Based on the same principle as the star anise candleholder, this is assembled round a yogurt pot, using a glue gun. The seeds used here do not require any advance preparation.

1 • Position the first row of *Hymenea courbaril* seeds on the base of the pot, without glueing it on, leaving less than $^1/_2$ in (1 cm) between the seeds. Glue the *Hymenea courbaril* seeds in a staggered row, using the cocktail stick to glue them on; your work will be more precise and neat using this.

2 • Assemble the seeds to the desired height, then let dry for 5 minutes.

3 • Carefully remove the yogurt pot and, as with the previous candleholder, check all the dabs of glue and make the candleholder stiff using the tip of a cocktail stick impregnated with glue.

4 • With a slightly glued cocktail stick, take up the lentils individually and glue them, rounded side toward the outside of the candleholder. A single lentil will be enough to fill each of the gaps between the *Hymenea courbaril* seeds.

Gourd candleholder

1 • With the drill and 3 fine but different-size bits, make several holes, either randomly or following a design, on the upper third of the gourd. Always drill from top to bottom, not sidewise or toward the top.

2 • Put a tealight inside; its light will reveal the drilled design.

SUPPLIES
Hymenea courbaril **and orange lentil candleholder**
• Empty yogurt pot
• 15 to 50 *Hymenea courbaril* seeds
• About 15 orange lentils

EQUIPMENT
• Glue gun
• Cocktail stick

SUPPLIES
Gourd candleholder
• $^1/_2$ gourd
• Tealight

EQUIPMENT
• Handheld drill

Square candleholder

Hydrangea lamp
Bedside lamp
(enlarge to 140%)

Flap to be glued

Crocheted fern lamp

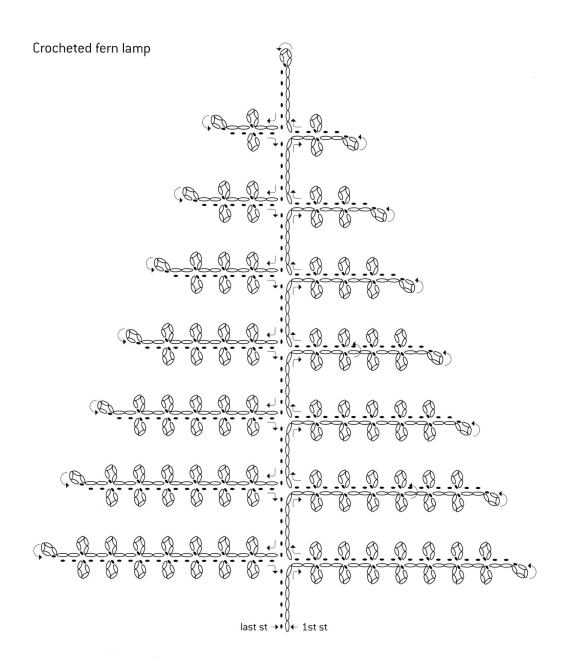

last st → | ← 1st st

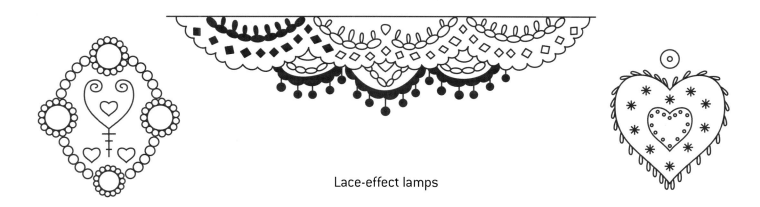

Lace-effect lamps

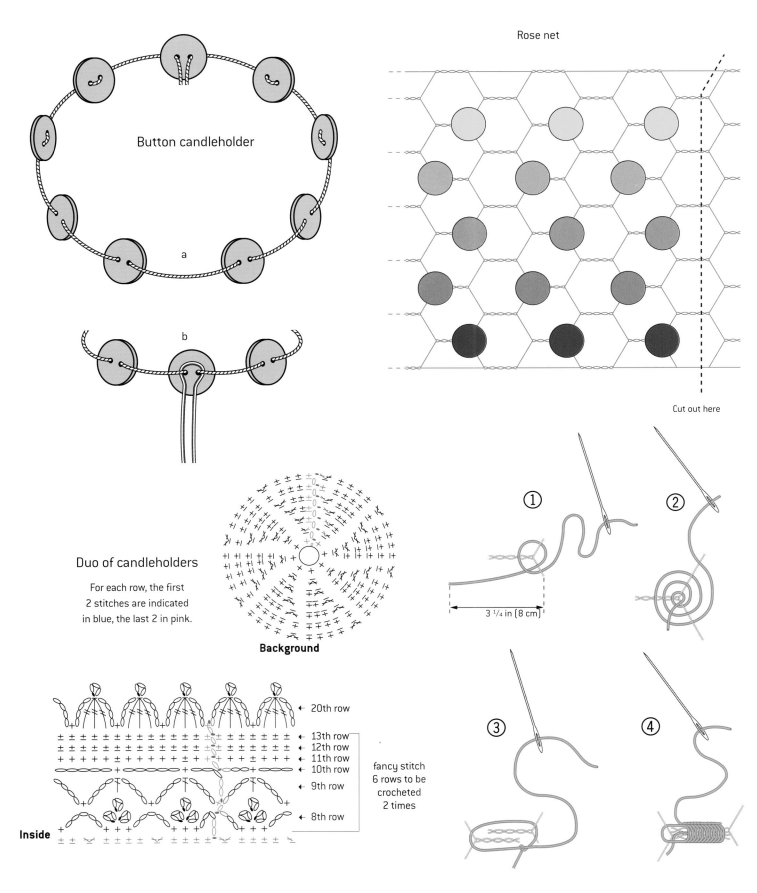

Button candleholder

a

b

Rose net

Cut out here

Duo of candleholders

For each row, the first
2 stitches are indicated
in blue, the last 2 in pink.

Background

Inside

← 20th row

← 13th row
← 12th row
← 11th row
← 10th row

← 9th row

← 8th row

fancy stitch
6 rows to be
crocheted
2 times

① 3 ¼ in (8 cm)

②

③

④

Button lamp
How to place the buttons

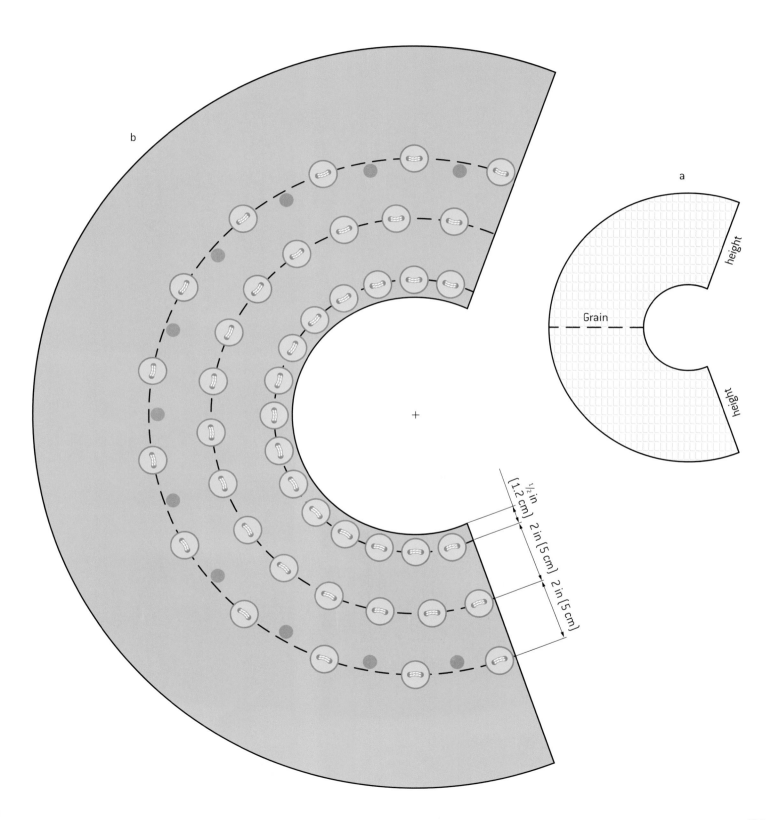

b

a

height

height

Grain

½ in
(1.2 cm)

2 in (5 cm)

2 in (5 cm)

Be practical
and organized

Week organizer

The week is organized in a flash on this very practical blackboard. You will not forget any important appointments!

SUPPLIES

• Slate measuring 8¼ x 12½ in (21 x 31 cm)
• Waterproof coating
• 7 pebbles, 1¼ in to 1½ in (30 to 35 mm) in diameter
• 2 pebbles, ⅝ to ¾ in (15 to 20 mm) diameter
• Satin varnish (optional)
• Clear superglue

EQUIPMENT

• Small drill with ¼ in (6 mm) carbide bit
• Ruler
• Soft cloths
• White or gray poster paint
• Flat paintbrush

1• Pierce holes in the slate at least ¾ in (20 mm) from the edge, following the photograph. Hold it flat in your hand to do this; this will enable the vibrations to be absorbed and will reduce the risk of breakage. *(A)*

2• Having thoroughly cleaned and dried the slate, draw 7 horizontal lines to divide it into 8 spaces, using the ruler and the poster paint. Then write the word "WEEK" in poster paint in the middle of the first strip. *(B)*

3• Apply 1 or 2 layers of waterproof coating with a paintbrush over the entire surface of the slate.

4• Once you have thoroughly cleaned and dried the large pebbles, write a day of the week on each of them. If you wish, varnish the Saturday and Sunday pebbles. Let dry. *(C)*

5• Glue these pebbles at the beginning of each line, then the small pebbles on each side of the word "WEEK," and let dry completely.

Tips

To make this project, you can use a roof slate or a school slate. To draw the lines on the slate, measure up and make pencil marks as a guide.

A

B

C

Grocery pots

These three little pots reveal a subtle intermingling of shades and textures: white and silver, smooth and rough.

Pots

1• Wrap each pot in Saran wrap fixed in place with adhesive tape.

2• Tear up the white paper and the crêpe paper into small pieces. Put them in the salad bowl, add a generous amount of water, then blend in a liquidizer.

3• Proceed in this way (instructions are given on page 30, steps 3 and 4). Cover the pots with the blended mixture *(A)*, then coat with wallpaper paste. Let dry for 2 or 3 days.

4• Varnish and let dry.

5• To unmold, slide the knife between the pot and the paper, and tear the latter on 1 of its sides. *(B)*

6• To wrap paper round the pot, secure the edges against each other with a few pieces of adhesive tape, apply a bit of the blended mixture on each of them, absorb the water with the sponge, and let dry. Repeat the process, removing the adhesive tape each time until the gap is entirely hidden.

SUPPLIES
- White photocopying paper
- Silver crêpe paper
- Silver silk paper
- Saran wrap
- Adhesive tape
- Wallpaper paste
- Food-safe varnish

EQUIPMENT
- 3 square pots with lids, in different sizes
- Ladle
- Salad bowl, bowl, glass pot
- Sponge
- Flexible silk bristle paintbrush
- Filling knife
- Cutter

A

B

C

D

Lids

1• Wrap each lid in Saran wrap fixed in place with adhesive tape.

2• Tear up the silk paper into squares measuring about ¹/₂ in (1 cm) on the sides.

3• Glue the outer surface of the lids with a paintbrush, then cover in paper squares. Overlap them slightly and coat each in wallpaper paste before you lay on the next. *(C)* Apply 2 or 3 layers of paper in this way. Let dry for 1 or 2 days.

4• Turn over the lids and cover their inner surface in the same way as before.

5• Varnish the 2 surfaces of each lid and let dry.

6• Engrave the inner surface of the 3 pieces with the cutter and remove the lids. *(D)*

7• To close the lids, secure the edges against each other with a few pieces of adhesive tape, glue the strips of silver paper between them, and let dry. Repeat the process, removing the adhesive tape each time until the gap is entirely hidden. Let dry.

8• Retouch the joins with varnish.

Tip

The pots will be more functional if their lids sit correctly in place on them. To achieve this, fill them with sand inside before closing them in step 7.

My personal mailbox

A photograph, some stamps, a few touches of imagination... and here is a mailbox that is personalized in an instant. A stunning effect is guaranteed!

Preparation of the transfers

1• Reproduce a photograph and some stamps in whatever size you wish on the photograph paper.

2• Reproduce 2 stamps for each key (height = the upper part of the key + ⅝ in [1.5 cm]; width = the width of the key + ½ in [1 cm]). For a nice finishing touch, reproduce the stamp that is behind the key with a mirror effect.

3• Cut out each image you have transferred, without any borders.

To finish the mailbox

1• Peel off the protective backing from the photograph paper and stick the photograph to the front of the mailbox, putting part of it inside the mailbox opening. *(A)* Add a few stamps, not forgetting the sides of the mailbox. Stick everything down well, pressing with a cloth.

2• Paint a few black spots and let dry for 12 hours. Apply a thin layer of varnish over the entire work to protect it.

To finish the keys

1• Stick the stamp transfers on each side of the keys. *(B)*

2• Machine-stitch them together ⅛ in (3 mm) from the edges.

Supplies
- Metal mailbox with keys
- Black metal paint (or cold paint)
- Round medium-size paintbrush
- Clear exterior varnish
- Large paintbrush
- Sewing machine and sewing thread (keys)

Equipment
- Photograph and used stamps
- Adhesive photograph paper
- Scissors
- Cloth

A

B

Ethnic photograph albums

Simple knotted thread on linen enables you to create attractive photograph albums in which to keep travel memories alive.

1• Cut the fabric to the same size as the photograph album it is to cover (front, back, and spine), adding 2 1/2 in (6 cm) to the height and width. Cut out a rectangle in the size of the front and back, less 3/4 in (2 cm) on the height and width.

2• Lay the large piece of fabric flat on your work surface and arrange pieces of string on top of the cover, following drawings 1 and 2 on page 282. Pin these. *(A)*

3• Make a stitch at every intersection. Afterward tie the string, following drawing 3, and sew the 1, 4, and 7 vertical strips of string on the intersections. If necessary, shorten the free ends of the pieces of string, but do not glue them. *(B)*

4• Spray the glue on the wrong side of the fabric and place this on the photograph album to be covered. Fold up the excess fabric inside the cover, notching the corners to obtain a neat result.

5• Spray glue on the 2 rectangles prepared in step 1 and lay them inside the cover, making a small hollow over the entire area.

Variation

You can also mix and match different types of string to create various shades or a harmony of colors.

Supplies
• Photograph album or notebook
• Linen fabric
• Kitchen string
• White thread

Equipment
• Measuring tape
• Dressmaking chalk
• Scissors
• Pins with heads
• Needle
• Glue spray

A

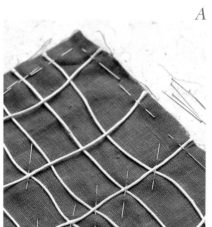

B

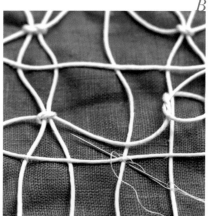

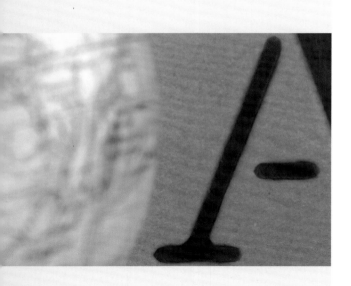

Letter files

Pyrographing the letters A, B, and C onto your files is an original and easy way to identify their contents.

SUPPLIES
• Cardboard files

EQUIPMENT
• Metal letter stencils, 4¹/₂ in (122 mm) in height
• Pencil
• Pyrograph machine
• Nib no. 24

1 • Position a letter stencil on 1 part of the cardboard file and trace it out in pencil. *(A)*

2 • Darken the inside of the letter with nib no. 24, exerting even pressure on the pyrography machine. *(B)*

3 • Repeat steps 1 and 2 for the other letters.

Variation
You can use smaller letter stencils instead and inscribe a whole word on the file.

A

B

Old-fashioned key ring

A rustic touch to keep your house keys safe, in which wood mingles with string and metal.

Preparation of the transfers

Reproduce the images of the keys on the photograph paper. Cut out each image you have transferred, without any borders.

To make the key ring

1• With a saw, cut strips of batten 6 in (15 cm) long. Cut out a piece at the tip of each of these.

2• Draw a pencil mark ³/₄ in (2 cm) from the edge of the piece of wood and make a hole in it with a drill.

3• Apply a little wood glue in the hole and insert an eyelet on each side of the wooden piece. *(A)*

4• Peel off the protective backing from the photograph paper and stick the key transfers onto the wooden pieces. Apply 1 or 2 thin layers of varnish. *(B)*

5• Thread the string into the hole and tie the ends up.

Tip

You can color the wood with a wood stain, such as a walnut stain, or with acrylic paint thinned down with a little water. Let dry thoroughly before applying the glue and varnishing.

SUPPLIES
• Piece of recycled batten, 2¹/₄ in (5.5 cm) wide and ³/₈ in (8 mm) thick
• Wood saw
• Drill and wood bit, ³/₄ in (6 mm) in diameter
• Metal eyelets
• Wood glue
• Clear matt varnish
• Paintbrush
• String

EQUIPMENT
• Old-fashioned keys (examples on page 283)
• Photograph paper
• Fine scissors
• Cloth

A

B

Letters for your organizer

To personalize your stationery and leather organizer quickly, here are some capital letters to be applied with a fine nib.

Leather

1 • Position the stencil on the leather cover of the organizer or pocketbook and trace it out in pencil. *(A)*

2 • With nib no. 22, make small evenly spaced-out holes close to each other, following the tracing. Make a test on a piece of leather before you begin work to gauge the pressure you will have to exert on the nib; leather is very soft and easy to pyrograph, so you will scarcely need to press down with your pyrograph machine. *(B)*

Paper

1 • As for the organizer, position the letter on the writing paper and trace its outlines out in pencil.

2 • With nib no. 22, make small holes in the paper following the pencil tracings. Protect your work surface by placing a piece of wood under the sheet of paper. *(C)*

3 • To make the envelopes, postcards, and notebook, proceed as for the writing paper.

SUPPLIES
• Leather organizer or pocketbook in a light color
• Piece of leather
• Writing paper
• Piece of wood
• Envelopes
• Plain postcards
• Notebook

EQUIPMENT
• Metal letter stencils, 1¼ in (30 mm) in height
• Pencil
• Pyrograph machine
• Nib no. 22

A

B

C

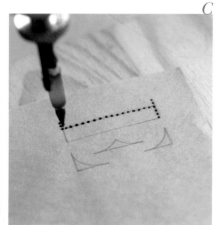

Memory hatbox

An attractive old-fashioned photograph beautifully personalizes this hatbox. The addition of a few beads makes all the difference.

SUPPLIES
- Round cardboard box
- Grosgrain ribbon, 1 in (2.5 cm) wide
- Velvet ribbon, $1/2$ in (1 cm) wide
- Textile glue
- Jewelry glue
- 3 rhinestones
- 2 different-size buttons
- Pencil

EQUIPMENT
- Portrait photograph
- Photograph paper
- Scissors
- Pair of compasses
- Cloth
- White printer paper

Preparation of the transfer

1• Reproduce your photograph on the photograph paper to the same size as the lid of the box.

2• Trace out a circle the same size as the photograph in the center of a sheet of white printer paper, then cut it out. Arrange this on the photograph, choose the centering, and trace the circle. Carefully cut out the photograph.

To finish the box

1• Arrange the paper circle in the center of the box's lid and lightly reproduce the tracing in pencil.

2• Peel off the protective backing from the photograph paper and stick the photograph to the lid. Press down with the cloth to make it adhere better.

3• Using the textile glue, stick the grosgrain ribbon onto the edge of the lid. Glue the velvet ribbon (leaving two 5 in [13 cm] lengths) on top of the grosgrain ribbon, as indicated in the photograph.

4• Make a loop with each of the 5 in [13 cm] lengths of velvet ribbon by folding the ends on the wrong side and gluing them down. Then glue the 2 loops in a cross shape on the upper end of the photograph. *(A)*

5• Lay 1 button on top of the other and glue them in the middle of the velvet loop. Finally, stick on 3 rhinestones with jewelry glue to make a hair slide to stick on. *(B)*

A

B

Fall leaf shelves

A small piece of wooden furniture decorated with fall-colored leaves is ideal for storing small garden tools and seeds or for filing your mail.

1 • Apply wood glue to the back of the leaves and stick them to the front of a drawer, some next to each other, and some slightly overlapping each other. *(A)*

2 • Cover the entire front of the drawer in this way. Let dry, placing a fairly heavy weight on top of the leaf-covered drawer, such as a pile of books.

3 • When the glue is dry, cut off any excess in the leaves with the cutter, flush with the edge of the drawer. *(B)*

4 • Repeat steps 1 to 3 for the other drawers, varying the colors and the shapes of the leaves.

Extra idea...

On the same principle, a hollyhock flower glued with wood glue and protected with two layers of acrylic varnish will transform a bamboo dish into an incense holder (see photograph above left). Make a small hole in the middle with scissor tips and stick your incense sticks on top. Clean your work with a damp but not too wet sponge.

SUPPLIES
• Piece of unpolished wood furniture with shelves
• Wood glue
• Dried leaves

EQUIPMENT
• Flat paintbrush
• Cutter

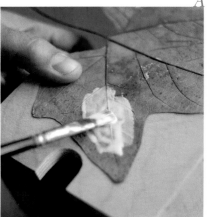

A

B

Corded plant pot

Ramp rope wound round a pot marries country and graphic styles. All you have to do is to place an elegant cactus or a few logs inside.

1• Following the drawing on page 282, mark out the position of the 48 holes on the pot in felt-tipped pen. Make the holes using the drill, applying pressure only lightly at the beginning to avoid any slipping.

2• Wind the hemp string round the ends of the ramp rope, at about ³/₄ or 1 ¹/₄ in (2 or 3 cm). In this way the ramp rope will not undergo any distress.

3• Cut 26 ft (8 m) sisal string and tie a double knot at 1 of the ends.

4• Wrap the ramp rope round the pot and thread the sisal string into the holes. To do this, start at the bottom and work in a spiral toward the top. Secure the sisal string with a double knot inside the pot. *(A)*

5• Finally, insert the sisal string between the rows of ramp rope that you have wrapped round the pot. Make a knot at each intersection with the vertical strands of sisal string in order to secure the last row of sisal string. *(B)*

Tip

If this is to serve as a plant holder, do not place your chosen plant directly into the plastic pot; the dampness of the earth would damage your work. Instead, place a saucer at the bottom of the pot and slide the plant and its pot inside the decorated pot.

A

B

Linen organizers

To sort your dish towels and towels and to tidy your household linen once and for all, these organizers have words pyrographed on them.

1 • Place your letter stencils on 1 of the small sides of the organizer, spacing them out at regular intervals and centering the word you have formed within the organizer's width.

2 • Use the metal ruler to arrange all the letters on the same horizontal line and stick them on the organizer with adhesive tape. *(A)*

3 • Draw the outline of the letters with nib no. 22 and fill in the inside with nib no. 21. *(B)*

SUPPLIES
• Wooden organizers
• Adhesive tape

EQUIPMENT
• Letter stencils, 1¼ in (30 mm) in height
• Metal ruler
• Pyrograph machine
• Nibs no. 21 and 22

A

B

Tool buckets

An inventive solution that can be freely adapted to all rooms in the house.

SUPPLIES

- 3 metal buckets, 4 in (10 cm) in diameter
- Plank of wood, 12 x 16 in (30 x 40 cm)
- Thin sandpaper
- White matt acrylic paint
- Large paintbrush
- Wood drill and $1/4$ in (4 mm) bit
- 60 in (150 cm) aluminum foil, $1/16$ in (2 mm) thick
- Cutting pliers
- 3 U-shape staples
- Hammer
- Clear matt varnish
- Ruler
- Pencil
- Eraser

EQUIPMENT

- Pictures of tools: pliers, spanner, screws, ruler (see examples on page 282)
- Photograph paper
- Scissors
- Cloth

Preparation of the transfers

1 • Reproduce the tool pictures on page 282 (pliers, spanner, screws) on the photograph paper. Do the same with those of the ruler, placing the lengths tip to tip to obtain 2 measurements of 12 in (30 cm) and 1 of 16 in (40 cm).

2• Cut out each image you have transferred, without any borders.

To make the display shelf

1 • Wash the buckets in warm soapy water to get rid of any traces of grease.

2• Sand down the plank of wood with sandpaper. Draw a horizontal line along its length, 4 $1/2$ in (12 cm) from the bottom. On this line, starting from the left-hand border, mark points at 2 in (5 cm), 4 in (10 cm), 6 $3/4$ in (17.5 cm), 8 $3/4$ in (22.5 cm), 12 in (30 cm), and finally 14 in (35 cm). Make a hole at each point you have marked, then glue the tracing down.

3• Thin down the white paint with 30% water and paint the plank of wood evenly, not forgetting the sides. Let dry.

4• Peel off the protective backing from the photograph paper and stick the tool transfers onto the pots and those of the ruler at the top and sides of the plank of wood. *(A)* Ensure they adhere well by pressing down with the cloth.

5• Cut a 17 $3/4$ in (45 cm) piece of aluminum foil. Thread it through the first 2 holes to form a loop, then place the bucket inside. Pull the thread behind in order to keep the bucket steady (do not pull too hard or the bucket will ride up again). *(B)*

6• Fold the ends of the foil by crossing them and stop them in the middle with a U-shape staple (see the diagrams on page 282). Repeat the process for the other buckets.

A

B

Bucolic notebooks

Notebooks in which you can catalog dried plants you have collected or just record the weather.

SUPPLIES

- Spiral exercise book or hardback notebook covered in craft paper
- Dried leaves and flowers
- Wood glue
- Double-sided adhesive tape, 12 in (30 cm) wide
- White silk paper or thin crystal paper
- Soft cloth
- Duct tape, 2 in (5 cm) wide

EQUIPMENT

- Cutter

1 • Stick the leaf or flower on the **notebook** using wood glue. Apply double-sided adhesive tape over the entire surface of the cover. Peel off the protective backing. *(A)*

2 • Cover the notebook with a sheet of silk paper or crystal paper. Smooth it down with the cloth. Cut off any excess paper with the cutter, level with the cover.

3 • Put a strip of duct tape on the notebook's spine, centering it well widthwise. Cut off any excess duct tape with the cutter, level with the notebook. *(B)*

4 • For the **spiral notebook**, carefully remove the cover and decorate it as before, following steps 1 and 2. Cut the perforations with the cutter once again before putting the cover back in place on the spirals.

Tip

For this collage project, use a spiral notebook which will enable you to remove and replace the cover without damaging it.

Variation

If you have no notebook or exercise book with a suitable cover to hand, you can cover your chosen notebook with chiffon paper, scrapbook paper, or any other kind of paper, using very wide double-sided adhesive tape. Afterward apply another layer of adhesive tape to your scrapbook paper in order to stick down the leaf or flower and the silk or crystal paper.

A

B

Linen pouch

This little pouch, which is decorated with tubes of paint and assorted ribbons, is ideal to tidy everything away!

Preparation of the transfer

1• Reproduce the picture of the tubes of paint on tracing paper. Allow a border of 5/8 in (1.5 cm) on each side, 3/4 in (2 cm) on top and 2 1/2 in (6 cm) below.

2• Transfer the picture (see page 283) with its borders onto a rectangular piece of linen. Cut the fabric round the borders so you end up with a rectangle of 8 1/2 x 6 1/4 in (22 x 16 cm).

Pouch

1• Cut a rectangle in the linen fabric of the same size as the picture (8 1/2 x 6 1/4 in (22 x 16 cm)) and a strip that is 2 1/2 x 20 in (6 x 50 cm) long.

2• Cut two 8 1/2 x 6 1/4 in (22 x 16 cm) rectangles in the silk and a strip that is 2 1/2 x 20 in (6 x 50 cm) long.

3• Cut the colored ribbons in 2. Glue them in 2s on the linen rectangles as a guide (see page 283).

4• Pin the strip of linen so its height and length are lower than each linen rectangle and prick it 1/2 in (1 cm) from the edge, right side to right side of the fabric.

5• Do the same with the silk strip and rectangles and pierce them 1/2 in (1 cm) from the edge.

6• Turn the linen pouch so the right side of the fabric is uppermost. Mark out a hollow 3/4 in (2 cm) (toward the inside) and a hollow 1 in (2.5 cm) at the top of the silk pouch (toward the outside).

7• Cut 2 magnetic strips 1/2 x 6 in (1 x 15 cm) and assemble them. They will inevitably become displaced— just ignore this and leave them as is.

8• Remove the adhesive from 1 of the strips. Glue the 2 strips that are side by side inside the linen pouch (on a hollow) and center the strips lengthwise 1/2 in (1 cm) from the upper border. Then remove the adhesive from the 2nd strip and glue it down so it faces the first strip.

9• Separate the magnetic strips and sew them by hand, surrounding them with thread at the center and the edges (see page 283,) so the fabric is on the wrong side, and sew invisible stitches along the edge of the silk pouch 1/8 in (3 mm) from the border of the linen pouch, underneath the magnetic strips. *(A)*

A

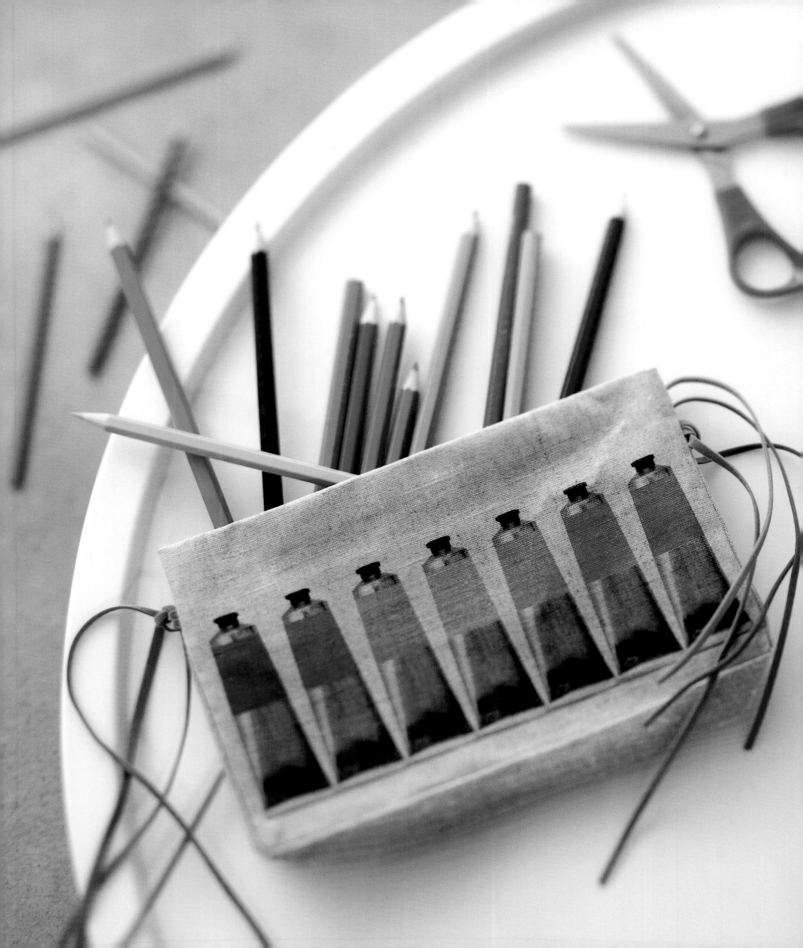

Two-tone boxes

Decorated with a mauve felt pompon, these boxes have much amusing allure and put color and tidiness into verse.

SUPPLIES
- Orange felt, ¼ in (5 mm) thick:
  – large box: 6¼ x 16½ in (16 x 42 cm) (body of box) + 1 square, 5¾ in (14.5 cm), and 2 measuring 4¾ in (12.5 cm) on the sides (lid and base)
  – small box: 4¼ x 17¾ in (11 x 45 cm) (body of box) + 1 square, 6½ in (17 cm), and 2 measuring 5½ in (14 cm) on the sides (lid and base)
- Mauve felt, 1/16 in (2 mm) thick:
  – 3¼ in (8 cm) on the sides to make 2 pompons
- Pale mauve braid (40 in [100 cm] for the large box, 34 in [85 cm] for the small box)
- Sewing thread in pale mauve

EQUIPMENT
- Pair of compasses
- Cutter
- Textile glue
- Sewing needle
- Punch
- Pegs
- Textile felt-tipped pen

1• Draw a 4¾ in (12.5 cm) circle in the orange felt with the compasses (for the base of the box). Cut it out with the cutter.

2• Using the punch, make 12 holes in the 6¼ x 16½ in (16 x 42 cm) sides of the rectangles. Place them on each side, but irregularly spaced out from the edges and from each other.

3• Assemble the edges by putting the mauve braid through the holes to form a cylinder.

4• Glue the sides of the bottom of the cylinder and put them on the bottom circle. Let dry thoroughly.

5• Draw 2 circles in the thick felt and cut these out: the 1st should be 5¾ in (14.5 cm) for the top and the 2nd 4½ in (12 cm) for the base of the lid

(if necessary, adjust this measurement so it matches the inside diameter of the box).

6• Cut 12 strips measuring 1¼ x 3¼ in (3 x 8 cm) out of the mauve felt. Fold each of these in 2 and sew them together at the center to make a pompon. Sew this securely onto the center of the large lid (the top) with the thread.

7• Afterward glue the base of the lid (the small circle) onto the large circle, centering it well. Let dry, keeping the work in place with pegs. *(A)*

8• Place the lid onto the box. By adjusting itself on the lower part of the lid, the box will keep its cylindrical shape well. Repeat the process to make an identical small box.

A

Extra idea...
To make stiffer and more solid boxes, slide a cardboard cylinder the same size as their inner diameter into each of the boxes.

Decorated shelves

A seaside photograph is transformed into a backdrop for a storage unit that celebrates nature.

SUPPLIES
• Small piece of furniture with drawers
• Acrylic paint in 2 colors that match the photograph
• Small roller
• Small and medium-size paintbrushes
• Clear matt varnish

EQUIPMENT
• Photograph
• Photograph paper
• Pencil
• Cloth
• Scissors or cutter
• Ruler

Preparation of the transfers

1• Reproduce your photograph to the desired size on 1 or 2 sheets of photograph paper.

2• Trace the template of the drawers onto the photograph, taking care that the 2 sides of the image match. To do this, place the front of the drawer on top of the photograph and draw its outline in pencil. Carefully cut out the pictures.

To finish the drawers

1• Using the roller, paint the piece of furniture evenly, not forgetting the inside and outside of the drawers. Let dry. *(A)*

2• Paint the simple designs in a different color using the small paintbrush. Let dry. *(B)*

3• Peel off the protective backing from the photograph paper and stick the transferred pictures onto the drawers. Ensure they adhere well by pressing down with a cloth.

4• Apply 1 or 2 thin layers of varnish to protect the work.

Tip

For an additional decorative touch, you can reproduce a detail of the photograph, cut it out, and stick it to the side of the piece of furniture.

A

B

Cotton penholder

A plastic bottle bottom is transformed into an embroidered penholder...ideal for decorating your office in blues and natural shades.

1• Empty and dry the bottle. Cut it to the desired height at a horizontal groove with the cutter.

2• Choose the thinnest possible embroidery needle to pierce the plastic without making holes that are too large. Embroider with long stitches using 2 blue threads of the blue cotton; start at the bottom of the bottle until you reach the first groove, sewing tight, large straight stitches, forming satin stitch. *(A)* Do not tie the thread at the beginning or end; instead, put the threads underneath the stitches inside the bottle.

3• Continue in this way by piercing from 1 groove to the other until you have gone along the pot.

4• For the last strip, situated between the last groove and the pot's edge, embroider long buttonhole stitches.

5• With a double length of natural-colored thread, embroider each groove in back stitch.

6• Sew on small buttons, working from the outside toward the center, to create small rays. *(B)* Use black thread for the light-colored buttons and natural-colored thread for the black buttons.

SUPPLIES

• Matt crochet cotton: 1 ball in blue and 1 ball in natural color
• Small 2- and 4-hole buttons in cream color, natural color, and black
• Sewing thread in black and natural color
• 2³/₄ pt (1.5 l) plastic bottle mineral water with horizontal grooves

EQUIPMENT

• Fine embroidery needle
• Thimble
• Scissors
• Cutter

STITCHES USED

• Satin stitch
• Buttonhole stitch
• Straight stitch

A

B

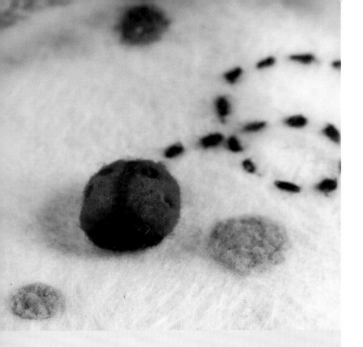

Ladybug hot water bottle

A soft hot water bottle cover is decorated with spots to attract a flying ladybug...

SUPPLIES
- White merino wool (2 oz [50 g]) and green merino wool (¹/₄ oz [10 g])
- Red and brown merino wool (a small amount of each)

EQUIPMENT
- Bubble wrap
- Synthetic tulle
- Soap
- Sponge
- Scissors
- Felting needles (1 with a fine point, 1 with a medium-size point, and 1 with a large point)
- Foam mold

1 • Lay the hot water bottle on the bubble wrap, then, following its outline, cut at 2 in (5 cm). *(A)* Lay this template on another large piece of bubble wrap.

2 • Lay 4 to 5 layers of white merino wool on the plastic template, overlapping at the top and sides and crossing these at every layer.

3 • Lay the tulle on top and rub it in hot soapy water. Rub for 10 minutes, remove the tulle, and turn the work over.

4 • Afterward shape the back of the hot water bottle by adding several crossed layers of wool. Do not let the wool overlap this time. Instead of that, join the 2 sides together. To do this, flatten the excess wool on the front and lay the merino wool on the back on top, folded toward the inside

on the edges. *(B)* As they are felted, the 2 parts will join together. Leave an opening at about 3 ¹/₄ in (8 cm) at the bottom, so you can slide the hot water bottle inside. Cover with tulle once again, then soap and rub for 20 minutes. Turn the hot water bottle so the front is uppermost and rub for about 10 minutes more.

5 • Roll everything (bubble wrap and work) for 10 minutes in 1 direction, then 10 minutes in the other direction.

6 • Remove the bubble wrap from the felted flap and beat the latter for 3 minutes, then rinse it in fresh water. Let dry.

7 • With the fine felting needle, pierce the brown wool on the right side of the front of the hot water bottle to amalgamate the brown wool and the white felted wool background and to

<table>
<tr><td>A</td><td>B</td><td>C</td></tr>
</table>

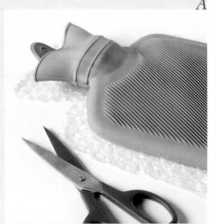

create the dotted path of the ladybug.

8• With the red wool, shape a small ball a little larger than the ladybug you wish to obtain, and roll it in the palm of your hand. Shape the ladybug, piercing the wool on the foam support with the large needle until you obtain the desired shape.

9• With the felting needle with a fine point, pierce some brown merino wool to shape the spots, head, and central line of the ladybug's body.

10• When the hot water bottle is thoroughly dry, slide the foam mold between the 2 thicknesses of wool (the front and the back), arrange a few tufts of green wool in the shape of spots, and pierce these with the felting needle with a medium-size point. *(C)*

11• Make a long strand of felt by rolling in your hand several strands of wool of the same length with warm soapy water. Rinse and let dry. Tie this strand attractively round the neck of the hot water bottle cover.

Supplies

- White cotton wool
- White silk paper
- Square white cotton wool balls to remove makeup (preferably embossed)
- Household string
- Adhesive tape
- Wallpaper paste
- Washable matt varnish

Equipment

- Sifter or other container, 6 to 7 in (15 to 16 cm) in diameter
- Cylindrical shape, 4 in (10 cm) high, the same diameter as the sifter
- Glass pot
- Flexible silk bristle paintbrush
- Pair of scissors

Cotton wool holder

With its adorable basket shape, this accessory will help you to begin your day with a light heart.

1 • Stretch and tear up the cotton wool into small thin pieces.

2 • Prepare the glue by diluting it a little more than is indicated. Glue the inside of the sifter (or other container) and cover it in cotton wool. Glue the cotton wool, then apply a new layer of it. *(A)* Repeat the process until you have obtained the desired thickness for the base. Let dry for 2 to 3 days before unmolding.

3 • Glue the outside of the cylindrical shape and cover it with small pieces of silk paper, overlapping these slightly.

4 • Glue the cotton wool balls (used to remove makeup) round the cylinder, spacing them out at $^1/_{16}$ or $^1/_8$ in (2 or 3 mm) intervals. *(B)* Glue them, then cover them with a layer of silk paper. Let dry for 2 or 3 days before unmolding.

5 • Join the base and body with strips of adhesive tape stuck onto the outside of the bag. Make everything consistent by gluing pieces of silk paper on the inside of the bag. Remove the adhesive tape and hide the join with strips of silk paper. *(C)* Let dry.

6 • Cut 18 lengths of string measuring about 12 in (30 cm) and, working 3 by 3, weave 2 handles. Tie a knot at each end. Glue the handles on either side of the bag, on the inside. Hide the free strands under the knots by gluing strips of silk paper. Let dry.

7 • Varnish the inside and outside of the bag.

A

B

C

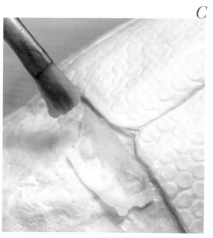

Ethnic photograph albums

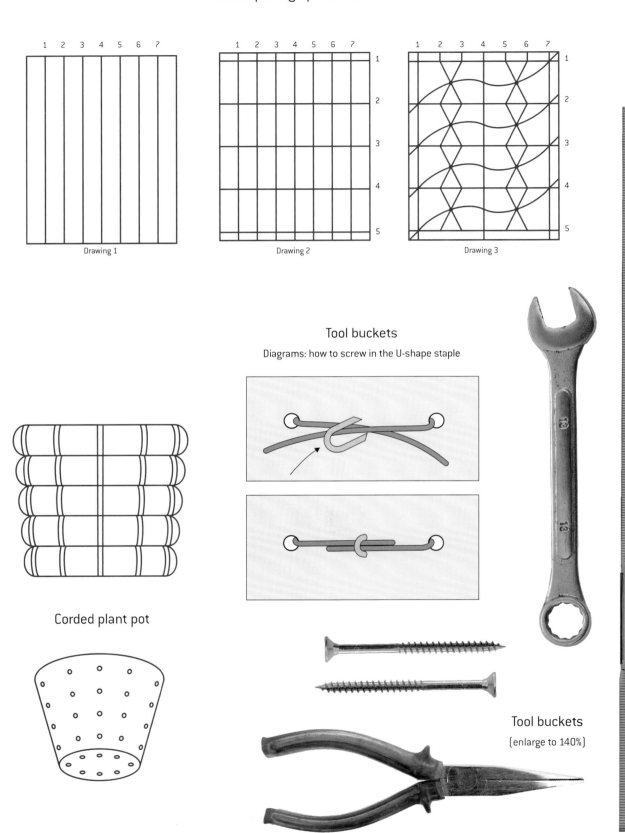

Drawing 1

Drawing 2

Drawing 3

Corded plant pot

Tool buckets

Diagrams: how to screw in the U-shape staple

Tool buckets

(enlarge to 140%)

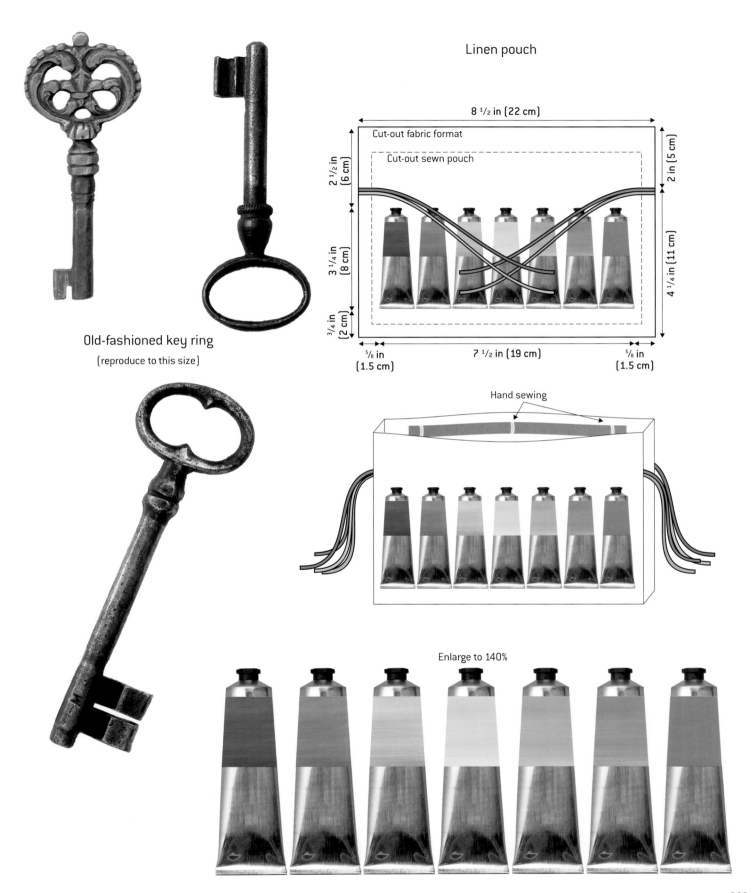

Linen pouch

8 ½ in (22 cm)

Cut-out fabric format

Cut-out sewn pouch

2 ½ in (6 cm)

2 in (5 cm)

3 ¼ in (8 cm)

4 ¼ in (11 cm)

¾ in (2 cm)

⅝ in (1.5 cm)

7 ½ in (19 cm)

⅝ in (1.5 cm)

Old-fashioned key ring
(reproduce to this size)

Hand sewing

Enlarge to 140%

The **art of**
fine **dining**

Floral tablecloth

Petals and hearts are crocheted separately, then arranged freely on the linen tablecloth in the style of a Matisse cut-out, fresh and joyous.

SUPPLIES

For a square tablecloth measuring 48 in (120 cm) on each side
- 2 oz (50 g) ball pearl cotton for crochet hook no. 2 in the following colors: green, yellow, red, fuchsia, orange, maroon
- Crochet hook no. 2
- 12/3 linen fabric in a dark natural color, 52 x 52 in (130 x 130 cm) for a square tablecloth measuring 48 in (120 cm) on the sides
- Basting thread, sewing threads to match the cotton yarn and the linen fabric
- Measuring tape, wool needle, sewing needle, pins with heads, pair of scissors
- Sewing machine
- Iron and thick flannel

To make the tablecloth

Fold the 4 sides of the cloth, wrong side to wrong side, by ¾ in (2 cm), then by 1¼ in (3 cm). Baste this, then pierce at 1⅛ in (2.8 cm) from the edges.

Crocheted designs

Large flowers. For each of these, crochet 8 large orange, red, fuchsia, maroon, or yellow petals, and a large green center (see stitches on pages 10–19 and the grids on page 338).

Small flowers. For each of these, crochet 6 small orange, red, fuchsia, maroon, yellow, or green small petals, and a small yellow or maroon center (see the grids on page 338).

Make as many flowers as you wish, arranging them on the tablecloth as required in order to judge their effect.

Assembly

Pull the yarns through to the wrong side. Lightly iron the designs on the wrong side. Pin them onto the tablecloth, then baste them. Sew the outlines of each of these by hand in back stitch (see page 19) or machine-stitch them. Spread out the tablecloth on the flannel, on the wrong side, and steam-iron it. Wait for an area to be dry before moving the fabric in order to iron the next area.

Mint tea

Both greedy and convivial, invitations to share a glass of mint tea are on the increase, giving free rein to dreams of jaunts away.

Large platter

1• Clean the platter thoroughly with the cloth soaked in white spirit to get rid of all traces of grease.

2• Trace your chosen designs (see page 338) as many times as you wish them to feature on the finished platter. Cut out each design, leaving a 1/4 in (5 mm) border all round.

3• Decide on a harmonious arrangement of the designs and secure them under the platter with adhesive tape. You could also use 1 or more smaller plates, the outlines of which traced on a sheet of tracing paper will serve as guides. All you then have to do is to trace the designs in the positions you have chosen. *(A and B)*

4• Engrave the designs, following their outlines, with the fine burr. When you go over them the first time, press only slightly to avoid slipping. Afterward you can go over them more firmly.

5• Once the engraving is finished, wash the platter in warm soapy water.

SUPPLIES
- Large blue glass platter
- Colored grooved glasses
- White spirit
- Soft cloth
- Tracing paper
- Adhesive tape

EQUIPMENT
- Measuring tape
- Pencil
- Photocopying machine
- Scissors
- Fine marker pen
- Electric engraver
- Fine and large diamond burrs

A

B

Glasses

1 • Clean the glasses thoroughly with white spirit to get rid of all traces of grease.

2 • Measure the circumference of the inside of the glasses. Enlarge or reduce your chosen frieze or design on a photocopying machine (see page 338) to adapt it to your size. If necessary, draw the same design several times. *(A)*

3 • Cut out the design. leaving a ¹/₄ in (5 mm) border all round. Make a few small nicks with the scissors to fit the paper better against the inside of the glass. Secure it with adhesive tape.

4 • Engrave the outlines that appear through transparency with the fine burr. When you go over them the first time, press only slightly to avoid slip-

A

ping. Afterward you can go over them more firmly. Having done this, fill in the surfaces, using the large burr if necessary. *(B)*

5 • Wipe repeatedly with the cloth to get rid of any glass dust.

Tip

For the simpler design you can draw freehand, directly onto the glass, with a fine marker pen. This will be a lot easier if the chosen glasses are grooved; that will enable you to repeat the designs correctly.

B

Bamboo tray

A geometric design covering the base of a bamboo tray; patience and precision will be your best assets here.

SUPPLIES
• Round bamboo tray
• Sandpaper
• Tracing paper
• Plastic sheet (e.g. a plastic envelope for a file)

EQUIPMENT
• Photocopying machine
• Pencil
• Pyrograph machine
• Nib no. 21

1• Sand down the tray on all sides with sandpaper to get rid of all traces of varnish. *(A)*

2• Enlarge the design on page 339 to the size of your tray, and trace it with tracing paper on the base of the tray.

3• Pyrograph the pencil-drawn lines with nib no. 21, placing the plastic sheet between your hand and the tray so as not to alter the design. *(B)*

Note

Bamboo is a very soft or fairly hard material, depending on its place of origin; take care to exert the correct pressure with your pyrograph machine in order to obtain even lines.

A

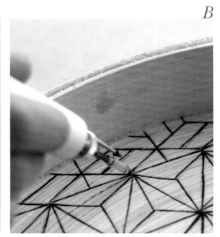

B

Salad bowl and servers

Simple materials and acid colors cheer up the pleasures of dining; you could use this salad bowl and servers to concoct sumptuous informal meals for your friends.

1 • Make a hole at the top of the handles of the salad servers.

2 • Sand down the outside of the salad bowl and the handle of the salad servers, then paint them in orange. Let dry. Afterward apply 1 or 2 layers of varnish; let dry completely once again.

3 • Load the glue gun and let it heat for 3 to 4 minutes. Drizzle a ribbon of glue at the top of the handles and on the base of the salad bowl, then stick on the sisal string. Proceed evenly and carefully in this way, tightening each row of string against the previous row. Finish with a border of string at the top of the salad bowl.

4 • Thread a piece of string through the holes in the handles and make a slip knot (see page 40).

5 • Draw the letters of the word "salad" on the salad bowl, then glue the string onto the letters with the glue gun. *(A and B)*

Tips

Slip a slightly smaller glass salad bowl into your wooden salad bowl. In this way you can prepare your salads without risk of damage to your work. The servers have a purely decorative function here. If you wish to use them for culinary purposes, paint only the top of the handles.

SUPPLIES
• Salad bowl and servers in unpolished wood
• Thin sandpaper
• Orange acrylic paint
• Clear matt varnish
• Sisal string, ¹⁄₁₆ in (2.5 mm) in diameter

EQUIPMENT
• Drill and ¹⁄₄ in (5 mm) bit
• Paintbrushes
• Glue gun
• Scissors
• Pencil

A

B

Pearly wood napkin ring
• 1 wooden napkin ring
• Gold pearl acrylic paint
• 8 ft (2.50 m) brass wire
• 80 tiny wooden beads
• 60 tiny glass beads
• Natural-colored felt
• Paste
• Paintbrush no. 12
• Cutting pliers
• Tape measure, ruler, fine pencil, scissors

Fish scale napkin ring
• Purple and orange felt
• 20 in (50 cm) orange ribbon, 1/2 in (1 cm) wide
• Basting thread, sewing thread in purple
• 1 tube purple sequins
• Paste
• 8 in (20 cm) purple bias binding
• DMC pearl cotton #5 in 608 color
• Sewing needle no. 9
• Paintbrush
• Fine felt-tipped pen, scissors, thimble, ruler, sewing machine

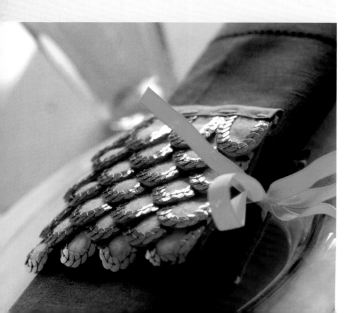

Napkin rings

Four very charming and decorative napkin rings to personalize your family's table.

Pearly wood napkin ring

1• Paint the napkin ring gold. Thread the wire first onto the outside of the napkin ring, then onto the inside (see drawing on page 338). Twist the 2 bits of brass wire to keep them attached to one another, then thread the wire lengthwise into the napkin ring, taking care to slide the fastening toward the inside.

2• Thread the beads, alternating them, all round the napkin ring. Then cut the excess thread, ensuring that you keep back a length to slide outside.

3• Cut a piece of felt the same size as the inside of the napkin ring, plus 3/4 in (2 cm) in length. Glue the inside of the napkin ring and put the strip in place. Overlap the 2 ends of the strip of felt, add a dab of paste, then lightly tap the inside of the napkin ring to make the paste adhere to the strip of felt. Let dry.

Extra idea...

You can also use seashells and glass beads to give this project a touch of elegant ethnicity.

Fish scale napkin ring

1• Draw and cut out two 4 x 3 1/4 in (10 x 8 cm) rectangles in the purple felt. Thread the orange ribbon between the overlapping felt rectangles, centering them well. Baste the rectangles, then machine-stitch them all round.

2• Draw 25 fish scales in felt-tipped pen on the orange felt, using the model on page 338 as a guide. Cut them out, then embroider the purple sequins all round.

3• Glue the fish scales, staggering and overlapping them (1 row of 4, 1 row of 3, and so on) on the visible side of the napkin ring. Let dry.

4• Hand-sew in saddle stich with the pearl cotton, keeping the slant by straddling the top and bottom edge of the napkin ring.

Extra idea...

On the same principle of embroidered fish scales tied together with a ribbon, you can convert this napkin ring to a belt, adjusting the length to your waist size.

- Pearl-grey felt
- No. 3 press stud
- Sewing thread in pearl grey, DMC pearl cotton # 5 in 415 color
- 2 green feathers
- 2 small blue flowers
- 19 transparent glass beads, 14 blue faceted glass beads, 13 iridescent blue glass beads, 1 tube transparent green glass beads
- Sewing needle, needle suitable for sewing on beads
- Fine felt-tipped pen, scissors, thimble, ruler, pencil

Pocketbook napkin ring

1• Draw and cut out two $8^{1}/_{2}$ x $4^{1}/_{4}$ in (22 x 11cm) rectangles in the felt. Sew one part (male or female) of the press stud $^{3}/_{4}$ in (2 cm) from a small side, in the middle.

2• Place the rectangle bearing the male stud in front of you. Sew 2 green feathers opposite the stud. Join together the flower stems and thread, alternating them, a transparent glass bead, a green glass bead, and so on. Leave an overhang of $^{3}/_{4}$ in (2 cm) in the stems and turn them round to finish. Sew the flowers into position.

3• Position the 2 felt rectangles, wrong side to wrong side, ensuring that the 2 parts of the stud are opposite each other. Sew the 2 small sides in cross stitch, $^{1}/_{4}$ in (5 mm) from the edge and every $^{1}/_{2}$ in (1 cm) in pearl cotton. On the long sides, sew every $^{1}/_{2}$ in (1 cm) a blue faceted bead, an iridescent blue bead, a transparent bead, and so on.

Supplies & equipment

- Linen fabric in silver, 20 3/4 x 4 in (52 x 10 cm)
- Sewing thread in dark brown, basting thread
- 29 iridescent glass beads
- 1 sheet Plexiglass in glossy brown
- No. 3 press stud
- Sewing needle no. 9
- Scissors, thimble, ruler, pencil, iron, sewing machine

Cuff napkin ring

1• Make a 1/2 in (1 cm) hollow on the small sides of the linen fabric and iron. Then fold the rectangle in 2.

2• On the part of the fabric that will be visible (the exterior part of the napkin ring), carefully draw a pattern of checks (see drawing on page 338), then machine-stitch this with dark brown thread. At each intersection of the grid, embroider on an iridescent glass bead.

3• Sew the Plexiglass sheet in the center of the lozenge, on the right-hand edge. Embroider 16 beads all round the sheet, to make a cameo design.

4• Sew the 2 parts of the stud onto the inside of the napkin ring, 1/4 in (5 mm) from each of the sides.

5• Fold the top and bottom of the napkin ring right side to right side. Baste the 2 long sides to join them together, then machine-stitch 1/2 in (1 cm) from the edge. Remove the basting thread. Turn your work over onto the right side once again and iron on the wrong side. Close the fabric rectangle by hand-sewing small stitches.

Ethnic table runner

This can either be a table runner or an individual placemat—all combinations are possible with this clever creation.

1• On the wrong side of the ridged fabric, mark out in the center, in white pencil, a 30 x 16 in (75 x 40 cm) rectangle. Inside this rectangle, 4 in (10 cm) from the small sides, draw 2 straight lines. The inner rectangle will thus measure 22 x 16 in (55 x 40 cm).

2• Wrong side to wrong side, fold the 4 sides of fabric at 1 in (2.5 cm) and mark out the folds with the iron. Afterward fold the small sides at 4 in (10 cm) following the lines, always wrong side to wrong side.

3• On the wrong side of the brown fabric, draw 2 straight lines in white pencil 1 in (2.5 cm) from the edges of the large sides to obtain an inner rectangle measuring 22 x 16 in (55 x 40 cm). Wrong side to wrong side, fold the 2 sides with the iron, following the drawings.

4• Open out the flaps of the ridged fabric and lay the brown fabric on top, wrong side to wrong side. Flatten the flaps, then pin the pieces together, taking up all the thicknesses. Sew the flaps, then the large sides of the placemat in running stitch.

5• Sew the buttons on the top and bottom ⅝ in (1.5 cm) from the right-hand edge and 2¾ in (7 cm) from the upper and lower edges of the placemat with pink cotton thread. Sew on the 3rd button in the middle, at ⅝ in (1.5 cm) from the right-hand edge. Repeat the process for the left-hand edge with the 3 other buttons. *(A)*

6• Make a second placemat in the same way. Cut the braid into 3 equal-size 16 in (40 cm) pieces. Place the 2 placemats side by side and join them, 2 buttons side by side with 2 other buttons. To do this, form a figure-of-8 with each braid round the buttons without tying a knot.

SUPPLIES

• For 1 placemat measuring 22 x 16 in (55 x 40 cm) (multiply the quantities depending on the number of placemats required or the length of your table if a table runner is being made)
• 6 exotic wood buttons, 1½ in (3.3 cm) each
• Black fabric with white ridges, 32 x 17¾ in (80 x 45 cm)
• Black and brown woven fabric, 22 x 17¾ in (55 x 45 cm)
• Fuchsia-colored cotton thread
• Black leather tubular braid, 48 in (120 cm) (to sew the 2 placemats together with 6 buttons)
• Sewing thread in black

EQUIPMENT

• Dressmaking scissors
• Tape measure
• White fabric pencil
• Iron
• Sewing needle, embroidery needle, pins

A

Star plates

Simple and stylized, a host of stars really brings colored plates to life. The trick is to arrange them harmoniously.

SUPPLIES
- Colored glass plates
- White spirit
- Soft cloth
- Tracing paper
- Adhesive tape

EQUIPMENT
- Dark felt-tipped pen
- Scissors
- Electric engraver
- Fine diamond burr

1• Clean the reverse of the plates thoroughly with the cloth soaked in white spirit to get rid of all traces of grease.

2• Here you are working on the wrong side of the plates. To arrange the designs harmoniously, you can draw 2 lines that cross at a right angle in the center of the plate. All you will have to do then is to stick down with adhesive tape a star in the 4 sections you have obtained or a star in the center of the plate. If you wish, you can repeat the process afterward, interspersing smaller stars. *(A)*

3• Trace the chosen designs (see page 340). For greater clarity, use a darker felt-tipped pen. Cut out the stars, leaving a border of ¼ in (5 mm) all round. Place the traced designs inside the plate and, by transparency, draw the designs directly onto the glass. *(B)*

4• Engrave, following the lines. When you go over them the first time, press only slightly to avoid slipping. Afterward you can go over the tracing more firmly. *(C)*

5• Turn the plate over. The design will appear through transparency. Once you have finished engraving, wash the plate in warm soapy water.

A

B

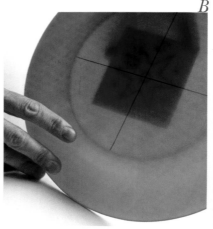

C

Bamboo bowl and saucer

A geometric design along a bowl is echoed in its saucer; this Japanese-style graphic effect will be sure to cheer up a traditional Vietnamese bowl and saucer set.

1• Place the small disk on the edge of the saucer and trace its outline in pencil. Starting from this circle, trace other circles adjoining each other. *(A)*

2• Go over the pencil lines with the pyrograph machine and nib no. 21, and draw more concentric lines, spaced out at $^1/_{16}$ in (2 mm) intervals, inside the circles. Only fill 1 part of the saucer's surface. *(B and C)*

3• Repeat steps 1 and 2 to make the bowl decoration.

SUPPLIES
• Bamboo bowl and saucer
• Small disk, about 1$^1/_4$ in (3 cm) in diameter

EQUIPMENT
• Pencil
• Pyrograph machine
• Nib no. 21

A

B

C

Seafaring tablecloth

Denim, rope, pebbles, and eyelets join forces to offer diners a tablecloth that is both original and practical.

(see page 340)

SUPPLIES

• Natural denim, 70 x 70 in (175 x 175 cm)
• Thread to match the tablecloth
• 28 gold plastic clip-on eyelets, 2³/₄ in (70 mm) in diameter
• 20 ft (6 m) hemp rope, ⁵/₈ in (14 mm) in diameter
• Linen string, ¹/₁₆ in (1 mm) in diameter
• 4 small brass eyelets, ¹/₈ in (3.5 mm) in diameter
• 8 medium-size pebbles
• 4 hooks, ¹/₈ in (3 mm) in diameter, with a ¹/₄ in (4 mm) opening

EQUIPMENT

• Tape measure
• Pins with heads
• Sewing machine
• Dressmaking chalk
• Pair of compasses
• Fine sewing scissors
• Grommet pliers

1• Pin a ³/₄ in (2 cm) hem all round the square of denim fabric, then machine-stitch this.

2• On the wrong side of the fabric, mark out 8 guides, spaced out at 7¹/₂ in (19 cm) intervals, on each side of the tablecloth lengthwise (see page 340). These guides indicate the center of the 2¹/₂ in (60 mm) circles you will need for the plastic eyelets. Trace these circles and cut them out with fine scissors. *(A)*

3• Clip on the plastic eyelets and thread the rope through them.

4• To keep the rope in place, tie linen string on each of its ends, ¹/₂ or ³/₄ in (1 or 2 cm) in. Tie a double knot, let the 2 strands of string overrun by 12 in (30 cm), and tie a knot at each of the ends.

5• Tie a bow, much as you would do with shoelaces, with the 2 strands of string to join the 2 ends of the rope together (in this way it can be removed for washing).

6• With the grommet pliers, put the 4 brass eyelets on the 4 corners of the tablecloth, ¹/₂ in (1 cm) from the edge.

7• Thread linen string round 2 pebbles and secure it with a double knot. Tie the 2 strands of string to a hook, adjusting their length so that the pebbles touch the ground. Attach a group of pebbles to each of the tablecloth's corners in this way. *(B)*

A

B

Romantic tray

A small tray for dainty young ladies; tea-time approaches with a touch of spring.

SUPPLIES
- Unpolished wood tray
- Thin sandpaper
- White acrylic satin paint
- Wood glue
- Dried flowers or petals
- Soft cloths
- Acetone
- Glass sheet the same size as the base of the tray
- Tube of white acrylic sealant

EQUIPMENT
- Flat paintbrush
- Small flat paintbrush

1• If necessary, sand down the tray and apply 2 layers of acrylic paint. Let dry thoroughly between layers.

2• When the paint is dry, stick the petals or flowers onto the base of the tray with wood glue, using the small flat paintbrush. Tap with a soft cloth to make the flowers adhere well. Let dry. *(A)*

3• Having removed any grease from the glass sheet and cleaned it, lay it on the base of the tray and fix it in place with white acrylic sealant between the glass edges and the wood of the tray. Remove any excess sealant by smoothing over with a damp finger and let dry. *(B and C)*

Tip
For a smooth seal, apply removable adhesive tape on each side of it, smooth it out, then gently remove the adhesive tape before the sealant is dry.

A

B

C

Engraved glasses

The most banal glass acquires a distinct character through a simple interplay of uneven lines—therein lies its whole strength.

SUPPLIES
- Tumblers
- White spirit and soft cloth (optional)
- Masking tape

EQUIPMENT
- Electric engraver
- Fine and large diamond burrs

1• Wash the glasses in warm soapy water to get rid of all traces of grease and clean them with white spirit. Dry them thoroughly.

2• Arrange the masking tape precisely. It will be used as a ruler. You can draw inspiration from the models suggested or invent others. *(A)*

3• Fit the fine diamond burr into the engraver and draw lines, following the masking tape; remove the tape and fill in the lines with the large burr. *(B)*

4• Once you have finished engraving, wash the glasses in warm soapy water once again.

Tip

To make squares or rectangles, position the masking tape in horizontal lines. Engrave and carefully wipe away any dust. Afterward repeat the process for the vertical lines.

Variation

For glasses with simple discontinuous lines, arrange the pieces of masking tape in a random fashion; these will serve as a guide and support to engrave straight lines.

A

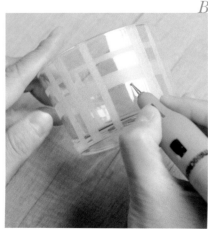

B

Embellished placemat

Spangled stripes are juxtaposed on this placemat,
creating an inventive and modern effect.

SUPPLIES

- 10 linen fabric in blue-gray
- Sewing thread, basting thread
- 1 strip wide striped braid, 14 in (35 cm)
- 2 strips narrow braid, 14 in (35 cm) each
- 1 tube charcoal gray tubular beads
- 1 package blue spangles
- 1 package gold spangles

EQUIPMENT

- Sewing needle, needle to sew on beads
- Scissors, sewing machine, iron, ruler, pencil

1 • Draw and cut out two 19 x 13 ³/₄ in (48 x 34.5 cm) rectangles in the linen fabric. With the sewing machine, oversew all 4 sides (top and bottom) in Bosnian stitch.

2 • Oversew 14 in (35 cm) narrow braid 2 in (5 cm) from the left-hand border at the top of the placemat. Do the same with the wide striped braid, then finish with the narrow braid. Iron.

3 • Embroider the central braid according to the design you have chosen. Sew the gold spangles onto the braid's 2 gold stripes, overlapping them, and finally sew the tubular beads horizontally onto the gray parts of the braid. *(A)*

4 • Oversew the top and bottom of the placemat right side to right side, then machine-stitch ¹/₂ in (1 cm) from each side. Allow for an opening of 6 in (15 cm) on 1 of the small sides to be able to turn the placemat round so the right side is showing. Having done this, iron the placemat on the wrong side, then close the opening with small stitches.

Tip
To keep the linen in better condition
you can attach fusible interfacing to
the back of the placemat.

Sage leaf transfers

Sage leaves, elegantly placed, enliven this natural-looking table runner.

SUPPLIES
- Linen fabric in white, 16 x 40 in (40 x 100 cm)
- Sewing thread in white
- Sewing machine and sewing needle
- Cotton thread in gray and white
- Silver seed beads
- Needle suitable for sewing on beads
- Embroidery needle

EQUIPMENT
- Pictures of sage leaves (see template on page 340)
- Transfer paper for light-colored fabric
- Iron
- Scissors

Transfer

1 • Enlarge the template of the sage leaves and reproduce it twice on transfer paper. Cut out, leaving a margin of ¹/₄ in (5 mm) round the picture, regardless of the type of paper you are using.

2 • Transfer the designs (see page 38) onto each end of the linen strip, placing them ³/₄ in (2 cm) from the edges.

To make the table runner

1 • Mark out a ¹/₂ in (1 cm) double hollow on the wrong side of the entire circumference of the strip of linen fabric and machine-stitch it. Over this stitching, embroider a row in basting stitch (see page 12) with 3 strands of gray cotton thread. *(A)*

2 • Embroider the veining on the leaves in straight stitch with 2 strands of white cotton thread. *(B)*

3 • Sew a few seed beads onto the sage leaves with the needle suitable for sewing on beads. *(C)*

A

B

C

Sunny bottle holder

This bottle holder will fulfill its function cheerfully, bringing a summery touch to your table.

SUPPLIES
• 5 linen fabric, 11 x 11 in (28 x 28 cm)
• Fusible interfacing, 8 x 10 in (20 x 25 cm)
• 3 handfuls opaque yellow glass beads, 3 handfuls opaque orange glass beads
• 1 large tube gold beads
• Sewing thread in gold, orange pearl cotton

EQUIPMENT
• Sewing needle no. 9
• Scissors, pencil, iron, sewing machine, ruler

1 • Fix the fusible interfacing to the center of the linen fabric with a hot iron. Oversew with the sewing machine in Bosnian stitch.

2 • Draw a circle, 3 1/2 in (9 cm) in diameter, on the linen side, using the pattern on page 342. Draw a line in pencil toward the inside of the circle, freehand, to form a spiral.

3 • Starting from the inside and working toward the outside, embroider the spiral by alternating yellow, orange, and gold beads, finishing with a series of gold beads. *(A)*

4 • Draw eight 3/4 x 1/4 in (2 cm to 5 mm) rays in pencil on the edge of the spiral. Embroider the rays by mixing yellow, orange, and gold beads.

5 • Overlap the small sides of the rectangle, right side to right side, and machine-stitch them, 5/8 in (1.5 cm) from the edge. Open out the hem and turn the work over to the right side. Make a 5/8 in (1.5 cm) hollow with the iron at the bottom and top of the bottle holder. Sew these hollows in cross stitch using orange pearl cotton, introducing a bead into each stitch.

Note
To obtain even cross stitches on the top and bottom of the bottle holder, draw guides in pencil 1/2 in (1 cm) from the edges to help you, spaced out at 1/2 in (1 cm) intervals.

Multicolored tray with wicker mugs

A tray full of geometric shapes in acid colors goes well with a touch of wicker.

Supplies

- Tray in unpolished wood and colored mugs
- Wood paints in mandarin, bright pink, turquoise, and lime-green
- Matt varnish
- 1 reel wicker cord, ¹/₄ in (4 mm) in diameter
- Glass sheet cut to the same size as the tray
- Silicone sealant

Equipment

- Pencil
- Ruler
- Paintbrushes
- Glue gun
- Scissors

Tray

1• Reproduce the design on page 342 in pencil on the base of the tray. Paint the tray, following the indications given in the drawing. Let dry, then varnish the tray. Let dry completely once again. *(A)*

2• Load the glue gun and let it heat for 3 to 4 minutes. Draw the spiral and figure-of-8 designs with a thin drizzle of glue, then glue the wicker cord, pressing down well on the glue. Carefully work each design separately. Finish with the design of the edges. Let dry. *(B)*

3• Lay the glass sheet on the tray and secure it with silicone sealant. Smooth out the sealant with a finger soaked in soapy water.

4• Hide the sealant by gluing wicker cord on it.

A

B

Mugs

1 • For the mugs, glue wicker cord round the handles with the glue gun. Work in short sections, tightening each row of cord well against the previous row. If the wicker cord is too large, you can divide it. *(A)*

A

Tip

To paint each area of color without the color going over into the adjoining area, limit the latter with masking tape. Apply the paint, let dry, then remove the masking tape. Work all the areas in the same color in this way before proceeding to the next color.

Beribboned table runner

Cross stitch is revisited here in order to draw a tartan design made up of vivid ribbons against a background of hessian. This project is very easy to make.

1• Baste a rectangle made up of 420 x 180 threads in the middle of the hessian (see plan). Start with the 2 central lines (vertical and horizontal), folding the fabric in 2, and count the threads on both sides.

2• Cross stitch is embroidered with a large blunt needle and ribbon yarn. If the yarn becomes twisted, let the needle hang down to untwist it. The ribbon yarn should be embroidered flat on the right side.

3• An embroidered line corresponds to 2 rows of cross stich in different colors (see the grid of 1 design).

4• Start by embroidering the 17 lines across the height of the rectangle. Prepare 60 in (150 cm) lengths of ribbon yarn to be able to make 60 half cross stitches from bottom to top

without a join. Come down again with a second length of the same size to end the crosses. Before you start a row, make a few basting stitches outside the basting thread and also at the end. *(A)*

5• Next embroider the lines lengthwise. You will need two 28 1/2 in (180 cm) lengths of ribbon yarn to proceed (and as much yarn to come back), the ends of which you will bring into the new embroidered vertical line (the middle line). At each intersection with the other vertical lines, thread the ribbon yarn underneath, then take it out in order to continue.

6• Once you have finished embroidering, machine-stitch the fabric all round with the thread that matches the fabric, close to the basting. Add 1 or 2 rows in Bosnian stitch, at about 3/4 in (2 cm) from the piercing. The ribbon yarn's basting stitches being well secured, cut off any excess, 1/16 or 1/8 in (2 or 3 mm) from the Bosnian stitch.

SUPPLIES
• Polyamide knitting ribbon yarn (such as Victoria by Anny Blatt): 1 skein in each of the following colors: pink, red, green, and pale green
• Hessian, about 28 x 52 in (70 x 130 cm)

EQUIPMENT
• 2 blunt needles (1 large and 1 smaller)
• Sewing thread in red and the same color as the hessian
• Sewing machine
• Measuring tape
• Thimble
• Scissors

STITCH USED
• Cross stitch

Plan and grid, page 341

A

Crocheted coasters

Vary the sizes and colors of these coasters to cheer up your table when you come to take refreshments. Don't hold back!

To make the coasters

Make a foundation ring, then crochet in the round (see page 18); begin each row with 1 chain and end with 1 sl st in the 1st stitch of the row (see page 15).

1st row: 8 sc

From the 2nd row on, crochet all the sc by stitching through the yarn behind the sc of the previous row (chain rib st, see page 18)

2nd row: 2 sc in each sc = 16 sc

3rd row: *1 sc, 2 sc in 1 sc*, rep from * to * = 24 sc

4th row: as for the 3rd row = 36 sc,

5th, 7th, 9th, 11th, 13th, 15th, 17th, 19th, 21st, and 23rd rows: 1 sc in each sc of the previous row.

6th row: *2 sc in 1 sc, 2 sc*, rep from * to * = 48 sc

8th row: 2 sc, 2 sc in 1 sc, 1 sc*, rep from * to * = 60 sc

10th row: *1 sc, 2 sc in 1 sc, 3 sc*, rep from * to * = 72 sc

12th row: *4 sc, 2 sc in 1 sc, 1 sc*, rep from * to * = 84 sc

14th row: *1 sc, 2 sc in 1 sc, 5 sc*, rep from * to * = 96 sc

16th row: *3 sc, 2 sc in 1 sc, 4 sc*, rep from * to * = 108 sc

18th row: *8sc, 2 sc in 1 sc*, rep from * to * = 120 sc

20th row: *4 sc, 2 sc in 1 sc, 5 sc*, rep from * to * = 132 sc

22nd row: *10 sc, 2 sc in 1 sc*, rep

from * to * = 144 sc

24th row: *5 sc, 2 sc in 1 sc, 6 sc*, rep from * to * = 156 sc

25th row: as for the 5th row.

For the large model, crochet 6 rows in lime-green, 3 rows in pale turquoise, 9 rows in medium turquoise, 1 row in dark turquoise, 6 rows in lime-green = 25 rows.

For the small, predominantly turquoise, model, crochet 8 rows in dark turquoise, 1 row in lime-green, 3 rows in medium turquoise = 12 rows.

For the small, predominantly lime-green, model, crochet 4 rows in medium turquoise, 2 rows in pale turquoise, 6 rows in lime-green = 12 rows.

To finish off

Fasten off the yarn. Lightly steam-iron on the wrong side.

SUPPLIES

For the 3 coasters

• 1 ball mercerized cotton for knitting needles or crochet hook no. 3, 2 oz (50 g) in each of the following colors: pale turquoise, medium turquoise, dark turquoise, lime-green
• Crochet hook no. 3
• Wool needle, pair of scissors
• Iron and ironing board

Personalized steak knives

For a picnic in the woods, these attractive personalized steak knives bear the name of each of the children; Hugo and Emma will no longer be able to fight over them...

1• Sand down all sides of the knives' handles with sandpaper to minimize the layer of varnish or stain that covers them.

2• Draw a small symbol and letters that will make up the name freehand on each knife's handle. *(A)*

3• Go over the pencil lines with nib no. 22. *(B)*

4• Varnish the handles with matt or satin acrylic varnish and let dry. This will protect the handles and will prevent them from blackening when they come into contact with water.

SUPPLIES
- Steak knives
- Sandpaper
- Clear varnish

EQUIPMENT
- Pencil
- Pyrograph machine
- Nib no. 22
- Paintbrush

A

B

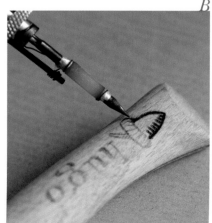

Geometric table mats

Astonishing and useful, these cork and wicker mats sport spirals, zigzag shapes, or straight lines. Anything goes!

1• With the cutter, cut out a 7½ in (19 cm) circle or a square measuring 8 in (20 cm) on each side in the mat, following the model you have chosen.

2• Following the drawings on page 342, mark out the position of the holes in ballpoint pen: at 1¼ in (3 cm) from the edge and 15 degrees' interval for the circular model; on 2 lines at ¾ in (2 cm), then 1½ in (4 cm) from each of the sides, and ¾ in (2 cm) intervals for the square model. Drill the holes with the drill. *(A)*

3• Paint both sides of the mat. Let dry.

4• Thread the wicker cord through the holes, securing the beginning and end of each length of cord with a dab of glue. *(B)*

5• For the round mat, coil some cord into a snail shape 2¾ in (7 cm) in diameter and position it in the middle. Afterward add 2 circles of cord side by side 1¼ in (3 cm) from the edge (see photograph).

Tip

To get rid of the small pieces of cork left over after drilling, lightly sand down the surface of the mat with thin sandpaper.

SUPPLIES

• Cork table mat
• 1 reel wicker cord, ¼ in (4 mm) in diameter
• Acrylic paint
• Superglue (or glue gun)

EQUIPMENT

• Ruler
• Pair of compasses
• Ballpoint pen
• Cutter
• Protractor
• Drill and ¼ in (5 mm) bit
• Flat paintbrush
• Scissors

A

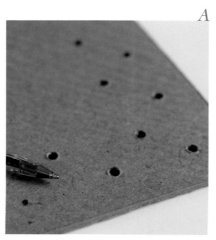

B

Ethnic placemat

Raffia with African designs and string braid, together with wood and copper beads, make a placemat that is ethnic in inspiration.

Supplies

• Raffia or matting with African designs, 19½ x 14 in (48 x 35 cm)
• String braid, 100 in (2.5 m)
• Sewing thread in cream color, tan-colored pearl cotton # 5, col. 738
• 1 tube white pebble beads
• 16 natural wood tubular beads, 4 tinted tubular wood beads, 12 coral-colored wood beads, 16 copper beads

Equipment

• Sewing needle no. 9, large-eyed needle
• Scissors, ruler, measuring tape

1• Oversew the entire circumference of the raffia placemat twice. Cut two 22½ in (56 cm) strips of string braid for the wide sides of the placemat and two 17½ in (44 cm) string braid strips for the small sides. Pull the ends of each strip a little in order to obtain fringing. *(A)*

2• Sew the small white pebble beads with pearl cotton on the edge of the string braid, just before the fringing. Hand-stitch the 4 strips of string braid in cream-colored thread onto the raffia placemat lengthwise.

3• Sew a coral-colored wood bead onto each corner, then 4 natural wood beads to make a star shape. Mark out the middle of the 4 strips of braid, then sew a tinted tubular wood bead and, on both sides, a copper bead and, on both sides, a copper bead, a coral-colored wood bead, and another copper bead. Sew on all these beads in pearl cotton. *(B)*

Tip

To ensure the beads are well aligned after you have sewn them on, pull some thread through the entire row, as for a necklace, and keep the ends of the thread under the placemat.

A
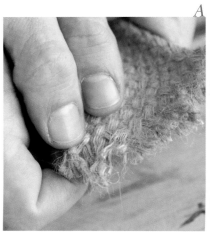

B

Coffee time

Letters and a host of coffee beans decorate this cafetière; time to have a break and share a comforting cup of coffee.

Cafetière

1• Mark out the surface to be engraved between the metal supports of the cafetière in marker pen. Separate the glass container from the metal frame. Clean it with a cloth soaked in white spirit to get rid of all traces of grease. Dry it thoroughly.

2• Stick a sheet of carbon paper inkside down against the glass, on the place where you are going to engrave.

3• Trace the drawing (see page 343). Cut it out, leaving a ¼ in (5 mm) margin all round. Stick the traced design onto the sheet of carbon paper. Go over the tracing, pressing firmly, with the ballpoint pen. Remove both the tracing and the carbon paper. *(A)*

4• Go over the design, with the thin diamond burr fitted to the engraver. When you go over the first time, press only slightly to avoid slipping. Afterward go over, pressing more firmly on the drawing, then fill in the inside of the designs with the larger diamond burr. *(B)*

5• Once you have finished engraving, get rid of all traces of ink by wiping the cafetière with a cotton cloth soaked in solvent, then wash the container with warm soapy water and replace it in the metal frame, centering the engraved design well.

Variation

To engrave glass cups, trace the design and stick the tracing paper inside the glass. Engrave, following the outlines of the drawing.

SUPPLIES
- Glass cafetière
- Glass cups
- White spirit
- Soft cloth
- Carbon paper
- Adhesive tape
- Tracing paper
- Solvent
- Cotton cloth

EQUIPMENT
- Marker pen
- Fine felt-tipped pen
- Scissors
- Ballpoint pen
- Electric engraver
- Thin and large diamond burrs

A

B

Delicate tablecloth

Embroidered with wool and beads, this white linen tablecloth is very easy to make and is an invitation to well-being and celebration.

1• Pin a hem on the 4 sides of the tablecloth, 8 in (20 cm) from the edge, and hand- or machine-stitch it.

2• Draw a line round the tablecloth 8 in (20 cm) from the edge in dressmaking pencil; this will form a rectangle.

3• Thread a generous length of mohair wool onto the wool needle. Insert your needle into 1 of the 4 corners of the rectangle, then make a straight stitch of about 6 in (15 cm), following the line. From there make 2 further straight stitches on 1 of the sides of the drawing to draw a first leaf. *(A and B)* (You can, if necessary, sew the top of the leaf on with nylon thread.) Proceed, as your inspiration dictates, by drawing a long gar-land of leaves.

4• Sew a bead and/or a feather at the edge of each leaf, then add a few beads here and there. *(C)*

5• Repeat the process for the other 3 sides of the tablecloth.

Note

The feathers should not be washed; they should be removed before each washing.

SUPPLIES
• Linen fabric in white, 100 in (2.5 m) wide, 13 ft (4 m)
• Thread in white
• White and green mohair wool
• Nylon thread (optional)
• Round iridescent beads and green faceted beads
• Drop glass beads
• White and green feathers

EQUIPMENT
• Pins
• Sewing machine or needle
• Dressmaking pencil
• Wool needle

A

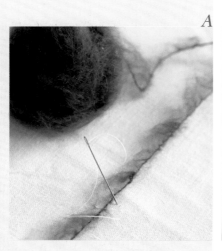

B

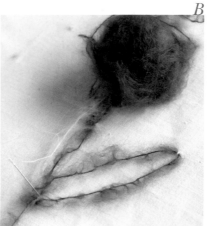

C

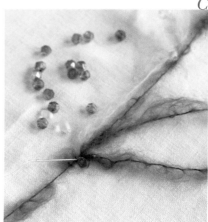

Decorated placemats

Overhand knots and lover's knots are repeated in unison on natural materials underlined with red.

SUPPLIES

Openwork placemat
- Linen fabric, 40³/₄ in x 14¹/₂ in (102 x 37 cm)
- Red cord, 1 in (2.8 mm) in diameter, 120 in (3 m)
- Thread to match the fabric
- Cotton thread in red

Lover's knot placemat
- Linen fabric, 40³/₄ in x 14¹/₂ in (102 x 37 cm)
- Strap, 1¹/₂ in (4 cm) wide, in red striped hessian, 35 in (88 cm)
- Thread to match the fabric
- 24 in (60 cm) red cord, 1 in (2.8 mm) in diameter
- 24 in (60 cm) linen string, 1 in (2.8 mm) in diameter

EQUIPMENT
- Measuring tape
- Dressmaking chalk
- Dressmaking scissors
- Pins with heads
- Sewing machine
- Needle

Openwork placemat

1• Cut 2 rectangles measuring 20¹/₂ x 14¹/₂ in (51 x 37 cm) in the linen fabric (see page 343). Cut out a 4 x 11 in (10 x 28 cm) window in 1 of these rectangles, 1³/₄ in (4.5 cm) from the edges. Fray the window all round for ¹/₂ in (5 mm).

2• Cut 3 lengths measuring 12 in (30 cm) of red cord, then pin these on the window heightwise, spacing them out at 1 in (2.5 cm) intervals.

3• Cut 10 lengths measuring 8 in (20 cm) of red cord, then pin these on the window widthwise, spacing them out at about 1 in (2.5 cm) intervals. To do this, pin them first on 1 side of the window, then proceed toward the other side by making an overhand knot (see page 40) at each intersection. Pin them on the other side. *(A)*

4• Machine-stitch the entire window, ³/₈ in (7 mm) from the edge, to fix this square cord pattern in place.

5• Sew the 2 sides of the placemat right side to right side, leaving an opening of 6 in (15 cm). Turn the placemat over and finish hand-stitching it.

6• Use back stitch with the cotton thread all round the window, on the hem.

Lover's knot placemat

1• Cut 2 rectangles measuring 20¹/₂ x 14¹/₂ in (51 x 37 cm) in the linen fabric (see page 343).

2• Pin these, then sew 20¹/₂ in (51 cm) of strap lengthwise in the placemat, 2³/₄ in (7 cm) from the edge.

3• Make lover's knots (see page 40), spaced out at 2 in (5 cm) intervals with the cord and the linen string. *(B)*

4• Sew these knots by hand on the remaining length of strap, centering them well. Pin them, then sew the strap thus prepared on the width of the placemat, 2³/₄ in (7 cm) from the edge.

5• Sew the 2 sides of the placemat right side to right side, leaving an opening of 6 in (15 cm). Turn the placemat over and finish hand-stitching.

A

B

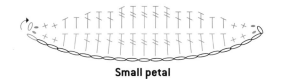

Small petal

Floral tablecloth

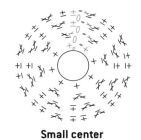

Small center

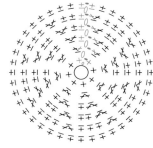

Large center

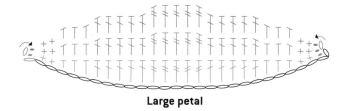

Large petal

- **Petals.** The 1st st of the chain is indicated in red.
Crochet the blue sts, the pink sts, then—for the large petals—the green sts.
- **Hearts.** For each row, the first 2 sts are indicated in blue, and the last 2 in pink.

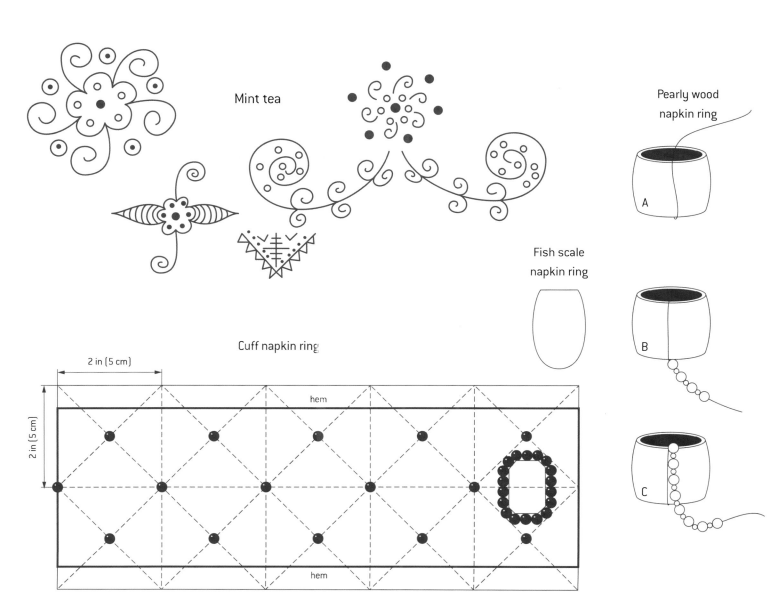

Mint tea

Pearly wood napkin ring

Fish scale napkin ring

Cuff napkin ring

2 in (5 cm)

2 in (5 cm)

hem

hem

A

B

C

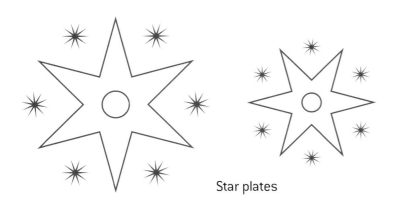

Star plates

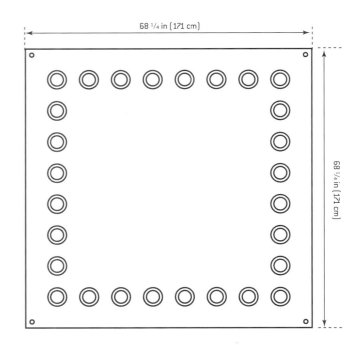

Seafaring tablecloth

68 ¼ in (171 cm)

68 ¼ in (171 cm)

Sage leaf transfers

(enlarge to 140%)

Beribboned table runner
Grid of 1 design

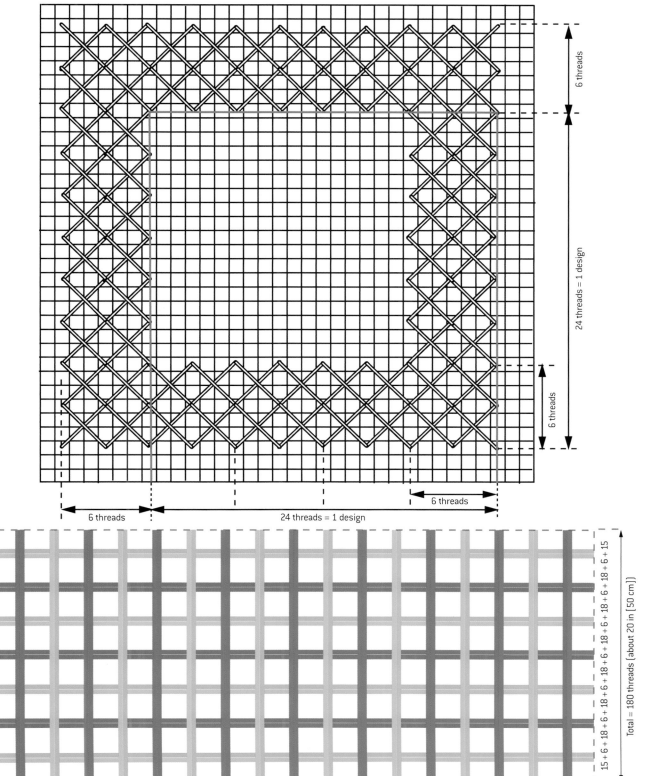

6 threads

24 threads = 1 design

6 threads

6 threads

24 threads = 1 design

6 threads

PLAN

15 + 6 + 18 + 6 + 18 + 6 + 18 + 6 + 18 + 6 + 18 + 6 + 15

Total = 180 threads (about 20 in [50 cm])

15 + 6 + 18 + 6 + 18 + 6 + 18 + 6 + 18 + 6 + 18 + 6 + 18 + 6 + 18 + 6 + 18 + 6 + 18 + 6 + 18 + 6 + 18 + 6 + 18 + 6 + 18 + 6 + 18 + 6 + 18 + 6 + 15

Total = about 420 threads (about 46 ¹⁄₄ in [116 cm])

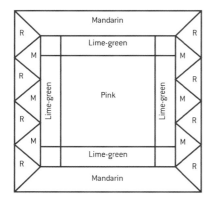

Multicolored tray with wicker mugs

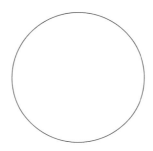

Bottle holder

(enlarge to the desired size)

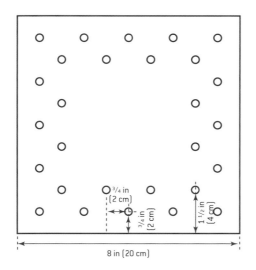
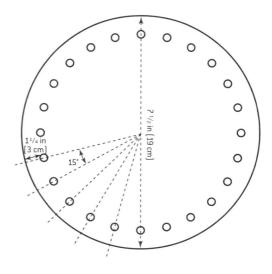

Geometric table mats

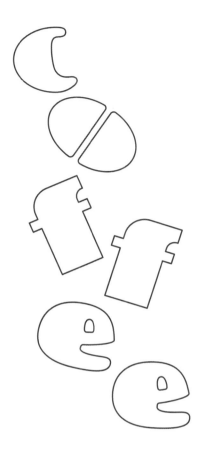

Coffee time

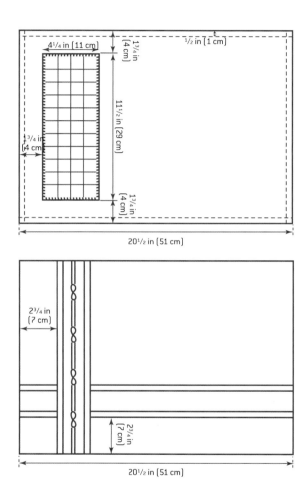

Decorated placemats

Little.
ideas

Buttons, buttons, buttons!

Little ideas that are very simple and quick to make, to achieve a successful decorative effect that is guaranteed.

Acid-colored tieback

If you like, you can improvise a tieback for your drapes in a flash! Thread transparent buttons with multicolored dots onto 3 strands of scoubidou thread, spacing them out at 2 in (5 cm) intervals. All you have to do after this is to tie the threads together, at each end, to hang this quick tieback to a hook.

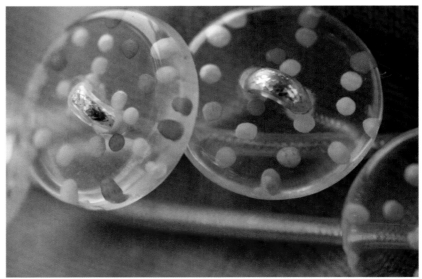

Key ring with colored beads

You can improvise a key ring with buttons threaded onto plastic thread and separated by colored beads. Create key rings in various shades of the same color, or in contrasting colors. The size and shape of the buttons can be varied for an even more original effect.

Colored magnets

Plastic buttons, sewn on in a trompe-l'oeil effect with colored thread, are actually glued onto a slightly smaller magnet.

Decorated stationery

Glued onto the Os of a note book decorated with printed letters, various buttons add a raised element to the cover.

In the wind

To make this decorative toy windmill, draw diagonal lines on a square sheet of paper, cut out half and flatten the points in the middle by gluing a button to keep them in place. Finally, glue the toy windmill onto a wooden stick and plant it in a small sponge cake.

Patchwork-style
The first page of this little exercise book is decorated with letters cut out of magazines and glued buttons so you can write the word of your choice.

Trompe l'oeil
Origami paper folded into a shirt-front shape is decorated with sewn-on buttons to make a highly original card.

At the office
Paper clips are invented anew by means of a button threaded onto colored wire, rolled up onto itself to form a double loop.

Creative beads

A luminous atmosphere for a summer's evening, a container with a timeless cameo: here are many simple ideas.

"Tulle flower" candleholder

A small glass pot can be turned into a candleholder in a trice. Overlap 2 squares of red tulle and 1 square of orange tulle. Tie them round the pot with a pretty ribbon and glue a few gold sequins on for a bit of luster!

Bird's nest

1 glass pot, 14 fuchsia-colored marabou feathers, paste, raffia, cable, crimp beads, 12 iridescent pink beads, 6 ceramic pink beads, 1 lead bead, 1 package gold sequins, flat-nose pliers, cutting pliers, scissors, tape measure.

1• Glue the feathers all round the pot. Let dry, then put raffia round the neck of the pot twice and secure it with a double knot.

2• Cut a 22½ in (56 cm) piece of cable. Fold it in 2. Slide 1 end of the cable through the raffia ties, then flatten it. Slide on a crimp bead. Thread an iridescent bead, a ceramic bead, an iridescent bead, and a crimp bead. Leave a 2 in (5 cm) empty space. Repeat the process twice. Leave a 4 in (10 cm) empty space, including the folded cable, and repeat the process 3 times as for the first side.

3• Finally, slip the thread first into a crimp bead, then in the raffia tie, slip it through the crimp bead once again, and in the first 2 beads. Pull gently. Crush the lead bead with the pliers, then cut off any excess cable.

4• Glue the gold sequins in staggered rows onto the raffia ties and onto the neck of the pot. Let dry.

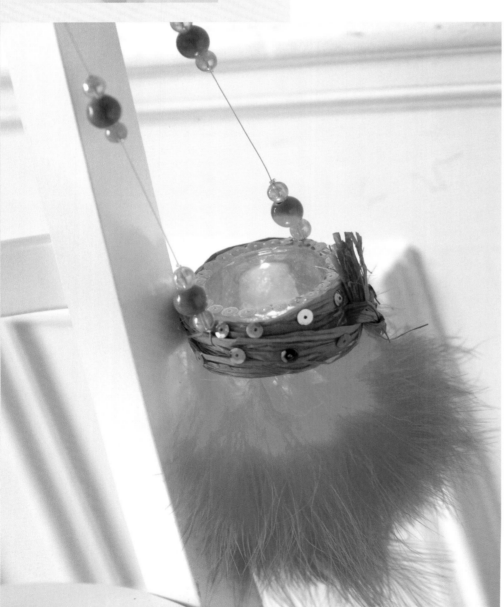

Cameo container

A simple container or earthenware pot is decorated with a cameo and a flange of beads.

Incense burner

1 small china bowl and 1 large square glass dish, 1 package silver and metallic blue glue dots, 32 opaque white grooved glass beads, 8 glass flowers, 8 flat white vinyl flowers, 1 tube blue seed beads, 4 blue faceted glass beads, mastic glue, superglue, cutting pliers

1• Glue some staggered rows of silver and metallic blue glue dots all round the china bowl with superglue.

2• Attach the white beads all round the glass dish with mastic glue. Let dry.

3• Glue the glue dots with superglue on the sides of the glass dish, alternating the colors.

4• Cut the flowers' stems, keeping only 1/2 in (1 cm) of the stems. Insert a flower into each bead on the corner and in each bead in the middle of the sides of the glass dish.

5• Create small flowers by sticking blue beads onto the flat white vinyl flowers or directly onto the white beads. Do this using superglue.

To keep the incense sticks firmly in the bowl, you can fill it with tiny seed beads.

Ideas with seeds

Photograph holder, bracelet, or napkin rings—here are ideas you can make instantly.

Incense burner
Pierce holes in an entada seed laid flat, without going all the way through. Place incense sticks in all the holes.

Drawer knob
Pierce a hole in a shea seed, without going all the way through, then position the screw in the drawer where the knob will be and fix the seed onto the screw.

Bracelet
Pierce holes in 6 *Hymenea courbaril* seeds lengthwise, then thread them onto a double cotton thread and tie.

Photograph holder
Make a small straight furrow in an entada seed with the blade of a small metal saw, deep enough to stick a photograph in.

Napkin ring
Pierce holes lengthwise in 5 butter beans, thread them onto stiff metal wire, close the whole thing on itself, and twist the wire. Cut off any excess wire.

Coconut vase
Choose a pretty coconut with fibers on it, cut and empty it out, then place a glass inside.

Inspirational raffia

Raffia can decorate or make everyday objects in a simple and quick way.

Water pitcher

• Glass bottle, raffia in different colors (white, yellow, orange, ver-milion, red, fuchsia), glue gun, scissors.

Load the glue gun and let it heat for 3 to 4 minutes. Drizzle a ribbon of glue round the bottle and stick on the raffia. Because the glue dries so quickly, arrange only a few strands of raffia at a time. Create strips of different widths and colors to make brightly colored stripes.

Pompon

• Blue and orange natural raffia, scissors.

Fold 3 strands of orange raffia in 2. Tie a knot 2 in (5 cm) from the fold, then another at 7 in (18 cm) (see page 355).

Prepare strands of raffia of the same length and fold them in 2. Thread them through the 2 knots, varying the colors, ensuring that the fold in each strand rests on the lower knot.

When the pompon is quite thick, secure it in position, surrounding it with a strand of raffia secured with a double knot.

Napkin ring with wooden beads

• Wooden napkin ring, red and orange raffia, 2 wooden beads (1 in natural color, 1 orange), glue gun, scissors.

Load the glue gun and let it heat for 3 to 4 minutes. Drizzle thin ribbons of glue onto the napkin ring, then stick on the strands of raffia, evenly spaced, horizontally and vertically.

Tie a knot in a different color of raffia at an intersection. Thread the beads onto the strands and secure them in position by tying a knot in each strand.

Napkin ring with glass beads

• Wooden napkin ring, purple and fuchsia-colored raffia, 10 to 15 purple, red, and orange glass beads, glue gun, scissors.

Load the glue gun and let it heat for 3 to 4 minutes. Drizzle the glue onto the napkin ring and surround this with purple raffia. Because the glue dries so quickly, work in small sections and put a few dabs of glue all over the napkin ring. Thread the glass beads onto the fuchsia-colored raffia and surround the napkin ring with this. Tie a knot in the raffia and place this inside a bead to fasten. Arrange the beads prettily on the raffia, then stick them on with a dab of glue.

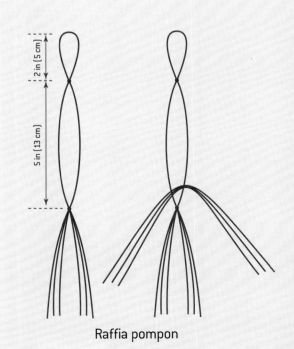

2 in (5 cm)

5 in (13 cm)

Raffia pompon

A garden paved with good ideas

• A pebble announces the name of the plant on a little zinc pot. Before you write the plant's name in white poster paint, carefully clean the pebble.

• To display long-stemmed plants attractively, use pebbles to support flowers in an old washtub.

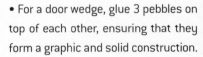

• For a door wedge, glue 3 pebbles on top of each other, ensuring that they form a graphic and solid construction.

- To identify fruit and vegetable seedlings and shoots in the garden, write the names of the plants on pebbles in white poster paint, then add a drawing of the fruit or vegetable in question.

- The soil has been covered with white pebbles in a zinc pot where horsetails grow.

Creation of projects

Agnès Petit: pages 26–31, 170–171, 194–195, 204–205, 230–231, 244–247, 280–281.

Nancy Waille: pages 10–13, 14–19, 52–53, 62–63, 68–69, 72–75, 80–83, 86–87, 98–99, 102–103, 152–157, 164–165, 200–201, 222–223, 228–229, 276–277, 286–287, 322–325.

Christèle Ageorges: 198–199, 334–335, 359–360.

Natacha Seret: pages 37–39, 88–89, 106–107, 110–111, 134–135, 248–249, 254–255, 258–259, 266–267, 270–271, 274–275, 314–315.

Christl Exelmans: pages 22–25, 48–49, 54–55, 84–85, 90–91, 94–97, 104–105, 108–109, 132–133, 142–143, 168–169, 206–207, 224–225, 272–273, 278–279.

Sabine Alaguillaume: pages 32–33, 130–131, 140–141, 182–183, 216–217, 288–291, 302–303, 310–311, 332–333.

Charlotte Vannier: pages 34–36, 46–47, 76–77, 92–93, 124–127, 136–139, 148–149, 176–177, 192–193, 202–203, 252–253, 256–257, 260–261, 264–265, 268–269, 292–293, 304–305, 308–309, 326–327.

Fabio Pane: pages 42–43, 160–163, 214–215, 242–243, 356–357.

Hélène Le Berre: pages 20–21, 50–51, 60–61, 64–67, 70–71, 78–79, 100–101, 166–167, 172–173, 208–209, 220–221, 300–301, 344–349.

Bernard Serra: pages 56–59, 158–159, 178–181, 218–219, 296–299, 312–313, 316–317, 330–331, 350–351.

Raynald Le Couls: pages 44–45, 144–147, 210–213, 226–227, 232–235, 352–353.

Lélia Deshayes: pages 40–41, 128–129, 150–151, 174–175, 196–197, 250–251, 262–263, 294–295, 306–307, 318–321, 328–329, 336–337, 354–355.

Styling

Lélia Deshayes: pages 16, 19, 62–63, 68–69, 80–81, 98–99, 152–157, 164–165, 190–191, 200–201, 222–223, 286–287, 324–325.

Christèle Ageorges: pages 3, 26–29, 31, 34–36, 40–41, 44–45, 56–59, 76–77, 124–129, 136–139, 144–147, 150–151, 158–159, 170–171, 174–175, 178–181, 192–199, 204–205, 210–213, 218–219, 226–227, 230–235, 240–241, 244–247, 250–253, 256–257, 262–265, 280–281, 285–286, 292–299, 304–307, 312–313, 316–321, 326–329, 330–331, 334–337, 350–355, 359–360.

Photographs

Julie Boogaerts: pages 37–39, 88–89, 106–107, 110–111, 134–135, 248–249, 254–255, 258–259, 266–267, 270–271, 274–275, 314–315.

Christl Exelmans: pages 22–25, 48–49, 54–55, 84–85, 90–91, 94–97, 104–105, 108–109, 132–133, 142–143, 168–169, 206–207, 224–225, 272–273, 278–279.

Florence Le Maux: pages 10–11, 20, 50–53, 60–61, 64–67, 70–75, 78–79, 82–83, 86–87, 100–103, 166–167, 172–173, 208–209, 220–221, 228–229, 276–277, 300–301, 322–323, 344–349.

Pascale Chombart de Lawe: pages 32–33, 130–131, 140–141, 182–183, 216–217, 288–291, 302–303, 310–311, 332–333.

Franck Schmitt: pages 4, 43, 160–163, 214–215, 242–243, 356–357.

Charlotte Bailly: pages 1, 47, 92–93, 148–149, 176–177, 202–203, 260–261, 268–269, 308–309.

Photographs

Frédéric Lucano: pages 3–4, 7, 10–11, 16, 19–20, 26–29, 31–33, 43, 48–49, 50–53, 56–59, 60–67, 68–75, 78–83, 86–87, 98–99, 100–103, 130–131, 140–141, 152–167, 170–173, 178–183, 190–191, 194–195, 198–199, 200–201, 204–205, 208–209, 214–223, 228–231, 240–241, 244–247, 276–277, 280–281, 286–291, 296–303, 310–313, 316–317, 322–325, 330–335, 344–351, 356–357, 359–360, back cover.

Thierry Antablian: pages 37–39, 88–89, 106–107, 110–111, 134–135, 248–249, 254–255, 258–259, 266–267, 270–271, 274–275, 314–315.

Fabrice Besse: pages 22–25, 54–55, 84–85, 90–91, 94–97, 104–105, 108–109, 132–133, 142–143, 168–169, 206–207, 224–225, 272–273, 278–279.

Claire Curt: pages 1, 34–36, 40–41, 44–47, 76–77, 92–93, 124–129, 136–139, 144–151, 174–177, 192–193, 196–197, 202–203, 210–213, 226–227, 232–235, 250–253, 256–257, 260–265, 268–269, 285–286, 292–295, 304–309, 318–321, 326–329, 336–337, 352–355.

Patterns

Laurent Blondel: pages 112–113, 114 t, 115 t and br, 118 br, 119, 120, 123, 184–186, 187 b, 188–189, 236, 237 b, 238 tl, 239, 282t and bl, 338–339, 340 t, 342–343.

Marie Pieroni: pages 113 tr, 115 m, 118, 122 t, 187 t, 188 b, 237 t, 238 bl, 338 t.

Natacha Seret: pages 114 b, 121, 282 r, 283, 340 b.

| **t:** top | **b:** below | **r:** right | **l:** left | **m:** middle |

Thank you to the companies that have so generously participated in the production of this book:

ASP Sérigraphie, Ateliers-Loisirs, Aventures Créatives, BHV, Bouchara, Bougies La Française, Captain Transfert, Casa, DMC, Entrée des Fournisseurs, Habitat, Ikéa, La Droguerie, La papeterie Saint-Sabin, Lin et petits points, Loisirs et Création, Mokuba, Moline, Muji, Perles Box, Phildar, 3 Suisses, Point à la ligne, Quartz Diffusion, Rougier & Plé, Designers Guild fabrics, Urban Nature.